Hugh Thompson (left) and Larry Colburn on their return trip to My Lai, March 1998.

What reviewers and readers think of *The Forgotten Hero of My Lai: The Hugh Thompson Story*

A jewel of reporting. . . an extraordinarily moving book.

– Seth Lipsky
The Wall Street Journal

An important contribution to the growing body of Vietnam War accounts and histories. . . painstakingly researched. . .

–The Midwest Book Review

Angers . . . presents a compelling journalistic investigation – readers will be affected by this story of heroism and rehabilitation. . . . The story of this authentic American hero and "warrior for humanity" is movingly portrayed in this first-rate biography.

– Karl Helicher
ForeWord Magazine

. . . a provocative and compelling story of a man whose courage and moral responsibility make him a true hero . . .

– William D. Bushnell
Independent Publisher

The heroic actions of Hugh Thompson, Larry Colburn and Glenn Andreotta have finally been recognized and appreciated by the government of the United States. This book proves that it is never too late to correct a wrong and that true American heroes live among us. Every parent concerned about the dangerous effects of negative peer pressure should buy this book as a gift to their children.

– John Cavanaugh
Political Scientist
Dayton, Ohio

It is impossible not to be moved by this great story. . . . Humanity needs heroes we can look up to and to lead us in difficult moments. . . . This book is an impressive and important milestone. My compliments and highest recommendation.

– Terje Lund
Major, Royal Norwegian Air Force; attorney at law; and special advisor on international humanitarian law to the Norwegian Red Cross
Oslo, Norway

This story of ordinary men taking an extraordinary action is destined to become a classic in the literature of the Vietnam period. . . . Thanks to the clear reporting of Hugh Thompson's story, we know the full story of the undaunted courage and bravery of Thompson and his crew. . . . Author Angers brings to light events leading up to and following My Lai in vivid detail and the development of the ethical foundations of Thompson and his crew that didn't allow them to look the other way on that fateful day.

– Bill Cavanaugh
U. S. Army (Retired)
Natick, Massachussetts

I read the book in two nights, reading and re-reading pages of unbelievable courage and heroism. . . . I strongly urge every parent to present this book to their sons and daughters for them to use Hugh Thompson's example of valor, compassion and love of mankind as a role model. . . .

– Frank Robles
U.S. Army veteran (1945-46)
Diamondhead, Mississippi

The Forgotten Hero of My Lai

The HUGH THOMPSON Story

TRENT ANGERS

Acadian House
PUBLISHING
Lafayette, Louisiana

For information, contact Acadian House Publishing, P.O. Box 52247, Lafayette, Louisiana 70505.

Library of Congress Catalog Card Number: 99-63662

ISBN: 0-925417-33-5

- **Published by Acadian House Publishing, Lafayette, Louisiana (Interior pre-press production by Ron Domingue and Brent Leger)**
- **Jacket design and production by Angers Graphics, Lafayette, Louisiana.**
- **Cover illustration and inside illustrations by Wei Li (Willy) Wang, Houston, Texas**
- **Printed by Sheridan Books, Fredericksburg, Virginia**

Introduction

Back in 1969, I interviewed a young Vietnam veteran, Paul Meadlo, for Walter Cronkite's CBS Evening News. In an eerily quiet voice he told America one of the most horrific war stories we'd ever heard. A shameful story. How American soldiers, in March 1968, gunned down hundreds of unarmed Vietnamese civilians at a village called My Lai, under orders from Lieutenant William Calley.

I asked Paul Meadlo how many people he killed that day.

Meadlo: Well, I might have killed about ten or fifteen of them.
Wallace: Men, women and children?
Meadlo: Men, women and children.
Wallace: And babies?
Meadlo: And babies.
Wallace: They weren't begging or saying, "No, no"?
Meadlo: Right, they was begging and saying, "No, no," and the mothers were hugging their children and – but we kept right on firing.
Wallace: Why did you do it?
Meadlo: Why did I do it? Because I felt like I was ordered to do it. At the time, I felt like I was doing the right thing. I really did because, like I said, I lost buddies.
Wallace: You're married?
Meadlo: Right.
Wallace: Children?
Meadlo: Two.
Wallace: Obviously, the question that comes to my mind: The father of two little kids like that, how do you shoot babies?
Meadlo: I don't know. It's just one of them things.

It was a story that stunned America. But, what I didn't hear until nearly thirty years later was Hugh Thompson's story. How this chief warrant officer and his door gunner, Larry Colburn, observed the massacre in progress from their Scout helicopter above My Lai. They set their chopper down to try to intervene, to keep more of the senseless, cowardly murders from taking place. You will learn more about all of it as you read this book.

Back in 1969 the Pentagon didn't know what to do about Hugh Thompson and Larry Colburn, or about their crew chief, Glenn Andreotta, who died in battle just weeks after the My Lai massacre. In fact, it took the Pentagon a full thirty years to acknowledge the heroism of these three men and to acknowledge the U.S. Army's shame at what had happened. The three men were finally awarded the Soldier's Medal in a public ceremony, at the Vietnam War Memorial in Washington in March of 1998.

Shortly after that, I accompanied Thompson and Colburn back to My Lai for the 30th Anniversary of the massacre for a "60 Minutes" report. They wanted to meet some of the women and children whose lives they'd saved thirty years before. And they did, in a stunningly heartwarming reunion. Beyond that, they were able to see a My Lai restored to bucolic, serene peace.

My admiration for Hugh Thompson and Larry Colburn runs deep, for their courage and compassion, for their integrity and their understanding of American ideals and the willingness to fulfill them at great danger to their own lives.

Hugh Thompson asked me in My Lai: "Has the United States ever apologized? Or are we too big to apologize?" It was a war crime, plain and simple. And we haven't yet apologized for it. Now would be a good time to do so.

– *Mike Wallace*
CBS News

This book is dedicated to the memory
of the 504 Vietnamese people who died
in the My Lai massacre on March 16, 1968.

(The names of the deceased are
presented beginning on page 223.)

Acknowledgements

Numerous people gave generously of their time and knowledge to help bring this book to fruition. I am indebted to the following for their contributions:

Those who helped edit the text and suggested ways to improve it: John Boudreaux, Jim Varney, Ed Moise, Cindi Angers and Mary Jones.

Those who helped in the research phase: Rich Boylan and Cliff Schneider of the National Archives in College Park, Maryland, who went above and beyond the call of duty to guide the author to a gold mine of historical documents dealing with the massacre, its cover-up and the politics of it all; Antonia Balazs, who extracted numerous valuable documents from the National Archives; Al Bethard at the University of Southwestern Louisiana Library, for guiding me to relevant material on President Nixon and Gen. William Westmoreland; Jack Epstein, who unearthed numerous important documents from the F. Edward Hebert papers at the Tulane University Library; Katie Jones whose research helped to show President Nixon's attitude toward the My Lai massacre.

Michael Bilton, co-author of *Four Hours In My Lai*, for sharing his considerable knowledge about the massacre, via e-mail from England, in response to the many questions sent his way.

The people of Levanger, Norway, for their courtesies during our visit to their fair city, particularly Mayor Martin Stavrum; Morien Rees, who headed up the Falstad Seminar; and Tone Jorstad, who works for the city.

The Norwegian and International Red Cross for their hospitality during our visit to Oslo, particularly Dr. Astrid Nokleby-Heiberg, Bernt Apeland and Terje Lund.

Le Dzung, press attache for the Embassy of Vietnam in Washington, D.C., for providing the names of the 504 Vietnamese people who died at My Lai; and to Nguyen Xuan of Lafayette, La., who helped assure the accurate reproduction of the names.

CBS News for their courtesies and cooperation while we were in Vietnam in March of 1998, particularly Mike Wallace and Tom Anderson.

Christopher Blakesley of the Louisiana State University Law School, Jordan Paust of the University of Houston Law Center, Matthew Lippman of the University of Illinois Law School, and Terje Lund of Army College in Oslo, Norway, for their contributions to the author's understanding and appreciation of the Geneva Conventions and international humanitarian law as they relate to the My Lai massacre.

David Egan and Lt. Col. Kevin Clement, who helped tell the story of the quest for Hugh Thompson's Soldier's Medal.

Neal Bertrand, Martin Back and Janet Guilbeau, who spent countless hours proofreading, transcribing taped interviews, and doing the seemingly endless job of fact-checking.

– T.A.

Contents

The Forgotten Hero of My Lai

The soldier, be he friend or foe, is charged with the protection of the weak and unarmed. It is the very essence and reason for his being.

–Gen. Douglas MacArthur, 1946

Chapter 1

A Special Gift From A Fellow Veteran

SPRINGTIME IS USUALLY MILD AND ALWAYS very green in semitropical south Louisiana. The sparrows and blue jays are out in force and the squirrels are chattering in the great live oaks which grace the lawns of the Bayou State.

During this moderate time of year, before the blistering heat of summer, the people of this region tend to spend more time outdoors than they do in any other season. Old men commune with nature in their tomato gardens, younger people jog about their neighborhoods, and friends and relatives gather for traditional backyard crawfish boils.

Hugh Thompson was looking forward to just such an outdoors gathering on the coming weekend as he left his office in Lafayette and headed for home in Broussard, four miles southeast of the city. On this particular day, May 5, 1993, he was also anticipating the arrival of a package of testimonial-type letters from a somewhat mysterious college professor who felt that Thompson had never gotten the recognition he deserved from the U.S. Army for his heroic deeds during the Vietnam War.

Thompson's white Bonneville zipped into Broussard and passed the little elementary school, St. Cecilia's, which is situated next door to the sizable Sacred Heart Catholic Church. In the lot between them, on the side of the road, a vendor had parked his truck under an oak tree, as was his custom, and was offering fresh strawberries at $5 for four little green basketsful.

Thompson stopped at the town's one traffic signal and combed his moustache with his fingers as he waited impatiently for the light to turn. In the window of the little grocery store on the corner was a sign announcing "*Boudin* $1" and another, "Louisiana Crawfish Only $4.99" – as opposed to the less expensive imported crawfish, which was getting to be a very touchy subject among local fishermen.

Two or three minutes after the light turned green, Thompson was home, his car was parked and he was heading for the mailbox. His package had arrived. It was from one David Egan, a Clemson University professor of architecture who lived in Anderson, South Carolina.

He didn't really know Egan, though he had spoken with him by phone the weekend prior. It seems that Professor Egan had been admiring him from afar and speaking highly of him for quite some time. More particularly, unbeknownst to Thompson, Egan had been on a three-year letter-writing and phone-calling campaign to convince the U.S. Army to award Thompson a medal for heroism for what he did at My Lai, South Vietnam, on March 16, 1968.

Thompson opened the package with his ink pen as he walked back up the driveway and toward his front door. He went to the refrigerator for a beer, kicked off his shoes, sat down on the sofa and began examining the contents of the package. He was a bit taken aback by what he saw. There were dozens of letters written by Egan on his behalf to senators, congressmen, the top brass of the Army, former members of Presidential cabinets, and others. Thompson smiled slightly as he read. This fellow, Egan, had nerve.

His letters were formal and polite, though passionate about the cause which he was espousing. They were well-focused and to the point. One could easily get the impression from reading them that Mr. Egan would prevail in his crusade, if for no other reason than his extraordinary willpower.

While grateful and even flattered by it all, Thompson was not optimistic that any medal for heroism would be forthcoming. A quiet, modest man of fifty at the time, Thompson wasn't seeking any kind of recognition for his actions at My Lai and never dreamed that anyone else would be either. He didn't look upon his deeds of that day as particularly heroic; he viewed them only as the actions of a soldier doing his duty, as any other man in uniform would have done, given the same set of circumstances.

But Professor Egan, who had been a U.S. Army officer in France in the early 1960s, knew a *bona fide* American hero when he saw one – and Hugh Thompson fit the description. The way Egan saw it, anyone who would risk his life, risk court-martial and risk the possible alienation of his fellow soldiers to save the lives of defenseless, innocent civilians, this was a hero, in the purest and most noble form.

While Egan had known for years about the infamous My Lai massacre, it wasn't until 1989, when he viewed a British documentary titled *Remember My Lai*, that he learned who Hugh Thompson was. And he felt strongly that the rest of the world should know, as well, about this forgotten hero of My Lai.

What Egan didn't understand, though, was why, in heaven's name, had the Army not recognized this man, one of its best and most courageous, in a manner befitting such an outstanding soldier. Why had they not held him up as a shining example of the caliber of men who served their country with honor in the Vietnam War? Was it because the Army was ashamed and embarrassed over what happened at My Lai? Were they afraid that any new publicity about anything to do with that dark day would only re-open painful old wounds in the American psyche?

Regardless, the fact remained that Thompson lived in virtual obscurity, his story little known to the vast majority of Americans, at a time when America could have used some good news.

David Egan was determined that Thompson would receive the medal to which he was entitled, and that the American people would learn – and take pride in – the true story of one of the many men who served their country with honor in the Vietnam War.

The first letter of Egan's campaign was addressed to Gen. Colin Powell, Chairman of the Joint Chiefs of Staff at the time. He had met Powell by chance at the Normandy American Cemetery in France in 1989. Powell wrote back:

> I appreciate your sincere interest in CWO Thompson's case and the desire to recognize him for his efforts. I am forwarding your letter to the Chief of Staff of the Army for review and appropriate action. As you noted, soldiers perform many acts of bravery during wartime, many of which pass unrecorded. Also, it is often very difficult to distinguish between a soldier's duty and an exemplary act of heroism during the demands and chaos of battle....

Egan also wrote to Dean Rusk, former Secretary of State under Presidents Kennedy and Johnson, and Melvin Laird, former Secretary of Defense under President Nixon. Both men wrote back and indicated that they saw merit in his proposal. Egan was encouraged.

As Thompson read the letters, his thoughts took him back to that dark day in March of 1968 when he witnessed a sight so horrible that his mind was unable to comprehend it at first. The content of the letters filled him with ambivalence: On one hand, there was pain and sorrow in remembering what happened at My Lai; on the other, a feeling of joy that someone would think enough of him to have gone to the trouble of seeking a medal on his behalf. He was touched by it all. His eyes teared up and he felt a lump in his throat. He put the letters down on his coffee table, got up off the sofa, and went outside to get some fresh air and to try to get Vietnam off his mind.

Chapter 2

Quest For The Soldier's Medal

HUGH THOMPSON FELT A STRONG SENSE of gratitude toward David Egan for what he was trying to do. And at the same time, he could not, in his wildest imagination, conceive of the U.S. Army going along with Egan's request to award him a medal for heroism for what he did at My Lai.

Thompson knew full well that for the Army to do so would draw the attention of the American public back to the Vietnam War in general and to the My Lai massacre in particular, two events that the Army, and a sizable number of the American people, would prefer to forget.

After all, the Vietnam conflict was the first war the United States ever lost (or gave up on), and the My Lai massacre was perhaps the most shameful chapter of the entire war, involving the slaughter of some five hundred unarmed Vietnamese civilians by U.S. soldiers. This was not the type of thing any civilized society could point to with pride. Moreover, the degree to which the American public had been divided over this war was unprecedented. Soldiers returning from World Wars I and II were welcomed home with open arms, while many men in uniform who returned from Vietnam were actually spat upon and jeered by some as "baby killers," even though this was a blatantly unfair characterization to use in referring to the vast majority of U.S. fighting men who served in Vietnam. A large number of U.S. military personnel had the feeling that they weren't welcome home, that their efforts overseas were misunderstood and unappreciated. This perception was not a figment of their imaginations. Many who were trying to re-enter the workforce in the 1970s were advised by fellow veterans not to write "Vietnam veteran" on their resumes, because many prospective American employers could read all sorts of things into that label that might or might not be true.

Being aware of this situation in general was one reason why Thompson felt the Army wouldn't be anxious to award him a medal for heroism in Vietnam., i.e., such an action by the Army might rekindle the fires of division within the United States.

A second reason was that the Army had previously awarded him a medal, the Distinguished Flying Cross, several months after the My Lai incident, in which it erroneously referred to his getting caught in a crossfire between U.S. and enemy soldiers at My Lai, when, in fact, there were no enemy troops to be found, only unarmed civilians. The omission of any reference to civilians being killed seemed to Thompson a deliberate attempt on the part of the Army to whitewash what really happened at My Lai. The citation that came with the Distinguished Flying Cross was tainted with false information, and Thompson had unceremoniously thrown away the medal, not wanting to be an accomplice in a coverup.

As pessimistic as he was about the Army awarding him a medal for heroism, he was, nevertheless, very appreciative of David Egan's efforts toward this end. So he called Egan the same night he received the package of letters.

"Professor? Hey, this is Hugh Thompson," he said in his deep, gruff voice.

"Well, Mr. Thompson, hello. Thank you for calling. Did you get the package?"

"Yeah, that's why I'm calling, to say thank you. I really appreciate what you did. That's the nicest thing anyone ever did for me in my life."

"Well, no problem. It was my pleasure. And I intend to keep on pushing until we get you that medal," Egan responded.

"I'm real grateful, but I'm afraid that you might be wasting your time. I don't think the Army is real interested in recognizing me. And they sure ain't interested in talking about My Lai again."

"Well, I can understand them not wanting to dredge up the My Lai massacre, but..."

"The medal that they gave me for what my crew and I did at My Lai was a damned lie, saying we got caught in a crossfire. There was no crossfire. The only ones firing were our guys, and they were killing civilians," Thompson said.

"Yes, I knew about the massacre. But, what's this about a medal? Tell me about your medal."

"The DFC."

"Oh, you *did* get the Distinguished Flying Cross."

"Yeah, but that's supposed to be for combat with the enemy. And there were no enemy there that day, just civilians."

"I understand."

"I think the Army was just trying to shut me up, to buy my silence, by giving me the DFC. This was part of the overall coverup, and I didn't want to have anything to do with that, so I threw it away."

"You threw the DFC away?"

"Yeah."

"You threw it away?"

"Yep, I just threw it away."

They chatted on for an hour about some of the time they spent in the Army, Thompson in Vietnam in '68 and Egan in France in '63. Thompson was curious about why Egan was making such an effort on his behalf.

"Professor, I appreciate your going to all this trouble. And I don't want to look a gift horse in the mouth, but can you tell me why you're so interested in getting me this medal?" Thompson asked.

"Well, it's just that what you did at My Lai was so noble, and I think our country needs to recognize you for it. Ya know, when the subject of My Lai comes up, I think most Americans feel ashamed of what our soldiers did there – as well they should.

They think of Lt. Calley and his men carrying on like Nazis," Egan began.

"That's exactly how they acted, like a bunch of Nazis, lining those people up at that ditch and mowing them down," Thompson chimed in.

"And, ya know, Hugh, I think hardly anyone in our country even knew what you and your men did there, trying to stop the massacre and everything."

"Yeah, you're right. The story didn't get out much," Thompson said.

"Another thing that motivated me to get involved in this is that when I was in the service stationed in France I stayed with a family who had relatives who were executed by the Nazis," Egan started to explain.

"What were they, part of the resistance or something?" Thompson asked.

"No, just boys and old men living in a little town out in the country. The Nazis were retreating through France and they just rounded up all the boys and old men and took 'em out, lined 'em up and shot 'em."

"Sounds just like what our guys did at My Lai."

"Then they raped the women and teenage girls, then went on their way, the cowards."

"Yep, sounds an awful lot like what happened at My Lai," Thompson said again.

"Hugh, I also wanted to tell you that when my troops and I were in France the French people treated us with respect, because for them the U.S. Army symbolized liberation from the brutality of the Nazis. And I guess I just wanted to say thank you for upholding our Army's tradition of honorable service while so many around you were disgracing the uniform," Egan explained. "It really means a lot to me, personally."

"Well, thank you, professor. I'm gonna need to run now. And thanks again for what you tried to do," Thompson said.

"*Tried* to do? I am nowhere near finished with this. I'm going to see them pin a medal on you if it's the last thing I do."

"I hope you're right. I'm not going to hold my breath, but I hope you're right."

Rather than being discouraged by Thompson's pessimism, Egan, an optimist by nature, was buoyed up by the lengthy conversation. He felt honored and privileged that this hero had talked with him for as long as he did. He was thoroughly impressed with Thompson's unpretentiousness.

And so Egan's letter-writing campaign continued. He was now more determined than ever to finish what he had started. With the assistance and encouragement of his wife, Jeannie, Egan would write more than a hundred letters to people in positions of influence, and most would respond favorably. By the fall of 1993 Egan's troops were lining up in support of Thompson's receiving the medal.

Egan enlisted the support not only of former Presidential cabinet members, congressmen and senators, but also retired Army officers, military historians, veterans groups and finally print and electronic news media. He mapped out a strategy as though he were supporting a candidate for high office – or planning a military operation designed to gain strategically important ground. He went about his task with a crusader's zeal. Armed with logic, determination and the power of the pen, he continued to storm the gates of the Pentagon and earnestly request that Thompson be recognized, that he be certified a hero. With the backing of the group he enlisted, Egan appealed to the Army's sense of fair play and fidelity – not only toward Thompson, but also toward the hundreds of thousands of veterans who could point to Thompson with pride and say that this man's ethical fabric was fairly representative of the majority of U.S. troops who fought in Vietnam.

On August 4, 1994, Egan wrote to General John M. Shalikashvili, who at the time was the Chairman of the Joint Chiefs of Staff:

> Dear General Shalikashvili:
>
> ...For several years I have tried to encourage recognition of CWO (Ret.) Hugh C. Thompson, Jr. for his heroic res-

cue of South Vietnamese noncombatants at My Lai. Some months ago, CWO Thompson was flown to My Lai by Netherlands TV in connection with a documentary prepared for the 25th anniversary of the tragic event. While in My Lai, CWO Thompson was reunited with villagers whose lives he had saved. The program also showed a small monument that indicated more than 500 villagers were killed by American soldiers....

As a U.S. Army veteran, I am saddened that the dozen villagers rescued by CWO Thompson are not acknowledged. This is perhaps understandable because even our own U.S. Army fails to officially recognize him for his heroic deeds....

Unfortunately, most of the U.S. media and academia recast historical events to denigrate our military, with My Lai often used to symbolize the "evil American presence in Vietnam." I resent these distortions. I firmly believe the American soldier helped give the South Vietnamese people nearly a decade of freedom and performed countless acts of humanitarian service such as medical aid, road construction, and building schools and hospitals.

Without the initiative of senior military leaders like you, the true story will never be widely known. For example, one straightforward message to America and the world would be the retroactive award of the DSC (Distinguished Service Cross) to CWO Thompson for his brave deeds at My Lai. This action by the U.S. Army would clearly affirm that our military stands for the highest humanitarian ideals.

I have corresponded on this case with your predecessor Gen. (Ret.) Colin L. Powell, so the JS should have a file of background materials. Included are letters-of-support by former Secretary of State Dean Rusk (1961-69), former Secretary of Defense Melvin R. Laird (1969-72), U.S. Senator Bob Smith (R-NH), and U.S. Congressman Billy Tauzin (D-LA). I would be pleased to provide you with further supporting documents or answer questions.

Thank you for considering this request that Mr. Thompson be officially recognized for his actions at My Lai, which reflect great honor upon himself, American soldiers, and our country.

The following year, on June 30, 1995, Egan penned a letter to

Secretary of the Army Togo D. West Jr., asking for help in correcting the language in Thompson's Distinguished Flying Cross and pointing out the benefits of his taking the initiative to recognize Thompson in an appropriate fashion:

> Dear Mr. Secretary:
> I am writing to ask your help in recognizing CWO (Ret.) Hugh C. Thompson, Jr. for his heroic rescue of South Vietnamese non-combatants on 16 March 1968 at the village of My Lai. I propose action be taken by the U.S. Army to correct the citation to Thompson's Distinguished Flying Cross (DFC) so it will describe his courageous actions at My Lai and *not* refer to "caught in intense crossfires," which did not occur.
> ...Immediate corrective action to reaward Thompson's DFC would clearly affirm that our U.S. Army stands for the highest humanitarian ideals. The presentation to him could be on the next anniversary or an earlier significant date.
> I believe recognition for Thompson should be initiated by the U.S. Army and not be due to media pressure or legislation by Congress....

While the appropriateness and wisdom of awarding Thompson the Soldier's Medal was a foregone conclusion in the minds of Egan and his troops, convincing the authorities in the Pentagon to award the medal would prove to be a challenge.

One of those in the Pentagon who did see things Egan's way was Lt. Col. Kevin M. Clement, a special assistant to Assistant Secretary of the Army Sara Lister. In an internal e-mail message to John P. McLaurin (his immediate superior), with a copy to Mrs. Lister, dated May 17, 1996, Clement wrote:

> Thompson was never recognized by the American Army for saving the lives of Vietnamese civilians on that day....
> The Vietnamese survivors remembered Thompson. I brought the subject up today during my visit at CMH (Center of Military History). The historian's response was the same as mine: He should be awarded the Soldier's Medal for his actions that day. They have the documents to substantiate his actions and strongly support the Army doing

> something to recognize his action....
>
> With permission of you and Mrs. Lister, I would seek to have the medal if/when approved presented to Hugh Thompson (whom I do not personally know or have any relation to) in front of the Corps of Cadets at USMA (U.S. Military Academy) – the place where I think it would have the most profound impact on tomorrow's officer corps. If scheduled in March of next year, USMA would have time to put together a seminar/symposium dealing with ethics, decisions in combat in conjunction with the presentation. All I need is your go-ahead.

A very different sentiment toward the awarding of the medal was expressed in another internal e-mail from Lt. Col. Peter Dagnes to Mrs. Lister. Dagnes took over Clement's job in the Pentagon in the summer of 1996. He wrote:

> ...We would be putting an ugly, controversial, and horrible story on the media's table. A story that has no good ending to it.... I'm specifically thinking of the election and sense that there is an associated risk with a Vietnam story. I think the country is supposed to be feeling good about where we are and where we are going. Any Vietnam story evokes too much emotion (and not a lot of it positive). It's just my two cents, but I recommend sitting on this completely until clear of the election.

He was referring to the Presidential election, wherein Republican Bob Dole was challenging incumbent President Bill Clinton.

After several months of discussion and debate among Pentagon officials and staff members, the issue was finally settled. On August 22, 1996, in response to Professor Egan's relentless campaign and solid reasoning, the Secretary of the Army issued orders that Hugh C. Thompson Jr. be awarded the Soldier's Medal for heroism for what he did to protect unarmed civilians at My Lai more than twenty-eight years earlier. The orders directed that this information be distributed to Thompson and Professor Egan.

It would have been a day of celebration for Egan and Thompson, except for one major detail: They were not informed. The order to distribute the information to them was not carried out; it was put on hold, indefinitely.

So Egan's crusade continued from outside the walls of the Pentagon.

The campaign also continued from within the Pentagon, thanks in large part to the efforts of Lt. Col. Clement. He advocated the cause which Egan was pushing, and in so doing found himself at cross purposes with more than one of his superiors.

Six months after the Secretary of the Army approved the award, Thompson still had not received official notification of its approval. Feeling that it wasn't right to keep Thompson in the dark on this matter, Clement faxed him a draft of the citation and the accompanying narrative.

Then, on February 18, 1997, Clement spoke his mind in a final e-mail message to John McLaurin, his immediate superior:

> I must relate to you that I have informed Hugh Thompson of his pending award of the Soldier's Medal. I know the last time we discussed this you had stated that, although the decision was up to me, you would prefer I did not mention it to him. The man has a very favorable feeling towards the Army. As such, I could not bear to string him out any longer.
>
> I have provided him with a copy of his orders and citation. He has agreed to not speak to the press prior to official notification....
>
> I have told Mr. Thompson that he will undoubtedly be receiving formal notification through official Army channels in the near future. He is content to wait until then. I have explained that the awards for his door gunner (Larry Colburn) and his crew chief (Glenn Andreotta) are still under consideration...hence the delay.
>
> LTC Dagnes had informed me in December that he could not find the award recommendations that I had prepared for them (citations) and sent to him via e-mail. I provided him with additional copies that same day....
>
> I have seen Pete's (Peter Dagnes') notes voicing his concern with the possibility of a negative news story by resurfacing My Lai. Hopefully, this has not influenced going forward with the award. I consider it a moot point. The

> board has met, the orders have been cut, the citation signed. I do not share LTC Dagnes' concerns. Thompson's is a good story – a soldier who did the right thing. He is a true-to-life hero. I am totally convinced that the Army has done the right thing in approving his award.
>
> Besides, I thought the criteria we applied was supposed to begin with the question, "Is it fair to the soldier?" – not, "How will this play in the press?"
>
> I do have one concern. The story should be about and remain focused on then WO1 Thompson and his actions in attempting to stop the slaughter at My Lai. I fear the longer the Army waits in getting around to notifying him and subsequently presenting the award, the greater the risk it runs in creating a new story: Why did the Army wait a half year or more since the orders were cut in August 1996 to notify Mr. Thompson?
>
> The longer the Army delays, the more it appears it does so to raise this story on the anniversary of My Lai (16-17 March). The perception becomes one of calculated manipulation of the award presentation. I fear the media would pick up on that right away. The focus of the story would then be less on Thompson's actions than on the Army bureaucrats' handling of the award. I would certainly hate to see that happen.
>
> I apologize if this is viewed as interference. I will inform Mr. Thompson tomorrow that I am no longer involved in this action and can be of no further assistance to him in this matter. Hopefully, that will appease all officials concerned. I will not contact you in regard to this matter again.
>
> I look forward to seeing notice of the award of the Soldier's Medal to Mr. Thompson in the near future.

While Clement's letter sent shock waves through several corners of the Pentagon, still no official word was forthcoming concerning when and where this medal might be awarded.

With Thompson and Egan now aware that the orders for the award had been signed, several aspects of unfinished business still remained: Where would the award be presented? Would it be a public setting or a private place? Would others besides Thompson be receiving an award, too?

Thompson let his wishes be known, in no uncertain terms, as

was his style: He gave the Army two dates when he would be available, December 10, 1997 and March 6, 1998; he wanted the ceremony to be open to the public, at the Vietnam Wall; he wanted the two men who were with him at My Lai to receive the award, as well, namely Larry Colburn and Glenn Andreotta. (Mr. Andreotta would receive the award posthumously, as he had been killed in action in Vietnam.)

Thompson stayed in touch with the Pentagon. As the months dragged on, the usually passive ex-soldier grew weary of waiting and anxious for the Army to set the date for the ceremony. The never-passive David Egan was also becoming concerned with what seemed to him an inordinate delay.

So, in April, some seven months after the award had been approved, Egan again wrote to Secretary of the Army Togo West Jr., urging him to present the award without further delay. But despite his urgings, nothing happened. Delay and postponement were the order of the day, as Pentagon officials debated issues of place and time: whether to have a public or private ceremony and when.

With no satisfactory result coming from Washington, Egan decided it was time to call in the reserves – a whole platoon of well-rested, letter-writing patriotic troops who were true believers in the righteousness of the cause. Accordingly, for the better part of a year (1997-98), Egan wrote to and called – or had his friends, associates and colleagues write to – more than two dozen U.S. Senators and Congressmen, representing the North, South, East and West of the United States, asking them to join the crusade to get the Army to do the right thing in regard to Hugh Thompson. The majority of them responded favorably. Some of them contacted senior military leaders in the Pentagon to urge that Thompson receive his award without further delay.

With all this political clout being brought to bear, one might expect that the Pentagon would have moved quickly in response, but such was not the case.

It was time to try a new strategy. Heretofore, Egan's campaign had been conducted privately, behind the scenes. But now it was time to go public, time to seek the assistance of the "fourth branch of government," the news media.

Being a well-informed citizen, Egan knew that people who work in governmental bureaucracies, be they elected or not, tend to sweat and to move with a bit more zip in their step when their performance, or lack thereof, is subjected to the bright, hot light of publicity. This is one of the natural laws of a free society. Another is that any journalist worth his salt lives to cover a good story. And Hugh Thompson's heroism, coupled with his government's inordinate delay in recognizing him for it, was a good story.

So, in an effort to help move things along, a thoroughly frustrated but still hopeful David Egan phoned Bob Timberg, a newspaperman whom he thought might have a strong interest in the story. Timberg, a Vietnam veteran and author of a book dealing with the haunting legacy of the Vietnam War, titled *The Nightingale's Song*, was an editor for *The Baltimore Sun*. As knowledgeable as he was about the war, Timberg had never heard of Thompson nor his heroic actions at My Lai. Egan gladly filled him in. After reviewing materials supplied by Egan, Timberg assigned a reporter to look into the matter.

The Baltimore Sun broke the story of the Army's foot-dragging in its November 14, 1997 edition. Under the headline, "My Lai still causes Army to flinch, delaying a medal," staff reporter Tom Bowman wrote:

> Nearly 30 years later, an effort to finally recognize Thompson's heroics is being stalled by Army politics. Approved for the Soldier's Medal in August 1996,...Thompson has not yet received the decoration or even been officially notified by the Army that it has been granted.

A few days later, a *Newsweek* article by Gregory L. Vistica pointed out:

> The Pentagon's official report on the (My Lai) massacre hailed Thompson...as a hero. But nearly three decades later the Army is still locked in a bitter feud over whether to give him the prestigious Soldier's Medal for his bravery.

The publication of these two articles alerted news organizations and caught the attention of journalists all over the world. TV crews and newspaper people from Germany, France, The Netherlands, Japan, Vietnam, Canada, England, the United States and other nations were now casting a very interested eye toward the Pentagon and this unrecognized, undecorated hero who seemed to be rising from the ashes of the Vietnam War. Here was the virtually unknown story of the silver lining around the dark clouds of the My Lai massacre. This was a story of pure, raw, unbridled heroism, a refreshing tale of man's humanity to his fellowman. It was about unselfishness, about the risking of one's life for the weak and the unarmed, the kind of story for which this cynical world was hungry. And news people in the United States and abroad were lining up to cover it as 1997 was drawing to a close.

Even a seasoned journalist with above-average powers of observation would never guess just by looking at Thompson that there was anything extraordinary about him. He is quiet, soft-spoken, usually a man of few words. He has never bragged about what he did at My Lai. Very few people in his own community even knew there were heroes at My Lai, much less that this guy was one of them. He appears to be a pretty average American male: mid-fifties, 5 foot 10, one hundred and eighty-five pounds, blue eyes, sandy-colored hair, glasses, somewhat handsome, divorced, three children, Episcopalian, employed by the Louisiana Department of Veterans Affairs, goes to work eight to five, five days a week, likes to have a few beers after work, watches NFL football religiously, loves his country and his aging mother, whom he cares for in his home. He is a Vietnam veteran who left part of himself on the battlefield and who thinks about the war every day of his life.

As he demonstrated at My Lai, he is a man of considerable courage, and he does have a temper. He can be stubborn and he can be aggressive, particularly when frustrated or treated disrespectfully. What happened with the awarding of his Soldier's Medal, with the Pentagon dragging its feet for a year and a half after the award was approved, angered him and drew out his aggression.

Thompson stayed in contact with the administrative people in the office of Secretary of the Army Togo West. He would call and ask about the date and place for the award ceremony.

"We're working on it, we're working on it," was the standard reply.

"I don't know what the hell you're working on! It's not that complicated; all you need to do is turn the papers over to the Military Awards Branch, and they can handle it from there," Thompson once responded angrily.

It was only after the *Newsweek* article came out (Nov. 1997) that Thompson was officially notified by the Pentagon that he was to receive the award. They called him on a Thursday and wanted him to leave Lafayette on Monday and fly to Washington. Someone would pick him up at the airport, bring him to a hotel, pick him up the next morning, bring him to Togo West's office for the ceremony, then drive him back to the airport.

The plan seemed simple, clear cut, concise – and not at all the way Thompson wanted it.

"What's the rush?" he asked. "Could it be…the *Newsweek* article?"

The fellow on the other end of the phone – J.B. Hudson, administrative assistant to Secretary West – sounded a bit indignant over what Thompson was insinuating. Then he tried to answer the question.

"The Secretary of the Army just found out about this and he's anxious to present the award," Hudson said.

"If that's the case, if he just now found out about it, then I'm convinced that the Secretary of the Army has surrounded himself with incompetent people," Thompson shot back.

"Why do you say that?"

"Because he's the one who approved the damned thing seventeen months ago! Don't tell me he just found out about it."

"Well, I mean he just found out that you wanted to have a public ceremony, at the Wall," Hudson said.

"Sir, I find that hard to believe," Thompson said dryly.

Then Thompson raised another sticky issue:

"What about my crew members?"

"What about them?"

"Have y'all made arrangements for them to receive the medal, too?"

"I don't know anything about that."

"Well, check it out and get back to me," Thompson said, adding that three days was just too short of a notice and that he wouldn't be able to be in Washington on the date requested.

Thompson's rejection of the proposal to have the award presented in a private ceremony – where neither media nor the public could attend – increased the pressure that was already on the Pentagon and reminded them of the kind of man with whom they were dealing. Another element of pressure which Pentagon officials felt was the rapidly approaching thirtieth anniversary of the My Lai massacre, March 16, 1998. Thompson and Colburn planned to return to Vietnam then, for a ceremony commemorating the victims of the massacre. Word around Washington was that the two heroes would be accompanied by CBS News, headed by veteran TV journalist Mike Wallace, who had covered the Vietnam War three decades earlier.

Superimposed over this developing drama was the possibility of Thompson creating an international incident that would have been a real embarrassment to the U.S. Army and the U.S. government in general. Thompson, who now had a photocopy of his Soldier's Medal certificate and the accompanying citation, compliments of Lt. Col. Clement, had told Secretary West's administrative personnel on more than one occasion that if the Army couldn't see its way clear to award the medal before he left for Vietnam, if they were still paralyzed by fear, uncertainty or embarrassment to even mention My Lai in public, then he would have the Vietnamese government make the presentation while he was in Vietnam. They had already said they would be honored to do so, Thompson reported.

The month of December 1997 passed, and still there was no word from the Pentagon concerning a date for a public award ceremony on U.S. soil. January came and went without any announcement either.

On February 20, less than two weeks before leaving for Vietnam, Thompson flew to Atlanta, Georgia, to meet with his old Army buddy, Larry Colburn (who lived in nearby Woodstock, Georgia), and CBS producer Tom Anderson. The purpose of the meeting was for Anderson to meet Colburn for the first time and for the three of them to discuss the details of their upcoming trip to Vietnam. They would fly from the U.S. to Ho Chi Minh City (formerly known as Saigon), then fly to Da Nang, take a bus to Quang Ngai and then to My Lai. The two veterans would be honored at the My Lai Memorial and would give brief talks to the crowd there. Arrangements were being made for them to be reunited with two or three of the women whom they had rescued from certain death during the war.

As they were discussing the plan, Colburn's pager buzzed. It was his wife, Lisa, calling to say that the Pentagon had called. It was urgent. He returned the call to the Pentagon and learned from a staff member named Col. Jimmy Jacobs that the award ceremony was set for March 6, that it would be open to the public and the press, that it would be at the Vietnam Wall, and that not only Thompson but also Colburn and Andreotta would be receiving the Soldier's Medal. Thompson had gotten everything he had asked for, everything.

While on the phone, Colburn appeared to be ecstatic about what he was hearing. A big smile was on his face and his eyes were tearing up as he looked at Thompson and pointed to him, then to himself, then to Thompson again, then held up three fingers, indicating that all three of them would be receiving the award. He held his hand over the bottom part of the phone and said, "March 6, at the Wall."

Colburn hung up, and both he and Thompson let out a yell, a victory chant, then embraced one another and patted each other's backs, as tears of joy dripped down their cheeks.

Chapter 3

A Day Of Triumph

THE DAY BEFORE HE WAS TO RECEIVE THE long-awaited Soldier's Medal, Thompson and his friend of fourteen years, Mona Gossen, flew out of Lafayette and headed to Washington, D.C. The flight was uneventful except for chatter about the details of the ceremony on the big day.

In his mind's eye, Thompson kept seeing the face of his buddy, Glenn Andreotta, and thinking of his name engraved on the Vietnam Wall, one of the tens of thousands of U.S. fighting men who came home in coffins. He wondered what Andreotta would look like today had he not died at the tender age of twenty, and how excited he would have been to be getting the Soldier's Medal, and how he had played a major role in the rescue of a little five- or six-year-old girl during the massacre at My Lai.

She was a South Vietnamese *child, one of the people we went to war to protect. She was somebody's little girl. So beautiful, so innocent. One of God's little children. At least we saved* her *from Calley and those other animals. I love the way Andreotta took her out of harm's way, without regard for his own life. I was so proud of him. I'll bet his folks were so proud, and still are. That's what soldiers are supposed to do, to protect the small, the weak, the defenseless... I miss him. I wish he could be with us to get his medal. He* will *be with us. He* is *with us...*

Thompson was filled with anticipation and excitement as the plane touched down at Ronald Reagan Airport in Washington. There, waiting for him and Ms. Gossen, was a military escort, who helped them with their baggage then drove them to their hotel.

Within a few minutes of the time they checked in the phone started ringing: media people wanting an interview, the Army calling to iron out some details about the itinerary, old war buddies calling to offer to buy him a drink. It would be like this the whole time he was in Washington, for three days. There were more than a hundred phone calls, gifts of welcome, gifts of congratulations, people wanting to shake his hand, to touch him, to be in the presence of this ordinary man who was becoming well-known for an extraordinary act of courage.

Heavy media coverage leading up to the awarding of the Soldier's Medal meant that more and more people around the U.S. were becoming familiar with Thompson's name. Before then, however, he was only vaguely remembered by relatively few as "the helicopter pilot who helped stop the My Lai massacre." And if Thompson's name was nearly forgotten or totally unknown to the majority of Americans, then the names of his crew, Larry Colburn and Glenn Andreotta, were even less recognizable.

Thompson felt strongly that if he were to be honored by the Army, and by the nation, then his whole unit should be, as well. It was his way of being faithful to his comrades, of sharing the spotlight, of acknowledging in all truth and humility that without their participation he could not have done what he did at My Lai. He viewed his unit as a three-legged stool, with three equally important parts; if one of those legs were broken or missing, the entire stool would collapse. The stool held together that day at My Lai, and as a result the massacre was stopped and some civilians were rescued.

Now U.S. and Vietnamese people were turning their grateful and admiring eyes to the men who had traveled to Washington to receive the Soldier's Medal, the recognition that was a long, long time in coming.

One of those men, who had arrived in Washington with his wife Lisa and son Connor about the same time as Thompson, was Larry Colburn, the door gunner on Thompson's aircraft.

Lawrence Colburn, a rugged-looking, sandy-haired guy with a heavy moustache, was born and reared in the Pacific Northwest and spent many years as a commercial salmon fisherman out of Alaska and a ski shop operator in the mountainous part of northeastern Oregon.

The only male among the four children of Harry and Catherine Colburn, he was reared in Mount Vernon, Washington. He was an altar boy and attended Catholic schools in elementary and junior high grades then moved on to a public high school.

Colburn lost his father at an early age. Harry was fifty-five when he suffered a third heart attack and died in 1964. Larry was fifteen at the time. An Army veteran who was overseas for three and a half years during World War II, Harry was a civil engineer who helped build the Grand Coulee Dam in the state of Washington.

Young Colburn was suspended from high school for two weeks in 1966 following a run-in with the assistant principal. Rather than going back to school after the allotted time, he decided not to return, opting instead to join the Army. Being only seventeen at the time, his mother had to sign a consent form before the Army would allow him in.

He went through basic training at Ft. Lewis, Washington, then moved on to Ft. Polk, Louisiana, for advanced training. From there he went to Ft. Shafter Army Base in Hawaii, where he earned his high school equivalency diploma before shipping out to Vietnam in December of 1967. For most of his one-year tour of duty he was a gunner, first on scout helicopters, then on the larger Huey gunships.

After being discharged from the service, in September of 1969, he returned home and spent a few months doing nothing in particular, except resting, dating, visiting friends and family, and enjoying his new sports car. He entered college on the GI Bill, studying and working for six semesters. But he struggled academically and financially and eventually dropped out, figuring that he didn't need a college education to make a living.

So, it was off to Alaska, where he would fish commercially for four or five months, earning enough money to carry him through most of the year. The rest of the time he would work at odd jobs and while away the days by dating and partying.

Concerned that he was drifting aimlessly through life, one of his sisters, Mary, asked him to come to her house for a while, in eastern Oregon, to help put a new roof on the place. He accepted the invitation and ended up settling in that area for seven years. He took a job at a ski shop, first repairing ski bindings and later managing the business.

He lived in the small town near his sister and her husband for a short while then moved to a secluded cabin on the mountain near the ski area where he worked. It was a rustic cabin without a phone or running water. The winter weather was frequently severe, sometimes getting to forty degrees below zero at night.

Colburn enjoyed the beauty of the winter, and the solitude. He had time to think about life, death, war, the future. His life was uncomplicated; his lifestyle was therapeutic. In the summers he would return to Alaska to fish.

In the winter of 1980, while working in the ski shop, he met and fell in love with the woman he would marry. Lisa Cale, a student at the University of South Carolina, was attending Eastern Oregon State College on an exchange program for a year. He was dead certain that this was the gal of his dreams, so when she left Oregon to return to South Carolina he went with her. They were married in 1985 and settled in the Atlanta, Georgia, area, where he would eventually own and manage a business dealing in orthopedic rehabilitation equipment.

The morning after their arrival in Washington, Colburn and Thompson were scheduled for a 7 o'clock interview with veteran TV journalist Mike Wallace of CBS News. Wallace would use some of the footage for a segment of "60 Minutes," which would air a few weeks later.

Wallace, who was approaching his eightieth birthday, came into the hotel bright-eyed and enthusiastic about the interview. With a welcoming smile and an air of cordiality about him, he greeted the people in Thompson's entourage. They were having coffee in a room next to the one where lights were being set up and the sound system checked.

Among other things, the interview dealt with how long it had taken for the U.S. government to get around to presenting the awards and who deserved the credit that this day had finally arrived.

"This day means a lot to you, doesn't it, Hugh?" Wallace asked.

"Yes, sir, it does. But mostly I'm happy because my crew will be recognized," he responded. "This award is also for the people who didn't make it back from Vietnam. It's for all the veterans who served honorably in Vietnam."

Wallace asked Thompson at what point he decided to go in and try to save the civilians, and Thompson explained that it was a joint decision.

"We did things as a team, normally. Everybody on the aircraft was upset about what we were seeing, and what was going on. We just couldn't explain it. We kept trying to analyze what was happening. And finally reality set in and we said, 'You know good and well what's going on down there. Quit fooling yourself!' "

"A massacre was going on?"

"Yes, sir, a massacre."

"You're getting the Soldier's Medal today, thirty years later. America, the Congress, apparently did not want to hear about this. Why?"

"Well, it's nothing that they're very proud of. These things just aren't supposed to happen – not with U.S. soldiers involved," Thompson responded, adding that the massacre of unarmed civilians is something he might expect from the Nazis, but not from Americans.

Thompson credited two news media with running the articles that forced the hand of the Army to award the medals.

"They never would have been given to start out with if it hadn't been for a *Newsweek* article by Greg Vistica and (a series) by Tom Bowman from *The Baltimore Sun*. The free press forced 'em into it.

"They wouldn't have done it. They did not like the publicity they were getting. So once the story broke, that's when the Army kind of wanted to usher me into the Pentagon seventy-two hours later (to receive the award in a private ceremony)," Thompson stated.

As Thompson and Colburn talked about the details of the My Lai massacre and the terrible things they witnessed then, one of the men in Thompson's entourage, who was observing from the next room, had tears running down his face. Charlie Poche of Lafayette, one of Thompson's best friends for fifteen years, wiped tears from his eyes as he explained that Thompson had never told him those stories in all the time they had known one another. Poche said he knew Thompson had helped to stop the massacre, but that he simply never talked about it.

Why hadn't he talked about it? For one thing, Thompson is a modest and humble man, and any talk that would seem like bragging would be out of character for him. For another, talking about it would tend to open old wounds, to bring back bad memories in more detail than he cared to remember.

But Thompson and Colburn were talking about it now, being drawn out by one of television's most skilled interviewers. With the award presentation ceremony only hours away, this was an appropriate time to recall the past, in some detail, and to relive it in their minds, and to mourn. It was also a day of joy, of celebration for receiving the Soldier's Medal, a triumphant day when courage and honorable service would be officially recognized and held in high regard by millions of people around the world who would watch the award ceremony on television or read about it in the newspapers. Many of those who would view it on TV would be moved to tears, as Charlie Poche was; many who would read about it would choke up with emotion.

After half an hour of pointed questions and answers, Wallace wrapped up the interview in the hotel, confident that he and his crew had gotten some valuable footage. The next segment of the interview was to take place at the Vietnam Veterans Memorial, the wall of names of fallen U.S. servicemen, so the CBS News crew, along with Thompson and Colburn, were driven to that site.

As they walked toward the wall, which bears the names of some 58,000 Americans who died in the Vietnam War, the men were discussing the significance of the monument, and its elegance.

They looked for Glenn Andreotta's name on the wall and when they found it, on Panel 48-E, they stopped there to continue the interview. Wallace sat down on the cool concrete. Thompson and Colburn squatted in front of him, their backs to the shiny black granite wall. The cameras began to roll as they talked about their fallen comrade and about heroism.

"I don't classify myself as a hero, and I don't think Larry does either," Thompson stated.

Colburn politely took exception to part of Thompson's statement.

"*I* classify *you* as a hero," he said to Thompson.

Wallace asked Colburn to explain.

"Hugh was the ranking man. He was a wonderful officer to fly with because he always discussed things briefly with his crew and wanted to make sure that we were all together on whatever we did. And we all decided that it was the right thing to do (to try to stop the massacre). Since there might be children who needed help or civilians that needed our help, we had to help them. But *he* was the man in charge."

Thompson seemed uncomfortable with Colburn's words of praise. He preferred to talk about Andreotta. It was because of Andreotta's keen sight, coupled with his compassion for the wounded and dying, that the crew was able to rescue a little girl of five or six during the My Lai massacre, Thompson pointed out. Had Andreotta not spotted the movement among the bodies in an irrigation ditch that was filled with villagers who had been shot, the child probably would have died, Thompson suggested.

Glenn U. Andreotta was a handsome man of twenty when he died, an all-American-looking guy from America's heartland, from St. Louis, Missouri. He was typical of the hundreds of thousands of young soldiers, in their late teens or early twenties, who went to war with their whole lives ahead of them, as their mothers prayed unceasingly for their safe return. These mothers lived in constant dread of hearing a certain knock on the door and seeing two military men in full dress uniform who were there to announce the bad news and to offer their sympathy. Such a knock was heard by Mrs. Ruth Andreotta on April 9, 1968. Glenn's father and Ruth's ex-husband, Joseph Andreotta, received the news a day later.

Born in New Jersey and reared in St. Louis, Missouri, Glenn was seven and his brother David was nine when their parents divorced in the mid-1950s. Their dad moved to Florida and remarried and had no contact with his children for the better part of a decade.

Ruth Andreotta was on her own to support and rear the boys following the divorce. She worked outside of the home, in a photo lab, for nine and ten hours a day. Glenn and David were given chores that included cooking, washing dishes, house cleaning, leaf raking and the like.

Twice while rearing the boys, Ruth had opportunities to be married, but she declined. While the financial support of a working husband would certainly have eased her burden, she did not want to run the risk of putting her children through the emotional trauma that she and they had experienced the first time around. The boys would be her companions. They would just have to get by with one parent, plus aunts, grandparents and friends.

The three of them lived in a small house that Ruth rented from her father. The house sat on five acres of land, and the yard was filled with apple trees. Ruth taught Glenn to make apple sauce, which he did well, except for the part about cleaning up afterward. Glenn also baked cookies and was said to be quite good at it. He would get mad at his brother David for snitching cookies just as soon as they came out of the oven.

In the wintertime, Ruth and her boys would sled down a big hill on the property. Glenn sometimes brought his little grey and white cat along for the ride. They spent many a winter afternoon speeding down the hill, but Ruth bowed out when the boys started getting reckless. After a few rides the cat hid when the boys took out the sled.

Ruth took the boys to church with her on Sundays when they

were young, but when they got older they began pulling away and wanting to attend services with their friends, a request which she found to be reasonable.

In the summer following Glenn's sophomore year Ruth had an opportunity to move her family into a better house, and she took it. Glenn was devastated because moving meant changing schools, which, in turn, meant leaving behind his friends. He rebelled. He was bound and determined not to go to the new school and finally, a few months into his junior year, he decided to drop out.

He quit going to school in October of 1963. He didn't ask permission of his mother to do so, nor did he bother to mention it to her. Nor did the school notify Mrs. Andreotta of her son's absence. Glenn just hung around the house and watched television. All this time, for three months, his mom and big brother were thinking he was in school, where he was supposed to be. He nearly got away with it.

When Mrs. Andreotta found out, she was understandably upset. She had no idea that her effort to improve their lot in life, by moving into a better house, would bring on such an adverse reaction, especially from this boy who had never given her any trouble. She did not realize how important it was to Glenn to be going to the same school as his best friends, who made up a major part of his emotional-support system. Glenn was one of a tight-knit, nearly inseparable group of eight boys who had been friends since they were nine or ten years old. They went to the same schools, were in Boy Scouts and Explorers together, even attended church together sometimes. There was a strong bond between these boys; all of them, to some degree, had a need to be with one another.

But, be that as it may, Glenn was going to have to do something with his life besides hanging around the house and watching TV. So, his mother gave him three choices: return to school, get a job, or join the service.

He chose option number two and went to work in the kitchen of a hotel in St. Louis. He held that job for two to three months, became disenchanted with washing pots and pans and chopping onions, and decided to pursue a job with a bit more adventure.

Glenn wanted to join the Army, but, being only 17, he would need his mother's permission, which she gave reluctantly. Glenn ended up in Vietnam for a one-year tour of duty. He was not involved in combat but spent his time behind the lines as a radio repairman.

After serving in Vietnam, Glenn returned to St. Louis in November of 1967, only to find all seven of his friends gone. They had joined the service, either Navy, Air Force or Marines. Since they were gone, and he had no girlfriend nor any other particular reason to remain in St. Louis, he considered returning to Vietnam. By signing up for another tour of duty, there would be certain financial incentives, and he figured when he was finished with his second tour he would return to St. Louis about the same time that all his friends were getting back.

Glenn's mother urged him not to go back to Vietnam. And so did his father. Ruth did not know that Glenn had been in touch with his father on and off for the previous two years.

After ten years of not communicating with his children, Joe had inquired and learned that Glenn was in the Army and stationed at Ft. Gordon, Georgia. He contacted his son and asked him to get a three-day pass, so they could spend some time together. Joe and his new wife, Cecilia, picked up Glenn in their Volkswagon Beetle and drove to Franklin, North Carolina, for the weekend.

"We were like total strangers," Joe would explain later. They got together several more times at Joe's home in Bellview, Florida, and continued trying to build a relationship. Father and son were getting to know one another.

While he was in St. Louis, in December 1967, Glenn spent an entire day visiting and talking with his mom. He had grown up a lot while in Vietnam. He was more a man than a boy. Mother and son reminisced about the recent past and discussed his plans for the future. Glenn seemed optimistic; Ruth tried to be, and pretended to be, but she was not. She felt in her heart that Glenn would not be coming home again. Somehow, she just knew it.

The following week, just before Christmas, she took a picture of Glenn and David clowning around, laughing over something or other. A few days later, Glenn was gone, headed back to Ft.

Gordon, then back to Vietnam, never to return.

Ruth keeps the Christmas picture in a frame on her dresser.

Joe flies an American flag in his front yard in memory of his son, and has since 1969, the year after he was killed.

After their interview at the Vietnam Wall, Thompson and Colburn returned to their hotel to rest and to review the prepared remarks they would give that afternoon during the award ceremony. They were nervous, anxious. They were not experienced public speakers, and they were afraid that they might choke up and be unable to speak, or possibly, in Colburn's case, get up there and forget what he was going to say. Thompson's remarks were neatly and carefully written; Colburn had only brief notes.

Trying to help calm their nerves, one of the members of the entourage told them not to worry, that they would do well because they had *earned* the right to speak on the subject of Vietnam and My Lai, and that no one alive today could tell their story with more authority and insight. That little pep talk seemed to build their confidence, until they learned a few minutes later that the management of Cable News Network (CNN) apparently deemed the ceremony to be so newsworthy, so significant, that they had decided to broadcast it live, in its entirety.

"Well, that's just great! Now we have a chance to screw up in front of five million people," Thompson cracked, in his customary self-deprecating way.

Colburn laughed nervously, then said his remarks would be very brief and to the point.

"How does the saying go? 'Be brief and be gone,'" Colburn asked.

"No, I think it's, 'Be sincere, be brief and be seated,'" Thompson chimed in.

They carried on in this fashion for a while, wise-cracking, making small talk, reviewing and editing their notes, saying parts of their speeches out loud. Consciously or unconsciously, this is how they calmed their nerves prior to the big event; but mostly just being together and feeling one another's support, the sense of camaraderie, helped them to feel that everything would be fine.

Before returning to the Vietnam Veterans Memorial for the ceremony, they and their entourage were driven in a motorcade to Ft. Myer, a few miles from their hotel, for a formal briefing and review of the itinerary. Among those present were Maj. Gen. Michael Ackerman, who would be master of ceremonies, and Maj. Gen. Donald Shea, the Army chaplain who would deliver the invocation.

While the briefing was in progress, Thompson motioned to his friend, Charlie Poche, to come over for a moment. Poche obliged him, then left the room, stepped outdoors, removed a cell phone from his coat pocket, and proceeded to call Thompson's ailing mother to tell her to switch her TV to CNN. She was in a hospital back home in Lafayette recovering from a mild stroke. If no one else in the world were to see him get the medal, he wanted his mom to see it. He felt that she, after all, deserved some of the credit for helping to build the character required to do what he did at My Lai.

After the briefing, the motorcade made its way to the Memorial, where the ceremony would be held. Thompson and Colburn had figured there would be a good number of people at the staging area, but what they saw startled them. A sizable crowd had gathered, made up of friends, family, Vietnam veterans, congressmen, senators, ambassadors and some of the top brass of the U.S. Army and other branches of the service. And off to the side was a large group of media people, representing fifty or sixty different news-gathering organizations, with video cameras set up, tape recorders at the ready, note pads out, and 35mm cameras pointed.

The men of the hour emerged from their cars and, with military escorts, marched up a little hill and through the crowd to take their place at center stage. They were blushing. They could feel people's eyes on them. They felt that the whole world was looking at them, and, in a way, thanks to the large contingent of media people, they were correct.

The ceremony began with a prayer, by Chaplain Shea.

Let us pray. Good and gracious God, we are here today before this solemn memorial to recognize three soldiers for their heroism. This is hollowed ground, a sacred wall, a wall that heals us and reminds us of the heroism and self-less service of those whose honored names are etched upon it, and those we honor who stand before it today.

We are humbled, gracious God, by the deeds of all these quiet heroes. Their lives and actions are the embodiment of our American hymn, *Who More Than Self Their Country Loved.* Their very lives proclaim the values we hold stronger than any philosophy espoused or creed confessed. Their personal heroism reflects all that we value dearly, all that we cherish, all that we hold to be good and right and just. We stand in awe of their heroism, and we have taken too long to recognize them. Remembering a dark point in time, we are now a richer nation as their personal heroic service is woven into the fabric of our history.

As You bless this ceremony with Your grace and presence, smile again on all the great heroes of our nation. May the legacy of their heroic actions be legends retold and models lived for generations to come. May they and their families experience our gratitude for their noble service to You and our nation.

In Your name, we pray. Amen.

After the invocation, Maj. Gen. Ackerman addressed the crowd and presented the awards. He used the occasion not only to praise the war heroes but also to speak about the core values which the U.S. Army promotes and tries to build in its soldiers.

We are here this afternoon to recognize the heroic actions of three former soldiers and also to recognize the importance of values – values that were clearly demonstrated by these great Americans nearly thirty years ago.

It is appropriate that this ceremony be conducted here at the Vietnam Memorial, a place that serves to heal as well as remind us of sacrifice....

Values tested in battle provide the ultimate test. Values that are deeply embedded remain strong during the most difficult hours....

Quality people are at the heart of everything the Army does, working together, with shared core values and a com-

> mon heritage. It is the Army's enduring values – loyalty, duty, respect, selfless service, honor, integrity and personal courage – that have allowed the Army to meet new challenges and missions in an era of change. They are values that inspire a sense of purpose necessary to sustain soldiers in difficult times.
>
> These same values were displayed by Hugh Thompson, Lawrence Colburn and Glenn Andreotta on the 16th of March 1968 in a village called My Lai, Republic of Vietnam.
>
> It was at that time and at that place that one of the most shameful chapters in the Army's history was recorded. The details of the events of that day were thoroughly investigated, and from those recommendations the Army was able to look at itself and take corrective action to ensure My Lai would never happen again. And it has not happened again.
>
> The leadership of the Army recognizes the responsibility to ensure that institutional values continue to be nurtured, reinforced and preserved in the face of ongoing change. And this ceremony provides a forum to do that.
>
> Early in the morning on March 16, 1968, an example of how values held up in the most demanding situation took place. Mr. Hugh C. Thompson Jr., Mr. Lawrence Colburn and Mr. Glenn U. Andreotta exhibited great personal courage and ethical conduct at the Vietnamese village of My Lai....
>
> It is clear that the crew saved the lives of at least eleven Vietnamese and initiated the report which saved countless others by bringing about a cease-fire. In his book, *The My Lai Inquiry,* Lt. Gen. William Peers wrote, "If there was a hero of My Lai, he (Thompson) was it."
>
> It was the ability to "Do the right thing"– even at the risk of their personal safety – that guided these soldiers to do what they did.
>
> This afternoon, we will finally recognize these men for their heroic actions....
>
> This award...is a tribute to these great soldiers, men who have become a legend in their own time, and whose actions on the 16th of March 1968 have set the standard for all soldiers to follow....

Following his remarks, Ackerman ordered the reading of the

citations which accompanied the Soldier's Medals, then pinned the medals on the proud but humble veterans, first on Thompson, then on Colburn. All who were seated stood up, and the newly decorated war heroes received a round of applause from the admiring crowd.

Thompson went to the podium to thank his supporters and especially to offer a word of encouragement to his fellow Vietnam veterans.

In a strong but quivering voice, he first thanked the U.S. Army for seeing fit to present him with the award.

"I proudly and humbly accept it, not only for myself, but for all the men who served their country with honor on the battlefields of Southeast Asia. And I see many of those brave men in the audience today. Welcome home, fellows," he said.

Thompson also thanked Larry Colburn for his support while in Vietnam and back here in the States; his mother Wessie Thompson, "for all your love and nurturing all these years, and for laying the ethical and moral foundation that would serve me well all through my life;" his crew chief, the late Glenn Andreotta, "who was with us at My Lai and who later died for his country while in Vietnam;" and Andreotta's parents, "who gave up such a fine son and who today still feel the heartache for the loss of their son in war."

He also recognized professor David Egan and Lt. Col. Kevin Clement for having played special roles in his receiving the medal, Egan for his eight-year crusade to have the Army award the medal, and Clement for pushing the medal through slow-moving channels within the Pentagon.

"And finally I'd like to recognize all Vietnam veterans – those who are alive today all across America, and those whose names are on the wall, just off to my left. I thank all of you who served your country with honor. In a very real sense, this medal is for you.

"Again, to my fellow veterans, welcome home," Thompson concluded.

Colburn stepped up to the microphone, thanking his family for their love and support and Thompson for his courage and loyalty to his crew. He acknowledged the Andreotta family for their sacrifice.

"It is my solemn wish," Colburn stated, "that we all never forget the tragedy and brutality of war."

He downplayed the "hero" label for what he and the others did at My Lai, saying that their rescue operation was only a matter of three soldiers doing their duty.

"I'd like to quote Gen. Douglas MacArthur regarding this: 'The soldier, be he friend or foe, is charged with the protection of the weak and unarmed. It is the very essence and reason for his being.'"

Following Colburn's remarks, the ceremony ended with the Army Band playing the official song of the U.S. Army, after which he and Thompson were greeted warmly and congratulated by approximately one hundred and fifty people of the hundreds in attendance.

Once they had shaken hands and/or hugged all the well-wishers, Thompson and Colburn, surrounded by a pack of cameramen and reporters, proceeded to the wall which bore the name of their fallen comrade. There they traced the etching of his name onto a piece of paper, intending to give it to his mother, possibly at the same time that she would receive his Soldier's Medal.

As the war heroes traced Andreotta's name, the cameramen pressed forward to get a clearer picture of what they were doing. Thompson was so crowded that he could hardly move. He felt trapped. He panicked.

"I gotta get out of here," he said with anxiety in his voice. The government bodyguards assigned to him and Colburn moved in instantly, took them by the arm and quickly escorted them through the crowd and to the cars that were waiting for them.

Thompson, Colburn and their entourage headed back to the hotel. With all the attention and adulation, both men were somewhat dazed, a little numb, considering the emotional energy they had expended. Thompson opened a crack in his window and lit a cigarette as his tired body sunk into the upholstery of the back seat. He looked out of the window with a vacant stare as the Washington landmarks zipped by. He was chatting with his friend, Mona Gossen, when he started to feel hungry, then realized that he had forgotten to eat lunch before the ceremony. It was a little after four.

Heroes at the Vietnam Wall

Prior to the Soldier's Medal ceremony on March 6, 1998, Larry Colburn (left) and Hugh Thompson visited the Vietnam Wall and located the etching of the name of their fallen comrade, Glenn Andreotta (inset), on panel 48-E. Andreotta was the crew chief on the helicopter piloted by Thompson when they rescued unarmed Vietnamese civilians during the My Lai massacre, on March 16, 1968. Andreotta was killed in action about three weeks later. He was 20 years old.

Glenn U. Andreotta

Glenn Andreotta of St. Louis, Missouri, was typical of the tens of thousands of young American men, in their late teens or early twenties, who went to war in Vietnam with their whole lives ahead of them but died in combat on the battlefields of Southeast Asia. **Right:** *Andreotta in the fall of 1966, prior to his first tour of duty in Vietnam.* **Below:** *Visiting his mother in St. Louis, in November 1967, after his first tour of duty.*

Glenn Andreotta with his dog in the winter of 1960.

Andreotta (right) with an Army buddy in Vietnam in the fall of 1966, during his first tour of duty.

Hugh Thompson

Hugh C. Thompson Jr. was a career man in the U.S. Armed Forces, serving first in the Navy then in the Army. He is credited with putting a stop to the My Lai massacre and saving the lives of unarmed Vietnamese civilians. **Clockwise, starting with photo at right:** *In his early years in the Army, circa 1966. With his parents, Wessie and Hugh Sr. while stationed in Hawaii, 1980. Off duty at U.S. military base at Chu Lai, Vietnam, in February 1968. On board his scout helicopter prepared for a mission over the Vietnam jungles in March 1968, just a few days prior to the My Lai massacre. While Hugh Jr. is in Vietnam in March 1968, his children, Brian (foreground) and Bucky, prepare for a ride on the back of Hugh Sr., as Palma, Hugh Jr.'s wife, helps steady the riders. Hugh Jr. as a youngster in Stone Mountain, Georgia, circa 1950.*

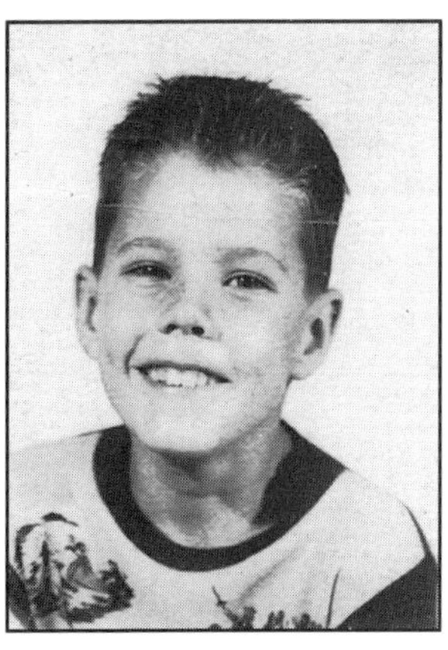

Larry Colburn

Larry Colburn was one of the three-man crew who intervened in the My Lai massacre in an attempt to stop the killing of defenseless Vietnamese civilians. After his tour of duty in Vietnam, he returned home to the Pacific Northwest, where he worked for a number of years before moving to the South and getting married. **Clockwise, beginning with photo at top right:** *Colburn, the salmon fisherman, off the Alaskan coast; the outdoorsman, in the mountains of Oregon; the grammar grades pupil, in Mt. Vernon, Washington.*

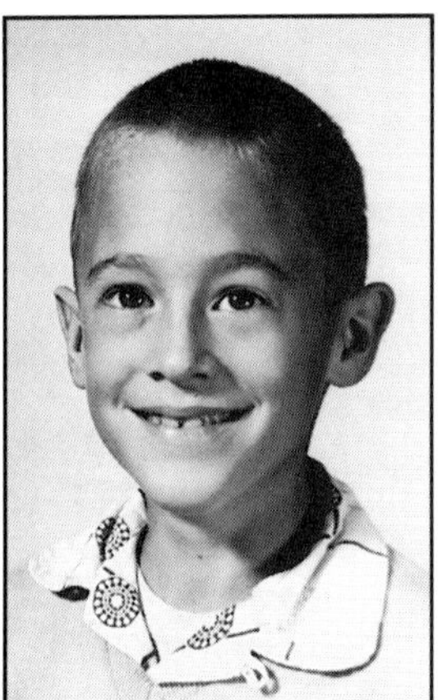

Soldier's Medal Ceremony

Larry Colburn (left) and Hugh Thompson (third from left) stand by anxiously as the Soldier's Medal ceremony is about to begin at the Vietnam Veterans Memorial in Washington, D.C. Between Colburn and Thompson is Maj. Gen. Michael Ackerman, who gave the keynote address. To Thompson's left is Maj. Gen. Donald Shea, the Army chaplain who delivered the invocation.

Thompson (left) and Colburn (center) are greeted by an old war buddy, Dale Mott, prior to the Soldier's Medal ceremony. Mott was one of the soldiers on board the Huey gunship that provided cover for Thompson and his crew when they rescued nine civilians from a bunker during the My Lai massacre.

Baltimore Sun photo by Chiaki Kawajiri

Hugh Thompson (left) and Larry Colburn give one another a hug after receiving the Soldier's Medal, as Maj. Gen. Michael Ackerman applauds.

When the group arrived at the hotel they headed for the bar on the mezzanine floor to have a few drinks, talk about the events of the day, and watch the big-screen TV to see what may show up in the news.

They didn't have to wait long, as CNN presented a segment which mixed footage of the day's awards ceremony with file footage and still photos of the Vietnam War in general and the My Lai massacre in particular. Midway through the segment, as CNN was showing close-up pictures of the victims of the massacre, Thompson turned his head from the television screen, spun around quickly and headed out of the bar, saying, "I don't need to see this..., I need to get something in my room." This was not the first time, nor would it be the last, that he would turn away from a picture of the carnage or divert conversation from the details of the terrible things that happened to the people of My Lai.

Later that evening Thompson and Colburn were guests of honor at a reception at Fort Belvoir's Officers Club. The event was emceed by David Egan, the crusader who wouldn't let Pentagon personnel rest until they agreed to give Thompson the recognition he deserved.

Egan introduced more than a dozen people in the room, one of whom was bearing a special gift from a former President of the United States. Brig. Gen. T.C. Mataxis, U.S. Army (Retired), a long-time supporter of Thompson's and an advisor on military affairs to U.S. Senator Lauch Faircloth of North Carolina, made his way to the podium, removed a letter from his coat pocket, and began reading.

> Hugh:
>
> ...You rightly take your place at history's table of glory, for you defended the cause of liberty with selflessness and resolve. The Soldier's Medal you receive today reminds us all that we owe a debt of gratitude to all the members of our Armed Forces, past and present, who have taken up the torch of freedom and answered their country's call to duty. We remember you with thankfulness and pride.
>
> My respects and best wishes,
>
> – *George Bush*

Thompson blushed. Surprised by the letter, he didn't know what to say. He folded his arms and stared at the floor as the audience rose to their feet in applause, signaling their wholehearted agreement with the former President's message.

Chapter 4

Growing Up In Stone Mountain, Georgia

THE MORNING AFTER THE LENGTHY CELEBRATION at Fort Belvoir, Thompson sat down at his hotel with reporters who wanted to know all about him: where was he from, where did he get that Southern accent, where did he get the moral courage to intervene at My Lai, what were his parents like?

Viewing his upbringing as very routine and unremarkable, and being a person who is not given much to idle chatter, when Thompson was asked to tell all about his childhood and adolescence, he responded, "I had a normal life," as though that pretty well summed it up. He was ready to move on to the next question.

Nicknamed "Buck," Hugh Clowers Thompson Jr. was born in Atlanta, Georgia, on April 15, 1943 and moved to nearby Stone Mountain (population 2,000) with his family when he was three years old. His father, Hugh C. Thompson Sr., spent four years in the service (Army and Navy) in World War II and thirty years or more in the Navy reserves; he died at age seventy-eight in 1987. His mother, Wessie Thompson, was a housewife who worked outside of the home very little when her children were growing up; she would turn ninety years old in December of 1998. Buck's one sibling, a brother named Tommie, was five years his senior; he spent twenty-two years in the Air Force, including two tours of duty in Southeast Asia.

Asked by reporters what valuable lessons he learned from his parents, the newly decorated war hero smiled slightly as his blue eyes darted left, then right, then left again.

"Do your chores. Don't lie. And don't run if you're about to get a whipping," he responded.

"Dad was real strict. If you didn't do what you were supposed to you got spanked, bare butt, nowhere to hide a book! But I got him figured out early on: Once he started giving you a whipping, start crying, and he'd stop," Thompson related.

One day, young Hugh decided to test his dad's resolve.

"I decided to run from him one time. That was a mistake! I didn't think the plan through all the way: I forgot I had to come home sooner or later. When I did come home, he hadn't forgotten, so I got it," he recalled, with a mischievous look in his eye and a slight grin under his sandy-colored moustache.

One of the reporters then asked Thompson how life was after Vietnam. The grin disappeared.

"I've had my ups and downs. Just a normal life, I guess," he answered in a dry tone. The way he said it, one could have gotten the impression that he didn't want to get into the details of the story about a life that was anything but dull and uneventful.

"Do you dream about what happened in Vietnam even today?" a reporter asked.

"Yes, uh huh," he responded, looking off into space. "There's a lot of sorrow there.... I probably need to go have it checked out," he said, hinting that these dreams and this sorrow were, in reality, not the minor concerns that he seemed to be indicating but rather painful aspects of his life that could, perhaps, be made less painful with the assistance of a counselor.

In response to questions about his family life, Thompson said he was divorced and had two children by one wife and one by another. The eldest was named Hugh ("Bucky"), age 34; then Brian, 32; then Steven, 18.

One of the reporters asked if any of his children had chosen a military career, to follow in their dad's footsteps.

"Are you on drugs?" he snapped back, which was his way of responding in the negative, emphatically.

Friends and neighbors remember Buck as a feisty child, constantly active, always outgoing and sometimes getting in trouble with his teachers for being sarcastic and for trying to be a comedian in class.

His first girlfriend, Gayle Brownlee, remembers him as being romantic, even when they "went together" in grammar school. They were next door neighbors, their houses separated by a big pasture. Buck would trot across the field, in his tennis shoes and short pants, and stand by Gayle's bedroom window and sing to her, which was his way of calling her to come out and play. The song which won her heart started like this:

"Hey, hey, good lookin', what ya got cookin', how about cookin' something up with me."

The romance lasted three or four years but faded with the passage of time as the young couple became interested in other mates.

Around the Thompson house, which was situated on forty-eight acres in the country, everyone worked. The boys' chores included feeding the cows and horses, weeding the vegetable garden, gathering eggs from the hen house, bringing in coal for the heaters and mowing the huge lawn. Buck remembers cutting seven acres with a push mower; he could get the job done in six hours if he ran with the mower.

The house was heated with coal-burning furnaces, and each bedroom had one. The one in the kitchen was the first to be lighted every winter morning; the boys would get dressed quickly in their bedroom then run into the kitchen to warm up.

They were taught to be polite at the table during meals, to say "Yes, sir" and "Yes, ma'am" when addressing adults, and to stand up for the "underdog." Buck's mom, Wessie, recalls her son "always taking up for the little guy" who was being picked on by bigger boys. She remembers receiving a report that Buck scolded a group of boys who were making fun of a physically handicapped child at school.

Buck's father was the same way. He could not stand to see anyone bullied by a bigger or stronger person. And he had a special place in his heart for the Native American Indians of Georgia, partly because of his own Indian lineage. His ancestors on his father's side were one hundred percent Cherokee; they had been forced off their land in North Carolina by the U.S. Government in the mid-1800s and had resettled on a farm in Georgia.

Once, in the 1950s, Hugh Sr. stood up for the Indians who were being discriminated against in an archery tournament in the Atlanta area. The officials were attempting to segregate the Indians from the other contestants, until Hugh Sr. protested. A champion archer himself, he argued successfully that all contestants should be divided only by their level of skill with a bow and arrow, and not according to the color of their skin.

Hugh Sr. was a Scout Master, so when the boys came of age they naturally became Cub Scouts and then Boy Scouts. They learned about pitching a tent and camping out, how to make a campfire, how to safely handle a knife and a hatchet, and a little about cooking over an open fire. They also learned the Boy Scout Law, that a scout should be "trustworthy, loyal, helpful, friendly, courteous, kind, obedient, cheerful, thrifty, brave, clean and reverent."

The Thompson family were regular church-goers, attending services every Sunday, religiously, first as Baptists, then as Episcopalians. The boys served as acolytes in the Episcopal Church. All three males in the Thompson clan helped to build St. Michael and All Angels Episcopal Church in Stone Mountain. Hugh Sr., a seasoned electrician, did the electrical work, while Buck and Tommie served as carpenters' helpers.

The boys were taught to take their religion seriously, particularly the Ten Commandments. They were also impressed with the importance of the Two Great Commandments, to love God above all things and to love their neighbor as themselves. Likewise, they were regularly admonished to tell the truth, always, and they faced dire consequences for deviation from this rule. In the Thompson house, the Eleventh Commandment was "Thou shalt not lie," a rule which the man of the house enforced with a belt. To him, being truthful was the very foundation of integrity;

he felt he owed it to his children to teach them this pivotal virtue.

Another virtue which Hugh Sr. tried to teach his boys was kindness toward their fellowman. A poor, black family who lived in a little house on the Thompson property had no car and no way to get to church on Sundays, so Hugh Sr. would provide transportation. He and the boys would pick them up, bring them to the Baptist church and come back ninety minutes later. Sometimes they would return early, while services were still underway. Buck would listen to some of the tunes they were singing and after a while grew fond of the music. He learned a few of the old Negro spirituals as he waited outside the church. He hummed along at first and later was singing full voice as he sat on the hood of his dad's car. One of his favorite verses, which reflected the singer's belief in an afterlife, was, "Swing low, sweet chariot, comin' for to carry me home." Another, which expressed a firm determination to overcome obstacles, was, "Ain't gonna let nobody turn me 'round, turn me 'round, turn me 'round. Ain't' gonna let nobody turn me 'round."

Though Buck's mother worked as a telephone operator in the evenings for a number of years, she was primarily a stay-at-home mom who was almost always home when her boys got off the bus, right in front of their house, in the afternoons. Her boys were usually accompanied by some of the neighborhood children, who followed them into the house and made themselves comfortable in the den. They never turned down an offer of cake, pie or cupcakes. Another attraction of the Thompson property was that there was always an after-school football or baseball game going on in the open space between the barn and the house. Oftentimes one or more of the boys would end up staying for supper.

Wessie was like a second mom to some of the boys and girls. They sought her advice and counsel on all manner of weighty questions which their own parents didn't have the time to discuss with them or which they simply refused to address. Most notable was the cluster of topics involving love, dating, marriage, and babies.

She also discussed these things with Buck and Tommie. She let it be known that they could always come to her with any problem or question they might have.

But as open-minded and approachable as she seemed to be, Wessie was strict with her boys when they began to have dates with girls. She would impose curfews when they went out, and she watched them closely when they brought dates home. She didn't want them doing anything she wasn't allowed to do when she was in her formative years.

Feeling his parents were watching him too closely, young Hugh once rebelled and told them that they were "the meanest, strictest people in Stone Mountain." Hugh Sr. took exception to that characterization.

"You don't know what strict is, boy. You should have known your Grandma Elmore (Wessie's mother)," he said, proceeding to tell Hugh Jr. how hard he had it.

"When I was dating your mother, Grandma Elmore would come looking for us if we were even ten minutes late coming back from the show. She'd track us down at the soda shop and walk back home with us, to be sure we didn't do anything she didn't approve of."

Buck's first paying job was plowing and tilling his neighbors' corn fields and vegetable gardens, with a tractor. His father showed him how. Beginning this work at age twelve or thirteen, he would earn $4 to $5 per hour. Later, in high school, he worked for the town's funeral home as a means of earning money. This job involved assisting in the embalming process and helping to move accident victims into the ambulance to be transported to the local clinic. Speeding down the highway in a slick, black Cadillac ambulance with red lights flashing and sirens blaring was rather exciting to this country boy who was now in his mid-teens. He was part of a life-or-death operation, a medical rescue mission, and it made him feel important.

The enterprising teenager used the money he earned to treat his dates to the movies (admission: sixteen cents) and to buy a motorbike, which was the rage in Stone Mountain and much of the South at the time.

His parents had reservations about the safety of motorbikes, but they agreed to allow him to have one, provided he paid for it with his own money. Then one day, as his parents had feared, he and his week-old Simplex got into a wreck with a truck. The story goes that his brakes were squeaking so he oiled them and some of the oil seeped onto the brake lining, causing his brakes to fail when he tried to stop at an intersection. His bike was subsequently struck by a pickup truck. Buck ended up on the hood of the vehicle, and his prized new motorbike was smashed beyond repair. An ambulance came for him and brought him to a hospital in Atlanta. His motorbike was dragged to the side of the road by his best friend and fellow 'bike rider, Don Carter. Buck sustained a head injury that left him unable to see out of his right eye for two to three months.

He bought another two-wheel vehicle, this time a small BMW motorcycle, and he and Don continued to cruise the rural dirt roads and paved streets in and around Stone Mountain.

Among their favorite destinations was a short-order drive-in cafe called Jack's. It served hamburgers, hot dogs, malts, soft drinks and the like. They would sometimes stop for an after-school snack, but more often than not they would just drive around the place, to see who was there, especially "the chicks," as they referred to the girls. They were like a couple of homing pigeons, and Jack's was like home. Their day just wasn't complete until they drove around Jack's after school, to see and to be seen. It was a teenager's ritual, performed frequently by practically every high school student in town.

When Buck turned sixteen, he got his license to drive a car and was allowed to use the family vehicle for dates from time to time, provided he was careful and courteous in his driving. He never wrecked the car, though the same cannot be said for his friend, Don.

One Sunday night, the two were rushing to church to meet a couple of girls – or so they claimed – when they got into a wreck. Don was driving his family's car. A car was stopped in the middle of the road with its lights out. When Don spotted the car, he pulled the steering wheel hard but was unable to avoid hitting the stalled vehicle. No one was seriously injured, but both cars would have to be towed. In the excitement, Buck lost the cigarette he was smoking. It was bad enough that they had gotten into a wreck, but if Don's dad found evidence that the boys had been smoking, and word got back to Buck's dad, there would be big trouble. They searched frantically for the cigarette, but were unable to locate it. They concluded that Buck had swallowed it, which was bad in one way but good in another. Had Buck's dad found out he was smoking, he would have been punished, possibly whipped, even at the age of sixteen. Moreover, his football coach would have made him run laps around the practice field until he dropped.

Buck and Don were on the Stone Mountain High School football team. Don was a lineman and Buck was a receiver. They participated throughout high school, playing both offense and defense. There were only sixteen or eighteen boys on the team. Buck became a hero one Friday night when he caught a pass for a touchdown that won the game in the last minute, giving his team its first winning season in many years.

As his brother Tommie had done on his seventeenth birthday, Buck took a ride with his father and signed up with the Navy reserves when he turned seventeen. There was no doubt in the boys' minds that they would spend time in the service of their country, as their dad had done and was continuing to do in the Navy reserves. It seemed only natural to them that they would imitate their father in this regard.

In addition to cruising around Jack's Drive-In, attending the monthly "sock hop" at the local high school gymnasium was a must for practically every adolescent in town. The boys and girls danced to the tunes of Elvis Presley, Chuck Berry, Chubby Checker and The Drifters. Some of the youngsters were so taken with the ambiance of the event that they thought they were in love with their dance partners.

Such was the case with Buck Thompson and Dolores Moore. He was a senior and she was a sophomore. They wanted to get married. Getting married shortly after graduation from high school, and even before, was not uncommon in the Southern

United States in the 1950s and part of the '60s. The girl's parents didn't seem to object, but the Thompsons had a fit when their boy told them of his intentions. They wanted him to go to college for at least two years before he tied himself down with the commitments and responsibilities of marriage. But Buck was in love, or so he felt, and the more his parents resisted his inclination the more determined he became to go through with it.

Then one afternoon, just after his eighteenth birthday, Buck told his mom he wouldn't be coming home that night, that he'd be sleeping at Don's house. Wessie was suspicious; something told her he might elope. She was correct.

Buck and Dolores sneaked away to nearby Ringgold, Georgia, to get a marriage license. When they returned to Stone Mountain, they were legally married. They wanted to live at the Thompson's house, but Wessie had made it clear to Buck beforehand that if he were to run away and get married then he could just come and gather up his clothes, because his days of living at home would be over. After all, she once said, if he were man enough to get married, then he could certainly find his own place to live.

The newlyweds stayed with the bride's parents for a month or so, until Buck graduated, on June 5, 1961. In a matter of a few days, he left Stone Mountain and headed to Atlanta Naval Air Station, where he began a three-year stint of active duty in the Navy. Shortly thereafter, Buck began to realize that getting married had been a mistake. Dolores realized it, as well, and the marriage was annulled within a few months of its inception.

Buck's time in the Navy would be spent in the Seabees, in the construction battalion. His specialty was listed as "heavy equipment operator," though he spent much of his time taxiing Navy officers to and fro. He spent many of his off-duty hours courting a pretty blonde-haired woman named Palma Baughman, and they were married in 1963.

When he completed his time in the Navy, in the summer of 1964, he returned to Stone Mountain and went to work as a funeral director at the local mortuary. He took courses in mortuary science and soon became a licensed funeral director.

But this field did not hold the satisfaction and excitement that the now-maturing Hugh Thompson Jr. wanted in life, so his mind was constantly wandering to other lines of work. After a year with the funeral home, he resigned to join the U.S. Army, signing up for the Warrant Officer Flight Program. The Army needed helicopter pilots to help fight the war in Vietnam, and the prospect of being part of that effort was attractive to him.

Chapter 5

Mission To My Lai

LESS THAN A WEEK AFTER RECEIVING THE Soldier's Medal in Washington, D.C., Thompson and Colburn were on a plane headed for Vietnam. They were to participate as honored guests in the Thirtieth Anniversary ceremony commemorating the victims of the infamous My Lai massacre. They were looking forward to being reunited with some of the people whose lives they had saved.

Arriving at the airport in Ho Chi Minh City (formerly known as Saigon) shortly after noon on Thursday March 12, Thompson, Colburn and a buddy of Colburn's were met by CBS News producer Tom Anderson, who was there to direct a camera crew for a special segment of the TV magazine show "60 Minutes."

Within minutes of the time they got off the plane, Thompson and Colburn were surrounded by reporters and photographers who wanted to get comments and pictures of the men who had risked their lives to save Vietnamese civilians in an earlier generation. The media people followed the war heroes to the baggage claim area, through the crowd that was clogging the entrance area, and to their taxi cabs, asking questions, taking pictures and jockeying for position all the while.

If the airport was crowded, so was the downtown area that they saw as they rode to their hotel. There were people everywhere. The traffic was heavy, quick moving and seemingly chaotic, a hodgepodge of overloaded trucks, bicycles and carts of every description, Mercedes Benz cars, Federal Express vans, compact cars, taxi cabs by the dozens and motorbikes by the thousands. Motorbikes are now an affordable and very popular means of transportation throughout Vietnam's metropolitan areas, a quantum leap forward in mobility for hundreds of thousands of people who were formerly on foot or on bicycles. The American visitors noticed that many of the motorbikes were carrying from one to three passengers at a time, including toddlers, teenagers and old folks. Many of the drivers wore handkerchiefs or bandannas over their noses and mouths, to filter out the fumes and smog, as they maneuvered through the streets of this sprawling Asian metropolis.

After checking into the hotel, the Omni Saigon, the two Americans had their bags brought to their rooms, freshened up a bit and headed downstairs to the lobby to relax over a cold beer or two. Thompson went into the bar that was adjacent to the lobby to buy a second round, and when he did the barmaid recognized him from his picture in a local newspaper. She viewed him as a celebrity, a famous man, and asked him to autograph her paper. He gladly obliged, and stayed to talk for a few minutes. Colburn came looking for him, wondering what had happened to the beer he was waiting on.

They returned to the lobby to wait for other members of their entourage to arrive. Soon they were joined by two newspaper reporters from the States, one from *The Times-Picayune* of New Orleans and another from *The Atlanta Journal-Constitution*, as well as a woman from a German television station.

As they sat and talked they were being observed by a desk clerk who, like the barmaid, had recognized Thompson from his picture in the newspaper. She and another young woman were giggling as they looked at the newspaper and then at Thompson and then at the paper again.

They were saying something about "Mister Thompson" in Vietnamese. They seemed shy, as though they would not have the nerve to approach Mr. Thompson and speak with him. Seeing this, one of the Americans in the group walked over to them and asked if they would like to meet Mr. Thompson. One agreed to do so while the other declined, blushing as she did.

"Hello, Mr. Thompson. I am very happy to meet you," the young woman said, speaking in English and bowing to show her respect.

"Well, hello, I am happy to meet you, too," he responded in a kind tone of voice as he reached out, shook her hand and bowed to her.

"It is an honor to meet an American war hero. And..." She stopped in mid-sentence as she choked up with emotion. "And, and you are a hero to my people, too."

Thompson, too, choked up for a few moments and hesitated before he spoke again. He had never looked at things the way this woman had just described them. He had never thought of himself as a hero to the Vietnamese people.

"Oh, no ma'am. Don't think of me as a hero, but as a friend of the people of Vietnam," he said.

"Oh, no, you are a hero to my people, Mr. Thompson."

"Well, thank you anyway, but I'm no hero. I was your friend that day and I'm still your friend."

"We are your friend, too," she responded.

"You see, to me, heroes are people who do something above and beyond the call of duty. We didn't do anything besides our duty that day – nothing that the average American soldier wouldn't have done. I'm just an average guy, no better than anyone else who fought honorably in Vietnam, and worse than some."

The desk clerk didn't seem to share Thompson's viewpoint on that subject, though she continued to be polite and extremely respectful. She was awestruck. She seemed to be feeling that she was in the presence of a great man. It showed on her face.

After this pleasant exchange, the Americans all piled into a small chartered tour bus, which took them to lunch at a restaurant that had been recommended by one of the hotel staff. As they disembarked and walked toward the entrance of the restaurant they were approached by four beggars, three of whom were children and one frail, hunchbacked elderly woman dressed in rags. Some of the Americans gave them money, and they expressed their gratitude in their native tongue.

The group had a few more stops to make that afternoon, the first of which was the Rex Hotel, a famous wartime landmark. The tour bus made its way through the heavy traffic, through the thousands of motorbikes that streamed through the arteries of the city. When they arrived at the Rex, they were again approached by beggars, as well as street vendors hawking sunglasses, cigarette lighters, jewelry and newspapers, published in Vietnamese, English and Chinese.

The Americans went into the Rex and then to its open air bar for a beer and a bull session. It was in a building next door to the Rex during the Vietnam War that U.S. Army information officers would give press briefings about the day's activities on the battlefield, the so-called "body count" of men and women killed on both sides, and how the war was going in general. These briefings came to be known as "The Five O'Clock Follies" because the positive information was almost always exaggerated and embellished and therefore not very useful to journalists who were trying to do a credible job of reporting on the war. When the briefings were completed some of the military people and war correspondents would walk next door to the bar at the Rex and the dialogue would soon degenerate into beer-drinking, tough-talking bull sessions that frequently went on for hours.

So, in the spirit of "The Five O'Clock Follies," Thompson and Colburn sat down at a table and had a beer or two with the reporters, then proceeded to tell a few war stories of their own. Whether these were true war stories, or just tall tales being made up as they went along, was not completely clear.

After leaving the Rex, the group headed for the War Remnants Museum, one of several war-related museums in Ho Chi Minh. They were responding to an invitation received by Thompson and Colburn prior to their arrival in the country.

On the grounds were old U.S. war planes, tanks and bombs, while inside were guns, maps and photographs depicting the trauma and devastation of war. Being brought face to face with so many reminders of war, Thompson and Colburn became noticeably uncomfortable and nervous. When the guide brought Thompson to the My Lai massacre display, which included a huge, nearly life-size photograph of dead women, children and old men lying on a dirt road, Thompson turned away and walked briskly to another part of the museum.

If Thompson was upset over the My Lai pictures, Colburn was equally disturbed over what he saw for sale in the museum's souvenir shop. Among several other items, he spotted a row of "dog tags" which ostensibly had been taken off the bodies of U.S. military men killed in the Vietnam War. If these tags were authentic – and he wasn't sure they were – he felt that offering them for sale was exploitive and disrespectful, so he bought them all in order to remove them from public display. He paid $4 each for the thirty-nine tags, which included names such as A.F. Stewart, #2022697USMC, Catholic; Bernard P. Schultz, #389466994, Lutheran; Donald L. Parker, #403441399, Baptist; John Crassel, #RA18361815, Catholic; Earl Johnson, #RA16777254, Baptist. Colburn planned to check the tags against the official list of U.S. soldiers missing in action and return them to the deceased servicemen's families if he could locate them.

The next morning early, the two war heroes and those traveling with them flew out of Ho Chi Minh City and landed in Da Nang, where they were met by a throng of reporters who, like the ones they encountered the day before, seemed excited to have these celebrities in their midst.

Thompson and Colburn made their way through the crowded airport terminal to a small chartered bus, which was to take them to Quang Ngai City, where they would stay in the Song Tra Hotel, just four or five miles from My Lai. Also on board the bus were a translator, the CBS News producer, and two teams of cameramen and sound technicians, who had flown in from Paris and Bangkok.

On board, too, was Mike Boehm of Madison, Wisconsin, and his Vietnamese partner, Phan Van Do of Quang Ngai, who were involved with several ongoing projects designed to improve the educational facilities and the financial condition of the people of My Lai. Among other things, these are the men who founded the Hanoi Peace Park and were to break ground for the My Lai Peace Park three days hence. Backed by a group of Madison area Quakers, Boehm also ran a small loan program which provided women in My Lai with the capital they needed to start and operate small businesses. He also initiated an art-exchange program between children of Madison and My Lai and had arranged for U.S. youngsters to make friendship bracelets for the Vietnamese kids. Another project the two were working on, and soliciting donations for, was the building of additional classroom space at My Lai so the children could attend class for a full day; as it was, some were going in the morning and the others in the afternoon, due to the limited capacity of the school buildings.

A few hours after arriving at their hotel in Quang Ngai, Thompson, Colburn and Anderson were to meet privately with a top local government official, Pham Hoài Hai, to firm up the itinerary for their stay in the area. But when they drove up to the building where they were to meet, the place was swarming with media people, from France, England, Germany, the United States, Canada, Vietnam and China, all of them wanting pictures of or statements from the men of the hour. One reporter had gotten word of the "private" meeting, and the news had spread like wildfire to the others.

Though the American guests and Pham Hoài were caught totally off guard and unprepared to have a news conference, they had one anyway, seeing how anxious the media people were to hear from them.

Speaking through a translator, Pham Hoài started off by welcoming his guests and spoke to them about their respective countries working together.

"We would like to forget the past and look forward to the future," he said. "We share a common point of view: that we'll never let anything like this (the massacre) happen again."

"Mr. Thompson and Mr. Colburn have made a valuable contribution by preventing more deaths, by managing to save several of our citizens. I hope the people here understand that it was not everyone who took part (in the massacre)," he added.

Colburn thanked Pham Hoài and said that he and Thompson were honored to be back in Vietnam.

"My only wish now is that the whole world will never forget the tragedy of all war. And I pray that diplomacy will prevent any such thing in the future," Colburn stated. "I am also very honored that we can take part in the Peace Park dedication, and I hope this park sends a very powerful message to the world about peace and reconciliation."

One of the reporters asked Thompson how it felt to be back in Vietnam.

"I feel welcome here. It helps me to be here," he answered.

Another asked him if it was true that he would be meeting some of the women he rescued thirty years earlier.

"Yes, we will, and I can tell you I will rejoice to meet some of the people who were there. I just wish we could have done more that day," he said.

The morning after the news conference the Americans boarded the little charter bus and headed for the grammar school in My Lai, four or five miles away. There Thompson and Colburn toured the overcrowded classrooms, visited with the children, and viewed drawings and paintings which children in Madison, Wisconsin, had sent to the pupils in My Lai.

The Vietnamese youngsters were warm and affectionate toward the war heroes; they had been advised of the kindnesses which these two men had shown to their people during the war.

Thompson and Colburn got along well with the children, posing for pictures with them, playing with them, speaking with them through a translator. Thompson was all smiles until one of the boys asked him, in English:

"Why your police kill my people?"

The question surprised him. He wasn't sure how to answer it because he had never quite figured it out himself. Looking at the little boy, he responded:

"It's a question that can never be answered. They just went crazy that day," he said as he began to choke up with emotion.

The boy's question jogged Thompson's memory, sending his

thoughts back to the day when U.S. ground troops went berserk and slaughtered not only unarmed adults but also innocent children who looked very much like the little boy who was standing there in front of him.

As Thompson and Colburn left the schoolyard, dozens of children followed them to the bus, some of them hanging on to the belts and arms of their kind, new friends from America. They didn't want them to leave.

The children were still crowded around the bus, waving, laughing and clowning around, as it pulled away slowly and headed down the road. Some of the men on the bus were behaving like the children.

A few minutes after leaving the school, the bus pulled off the road and parked in the dry grass next to a rice paddy, where farmers were harvesting their crop in very much the same way as it has been done for centuries. The CBS News crew walked fifty or sixty yards out into the field to set up their equipment. They began filming Thompson and Colburn as they came into the field, past a handful of farmers who were cutting and gathering the crop. Meanwhile, a dozen other photographers and videographers had gathered by the bus and were taking pictures from the road.

Thompson was pointing to an area where the My Lai villagers' huts and houses stood prior to the time they were destroyed by American troops thirty years prior. Painful memories were mounting as the two veterans talked and gestured and recalled the events of that day. Thompson then looked down at the ground and covered his face with one of his hands. Colburn put his arm around his friend's shoulders, then the two of them hugged and patted one another on the back.

Physically and emotionally fatigued, Thompson and Colburn dragged into the hotel late in the afternoon, hoping to lay down and rest for a while. Instead, they were met by a handful of journalists who were waiting for them and wanting an interview. So they sat for two hours and talked with reporters for French and British news agencies and other print media.

During the course of the interview, television journalist Mike

Wallace of CBS News arrived at the hotel, having left the United States two days later than the others. Wallace, who had spent some time in Vietnam as a war corespondent three decades earlier, had a special affinity for this story of wartime heroism. Even at age seventy-nine, he had traveled halfway around the world to witness the heartwarming events that were soon to unfold.

Sunday March 15 was to be a very emotional and memorable day for Thompson, Colburn and the news crew who accompanied them. Not only did the two war heroes have a pre-arranged meeting with two of the women whose lives they had saved but also they had an impromptu meeting and conversation with another survivor of the massacre that left everyone in tears – Thompson, Colburn, the survivor, her interpreter, the producer, the interviewer, the TV soundmen and even the cameramen, who viewed the scene through teary eyes.

The first meeting took place early in the morning, as Thompson and Colburn were reunited with Pham Thi Nhung, age 76, and Pham Thi Nhanh, age 36, and her two young daughters.

Thompson was the first to greet the two women, then he introduced them to Colburn. It was a joyful though slightly awkward moment for all involved, as Colburn wanted to hug the women while they, inhibited by custom, only seemed to want to shake hands. So, they shook hands, then Colburn hugged them anyway. He seemed to take a particular liking to the older woman.

The four adults sat down at a table outside the home of the younger woman, and they talked about their families as they sipped tea and ate fruit. Colburn sat by the older woman and held her hand for much of the time they were there. Nhanh's younger daughter hung on to her mother's arm as the child studied the men at the table.

Mike Wallace sat with them and, after the exchange of greetings and other pleasantries, got down to the business of interviewing his subjects and promoting dialogue among them.

"We sincerely thank you for what you did for my family," Nhanh said to the two heroes, speaking through an interpreter. "Today our family is so proud to welcome you here. And today is also just a very sad day for our family because my father died because of the American soldiers who killed him on that day thirty years ago."

"This man right here was the commander of the aircraft that rescued you," Wallace said, pointing to Thompson.

"Thank you for your help. You know, nine people survived because of what you did," said Nhanh. "We are alive now because of you. Thirty years has passed, and now we see face to face the person who rescued us and helped us on that day."

The older woman, Nhung, recalled that the ominous sounds of war permeated the village and the surrounding countryside for a prolonged period that fateful day. She remembered that she had eaten breakfast and was headed for a nearby hamlet to go shopping when American troops came in and started "arresting" the villagers. Her husband and child were among those arrested and later executed, she said.

Nhanh, the younger woman, told Thompson that she had been wanting to thank him for many years.

"I was quite young at the time of the incident, and I didn't think about it a lot after that. But when I grew up, and particularly after I was twenty years old, I thought, 'I have to thank the person who helped me and who rescued me on that day....' I often tell that story to my children."

Then she brought up an aspect of Thompson's rescue that has haunted him since the day it happened:

"If you had been there earlier, you would have rescued more people, not only the ones in my shelter."

Thompson swallowed hard and responded:

"I've thought about that often, and I wish we could have done more."

After the reunion between the two heroes and the two women whom they rescued from a sure death, Thompson,

Colburn and the news crew stopped at the My Lai Memorial to continue with the filming and interviewing. Wallace was interviewing Thompson when he got word that a third survivor of the massacre was there, standing by, and wanting to meet the American soldiers who helped her people that day.

Her name was Pham Thi Thuan, a woman in her early sixties. She was with her mother and eldest daughter when they were machine-gunned to death on the bank of an irrigation ditch. Thuan wasn't struck by bullets but was knocked into the ditch by the body of someone who was. She was covered by the bodies of her family members and several of her neighbors who were shot and killed. She managed to survive by remaining still so the soldiers would think she was dead.

Accompanied by an interpreter – a young Vietnamese woman who worked as a guide at the memorial – Thuan walked up to Thompson and Colburn, said hello and thanked them for what they had done.

"She wants to meet Mr. Thompson, a good man," the interpreter told Wallace.

"Very, very glad to meet you," Thuan, the survivor, said to Thompson.

"Hello, ma'am. It's nice to meet you," Thompson said, his voice beginning to crack as he took her small hand in his and patted it with his other hand. "I'm sorry we couldn't help you that day."

"Thank you very much," she said.

Then she posed two questions to him that brought tears to his eyes.

"Why were so many villagers killed that day?" and "Why were you so different than the rest of the Americans?"

"I saved the people because I wasn't taught to murder and kill. I can't answer for the people who took part in it. And I apologize for the ones who did. I just wish we could have helped more people that day," Thompson answered.

Then, through tear-filled eyes, the old lady and the young interpreter looked at Mr. Thompson with gratitude and admiration.

Just before the two Vietnamese women walked up to them, Thompson and Colburn were telling Wallace that one thing that would help to bring a sense of closure to the My Lai incident, and the Vietnam War, would be if the U.S. government would offer an official apology to the people of Vietnam for the massacre.

"I'm not a scholar, I'm not sure, but has the United States ever apologized? Or, are we too big to apologize? It happened. The United States knows it happened. It's embarrassing.... You can't go forward till you get it out of reverse," Thompson said to Wallace.

Thompson, of course, is the last person in the world who would have any reason to apologize, for without his decisive action the massacre would have claimed more lives than it did. His statement to the survivor, Thuan, i.e., that he apologized for those who took part in the killings, while an unofficial expression of apology, certainly represents the sentiments of many, many U.S. citizens and soldiers – if not the overwhelming majority – who were, and are, deeply sorry for what happened at My Lai in March of 1968.

On Sunday night the war heroes and the CBS crew had supper with local government official Pham Hoài Hai in Quang Ngai City Guest House. A fine Vietnamese meal was prepared, made up of several courses and of such a quantity that the men couldn't eat all that was placed before them. There was also beer and whiskey and several toasts, one of which was offered by CBS producer Tom Anderson.

"Thirty years ago these two men taught us all a lesson: that people are more important than politics. I cheer them for taking the stand that they did," Anderson said.

"Hear! Hear!" said several of the diners, and all at the table drank to the toast with enthusiasm.

As part of the hospitality, Pham Hoài sang two Vietnamese ballads for his American guests, and a young Vietnamese woman sang another. Then they asked the Americans to sing something from their culture. The hosts looked on with amusement as the

Americans sang in deep voices, "Swing Low, Sweet Chariot," followed by "Amazing Grace." For the latter song, everyone at the table held hands, and the Vietnamese hummed along as the melody went on and the men swayed from side to side.

A spirit of brotherhood and mutual respect filled the air throughout the evening, as the men learned more about one another's cultures.

As the sun came up over My Lai on the morning of March 16, 1998, Hugh Thompson was tossing and turning after a restless night. This was the exact date, thirty years earlier, when he and his crew witnessed the terrible sight that they would never forget.

He showered, shaved, got dressed and went downstairs to the little cafe in the motel and had scrambled eggs and french bread with Wallace and the TV crew. Then it was off to the My Lai Memorial for the Thirtieth Anniversary commemoration of the people who were killed in the massacre.

When the little bus arrived at 7:15 a.m. the road which runs by the memorial was clogged with Vietnamese people headed for the ceremony. Many of them were hoping to get a close look at the two heroes.

Thompson and Colburn were greeted formally, though warmly, by local and provincial government and business leaders before proceeding to the staging area for the day's event. As they did, photographers walked in front of them to get close-up shots of the men of the hour. Dozens of other photographers and reporters waited at the staging area, where eight hundred to a thousand Vietnamese people stood by for the beginning of the program. Mixed in with the Vietnamese people was a smaller number of citizens of the U.S., Canada and various European countries. A distinct mood of solemnity and reverence filled the air.

Behind the podium was a large concrete sculpture representing those who died and those who lost family members in the My Lai massacre. The most prominent feature of the monument is a tall statue of a woman holding a lifeless baby in one arm, with her other arm raised with a clenched fist of anger and protest, as though she were making a vow that the death of her baby would not go unavenged.

Toward the beginning of the ceremony uniformed Vietnamese soldiers carried wreaths of flowers forward and placed them at the foot of the sculpture, to commemorate the Vietnamese who died in the massacre. There were five or six wreaths brought forward, representing the people of five or six different villages.

The first speaker was Hoang Ngoc Tran, deputy chairman of the Quang Ngai Province People's Committee. He talked at length about the massacre, the injustice of it and about the future of Vietnam and the region. He thanked the Americans who risked their lives to put a stop to the killing.

At this point, Thompson and Colburn were introduced and asked to come forward. When they got to the podium the crowd pressed forward, wanting to get a better look at the men who were heroes not only to the American people but to the people of Vietnam, as well.

At Thompson's request, Colburn did most of the talking. He expressed sorrow over what had happened at My Lai three decades earlier and hope for peace and prosperity for the people of Vietnam.

"May we never forget the brutality of the crime," he said, pausing as a translator repeated his statement in Vietnamese. "If we can practice patience, understanding, cultural understanding, and love, I believe in my heart – and I pray to God – that we can achieve peace on earth."

Thompson stepped to the microphone and spoke very briefly. He said he appreciated the invitation to participate in the ceremony and regretted that he wasn't able to save more people's lives on that dark day in 1968.

He was visibly shaken, as the clock ticked up toward a few minutes to nine, the exact time thirty years before, to the day and to the minute, that he and his crew were spotting the bodies of dozens of Vietnamese civilians scattered about the land – a sight so foreign to anything he had ever seen that he literally couldn't believe his eyes.

As the ceremony ended, people lined up in front of the huge statue to pay their respects to the dead by lighting joss sticks and placing them in a vase on a stone marker which marked the place where some were killed in the massacre. (When lighted, joss sticks create a smoke that is believed by many in Southeast Asian cultures to be a medium through which the living can communicate with the spirits of their deceased ancestors.)

Meanwhile, a nervous Colburn and a highly stressed Hugh Thompson were making a beeline for one of the buildings on the grounds so Thompson could get away from the crowd, find some breathing room and try to compose himself.

Colburn had his arm around Thompson's shoulders as they walked up to and through the little building and onto the back gallery, where Thompson broke down and cried. Even the pursuing photographers lowered their cameras out of respect for Thompson's need for privacy.

I'm a nervous wreck. It was exactly thirty years ago – to the minute. Why did our soldiers do it? It wasn't necessary. What did it accomplish? It was meaningless. Did you see the faces of those beautiful children in the crowd? Those old people with the wrinkled skin, they were alive at the time of the massacre. These people are so small. That young woman they blew away wasn't a threat to anybody. Can we go home now? Larry, get me out of here.

"I gotta get out of here. Larry, we'd better go," Thompson said frantically. "Get me out of here."

"We're okay now, Buck," Larry kept telling him.

"Let's get out of here. Take me out of here," Thompson said again.

But they couldn't leave just yet. There was something else they had to do before leaving the little building.

Thompson presented a framed copy of his and Colburn's Soldier's Medal certificates to one of the local officials, to be hung in the My Lai Museum, a component of the My Lai Memorial. Hopefully, Thompson said, it will remind all who view it that not all Americans who were at My Lai that day were involved in war crimes.

Then Colburn presented the local official with a gold-plated, long-stem rose which he described as "an international symbol of love, a token of the love and appreciation which the people of the USA hold for the people of Vietnam." He asked that it be placed in the museum permanently.

When the brief presentations were completed, Colburn was feeling a strong urge to escort Thompson out of the crowd, but he couldn't get out of the little building. He and Thompson had literally been backed into a corner by TV, radio and newspaper people who had pressed forward and were asking questions loudly.

"Mr. Thompson, can you give us a statement? Mr. Thompson, how do you feel today about all of this?"

Thompson was in a state of high anxiety. His face was flush. He looked frightened.

Colburn stepped forward, toe to toe with the media people closest to Thompson, as though he were defending a wounded comrade in battle.

"How in the hell do you think he feels?" Colburn said forcefully. "He feels crowded, for one thing."

"Could we just have a few minutes to...," one of the reporters started to ask.

"No, you can't. Not now. We have to go somewhere," Colburn said as he took Thompson by the arm and muscled his way out of the corner, through the crowd, and out the back door.

They took a few minutes to catch their breath and try to compose themselves. Then they left the My Lai Memorial and began walking down the main road toward the site that would become the My Lai Peace Park. The half-mile walk was relaxing. The more Thompson walked the more relief he felt from the tension in his mind and in his back and neck.

Shortly after arriving at the site there was a brief ceremony, with some speakers representing the U.S. and others representing Vietnam. Mike Boehm, who was spearheading the project, said he hoped the park would be a permanent symbol of peace between Vietnam and the U.S., as they put the past behind them and look to the future in a spirit of cooperation. He said he envisioned the Peace Park as a tranquil place where people could go to relax, pray, and reflect on the beauty of peace and brotherhood.

After the speeches, Boehm, Thompson, Colburn and others took the next step in the development of the park: They planted and watered a small tree, and then another. They expressed hope that from now on the people of Vietnam would know only peace, good health and prosperity, and that they and their children, and their children's children, would never again know war.

Following the dedication of the Peace Park, Thompson, Colburn and the news crew boarded the bus and returned to their hotel in Quang Ngai. They packed their bags and checked out of the hotel and headed north on Hwy. 1 for Da Nang.

As it always is, the road was swarming with traffic, with bicycles, motorbikes, some cars and trucks, and carts and wagons of every sort being pulled by oxen or by people. Men, women and children walked on the shoulders of the road, carrying bulky loads that were larger than they were.

The driver of the bus would speed up, slow down, slam on the brakes, pull hard to the left to avoid hitting a pedestrian who wasn't watching where he was going. Some of the passengers on the bus were looking out of the windows at the sea of humanity through which they were passing. Other passengers, chatting over cold beer or bottled water, seemed oblivious to the world outside of the bus.

After three or four hours of weaving and braking, the bus rolled into Da Nang. The emotionally fatigued passengers disembarked to spend the night at the luxurious Furama Resort Hotel, with its marble floors, first class rooms and food, and a clear view of a sandy beach on the South China Sea. Thompson, Colburn and some of the news crew gathered in an open air lounge area next to a swimming pool and chatted over drinks and pretzels as night fell over the city.

The following morning Thompson was up early and walking

along the beach, thinking about the events of the previous three or four days. He was also remembering the time he was stationed in Da Nang, when the U.S. military base there was being bombarded by rocket fire coming in from a few miles out of the city. He recalled the search-and-destroy missions he had flown in an effort to protect the base, and how he nearly lost his life in the process. But that was then and this was thirty years later. It was a cool, sunshiny day on a sandy beach, and he had some time on his hands. No reason to rush, no bullets to dodge. It was good to be in Da Nang during peacetime.

By mid-morning the travelers were loading their belongings onto the little bus and heading for the local airport. The cameramen and sound technicians said good-bye at the airport and headed off for Paris and Bangkok, while Thompson, Colburn and Anderson were en route to Hong Kong, where they were to spend a final night on Asian soil. Wallace had left the day before to fly back to New York by way of Paris.

Thompson and Colburn were up and running again the next morning, boarding a United Airlines jet bound for America. They took their seats in the business class section, Thompson by the window and Colburn next to him. It felt good to be going home.

As the miles between the big jet and the shores of China increased, Thompson and Colburn settled down and began to unwind. The return to My Lai had been a hectic and somewhat trying experience.

"Well, what do you think, boss? Did we do okay?" Colburn asked Thompson after the plane had been airborne for an hour or so.

"Yep, I think we did fine," Thompson said, only half paying attention.

"It was so good to see all those little kids smiling again, not having to worry about being blown up, not having to be looking over their shoulders all the time, just being able to be kids," Colburn stated.

"Yep, sure was," a drowsy Thompson agreed.

"I think CBS shot some good stuff at the school and at the reunion," Colburn said, still trying to strike up a conversation.

"Yeah, those boys really knew what they were doing. Wallace was really into it. Anderson said it was turning out real well. He said it was some of the best footage ever shot for '60 Minutes.' They'll do a good job."

"I can't wait to see it. I hope they got a good shot of my new girlfricnd."

"Who?"

"My new girlfriend, the one I was sitting next to at the table at the reunion."

"Oh, yeah, she was sweet. Tiny little thing," Thompson observed.

"She was forty-six at the time of the massacre, so she'd be seventy-six now. Looks like she's had a real hard life, poor baby."

"Yeah, she was a sweet little thing. Couldn't have weighed eighty pounds."

"Did you notice we were holding hands for a lot of the interview?"

"No, I missed that."

"She was holding my hand and patting it as if to say, 'Thank you, thank you.'"

"Whoa! You'd better not let Lisa find out about that," Thompson said playfully, referring to Colburn's wife.

"I could feel her calluses. Tough, hard hands..." Colburn's voice faded. He could see that Thompson was about to fall asleep.

Colburn stayed with his thoughts of the woman's hands. They were coarse, bony, arthritic hands that had known hard work all her life. He remembered the big, strong hands of the men he helped capture for interrogation during the war, and the tender, little hands of the child he helped rescue at My Lai. Glenn Andreotta was handing the child to him, and the war was coming back to him real clearly. Here comes Lt. Calley and he's telling Thompson to get back in the chopper and mind his own business. Nearby all those Vietnamese people are lying in the dirt, killed, violated, blown to bits, some of them not dead yet. They are moaning, groaning in awful, awful pain, the voice of humanity crying out for mercy, begging for help. Colburn can hear their voices again.

Tears welled up in his eyes. He buried his face in the palms of his hands, bent over and began to cry. Thompson woke up.

"What's the matter, buddy?" Thompson asked, patting Colburn on the back.

Colburn continued to sob. He was unable to speak.

"It's okay, it's okay. I have an idea what you're going through," Thompson said, remembering the previous times he had returned to Vietnam after the war, once to aid in an investigation of the massacre and once to participate in a documentary by a Dutch television crew.

Thompson remembered boarding the plane to go home on a fourteen- or sixteen-hour flight with not much to do, lots of time on his hands to think and to reflect on what happened to the people of My Lai. He recalled being overcome with sorrow for those who died and for their loved ones, then feeling very angry toward the men responsible for the killing, then sad again, then crying. He remembered looking out of the window so the stranger sitting next to him couldn't see him crying, because the last thing in the world he wanted to do was explain to some stranger why he was so sad. And when he cried he tried to do so quietly, so as to not attract attention, though that didn't always work.

But this time, on this return flight, Thompson was ready for the strong emotions that he knew could sneak up on him and catch him off guard. His main defense was to refrain from thinking, to put his mind in neutral, to think of pleasant things back home. He would quickly get his mind off the subject if he found it drifting there, toward memories that would upset him and undo him all over again.

Colburn was now sobbing loudly enough for others in the immediate area to hear. A stewardess approached him. Her eyes met Thompson's and he shook his head. She understood and walked away.

On the flight over to Vietnam, Colburn had promised himself that even if he ran into some very disturbing circumstances or memories he would not allow himself to break down and cry,

Mission to My Lai

U.S. war heroes Hugh Thompson and Larry Colburn received a warm welcome when they returned to Vietnam in March of 1998 for the 30th anniversary of the My Lai massacre. Their mission was to participate in a ceremony commemorating those killed at My Lai and to be reunited with some of the people they saved during the massacre.

Visitors to Ho Chi Minh City (formerly Saigon) can't help but notice the large number of motorbikes streaming through the streets. The motorbike represents a quantum leap forward in mobility for hundreds of thousands of people who were on foot or on bicycles prior to the war.

Thompson (left) and Colburn visit the Rex Hotel in downtown Ho Chi Minh City. During the war, the open air bar at the Rex was a favorite spot for war correspondents and military people to drink and talk following official daily media briefings, which came to be known as "The 5 O'Clock Follies."

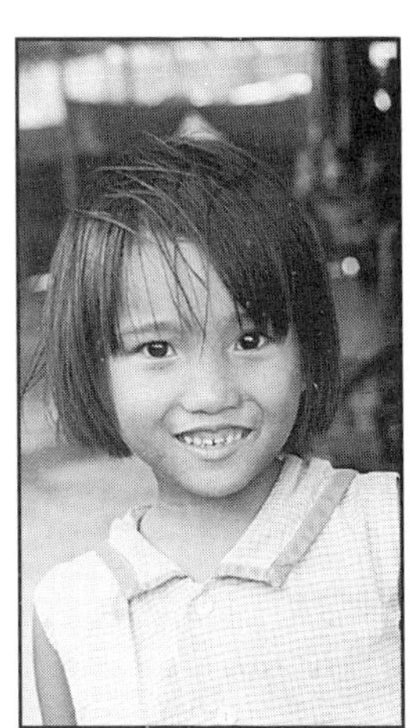

Surrounded by Vietnamese children who attend the grammar school at My Lai, Thompson (left) and Colburn enjoy a light moment while touring the school grounds. The war heroes proved to be popular with the pupils, who had been told of their acts of compassion toward the Vietnamese during the war. Colburn said it did his heart good to see the children smiling and playing and leading normal lives, rather than living in fear of being bombed or shot, as was the case during the war.

Mike Boehm (left) and his Vietnamese partner, Phan Van Do, visit the overcrowded grammar school at My Lai. Boehm, who is from Madison, Wisconsin, and a group of Quakers are engaged in an on-going project designed to improve the health, education and financial status of the people of My Lai.

My Lai pupils look over a panel of photos showing Madison children with whom they are engaged in an art-exchange program. The program is designed to build bonds of friendship between the pupils of two vastly different cultures.

The My Lai Memorial commemorates the 504 Vietnamese civilians who were killed by U.S. ground troops in 1968. The memorial includes a museum, statues, landscaped grounds, and the irrigation ditch where the bodies of 170 people were found after the massacre. **Right:** *A large concrete sculpture symbolizing the Vietnamese who died and who lost family members is the centerpiece of the memorial.* **Bottom right:** *A stone marker marks the spot where five people from the same family lost their lives. Joss sticks (like incense) are burned at these markers to produce a smoke that some of the Vietnamese believe to be a medium in which the living can communicate with the spirits of the deceased.* **Below:** *Bronze statue depicts mother and child killed in the massacre.*

After being reunited with two of the women whose lives they saved during the massacre, Colburn and Thompson, along with the women, were interviewed by Mike Wallace of CBS News for a segment of the TV magazine program, "60 Minutes." From left to right are Wallace, Pham Thi Nhung, Colburn, Pham Thi Nhanh and her daughter, and Thompson.

Colburn and his special friend, Pham Thi Nhung, one of the women he helped rescue from a sure death.

A third survivor of the massacre, Pham Thi Thuan (in coolie hat), escorted by an interpreter, approaches the spot at the My Lai Memorial where the war heroes were being interviewed by Wallace. She met and thanked Thompson and Colburn for what they did for her people.

Thompson shows photos of his children to massacre survivor, Pham Thi Nhanh.

Colburn (left) and Thompson (right) with CBS newsman Mike Wallace in Da Nang, Vietnam, following their trip to My Lai.

Vietnamese child looks on in wonder from the side of a road in the rural hamlet of My Lai as cameramen set up to film the war heroes.

especially in front of the cameras. He intended to hang tough and be there for Thompson in case Thompson needed someone to lean on. And a few such occasions did occur. Now the roles were reversed. Thompson was attempting to console his friend and comrade, but Colburn would not be consoled.

"Settle down, settle down. Everything's going to be alright," Thompson said, to no avail, as he continued patting him on the back.

Like Thompson and many other Vietnam veterans, Colburn had had sporadic bouts with anxiety and depression over the war and the terrible things he had seen and experienced. He had been holding in his pain and rage for the better part of thirty years. And, like many others, he had made little or no effort to seek the help of a counselor to cope with his heavy psychological burden.

After Colburn had stopped crying for a while and had composed himself, more or less, the subject of counseling came up.

"You okay, man?" Thompson asked.

"Yeah, I'm okay," Colburn said, not sounding okay.

"You sure?"

"Yeah, I'm okay. I don't know what came over me."

"I do. It was the same thing that came over me last time I went back to Vietnam."

"What am I, crazy?"

"No, you ain't crazy, you're just human. Or, if you're crazy, then the rest of us are, too."

"I don't know what came over me. I haven't cried like that since my father died; in fact, I didn't cry as hard as that when he died."

"Larry, look, when we get back, I think you ought to go see someone about that."

"Like a shrink?"

"Yeah, like a good counselor," Thompson said.

"Well, maybe we both ought to," Colburn suggested rather pointedly.

"I've been giving it a lot of thought myself lately, to tell you the truth."

"Well, I'm not too keen on counselors."

"Why's that?"

"I went once, in 1983, to a shrink at the VA. He asked me to tell him what was troubling me, so I talked for forty-five minutes. He'd ask a few little questions and I'd keep talking. The man never looked at me once while I was pouring my heart out to him! Then he gave me three prescriptions for some pills and said to take these twice a day, and that was all he had to offer. I crumpled up the prescription slips on the way out of his office and threw them in the trash. And I haven't been back since."

"Sounds like you got ahold of a real doozie!" Thompson observed.

"A real jerk. He could have cared less."

"But, I wouldn't judge 'em all by that one guy."

"No, I guess I don't."

"Larry, look, promise me you'll go see someone when you get home."

"Okay, I'll make you a deal: I'll go if you go."

"Okay, it's a deal."

The conversation faded and Thompson picked up a newspaper to read about their visit to Vietnam. Colburn leaned back in his seat and closed his eyes. Twenty minutes later he broke down again. Between sobs he was cursing Lt. Calley and the others responsible for the killings at My Lai.

"Settle down, settle down," Thompson said in a comforting voice.

"Glenn didn't have to die! Why in the hell did he have to die? He never hurt anyone," Colburn blurted out.

"No, he was one of the good guys," Thompson chimed in.

"And all those poor Vietnamese people, even little kids and babies, five hundred people, slaughtered like sheep, but worse."

"I know."

"The Vietnamese are good, decent people," Colburn proclaimed. "They are as gentle as they come. Their lives have been torn apart by one war after another after another. And for what? All they want to do is to be left alone to raise their crops, raise their families, see their children grow up. They don't care about communism or capitalism or socialism."

"I think you're right."

"I know I'm right. It's always the civilians who suffer. They're the ones who get killed and watch their children suffer and die. We lost sixty thousand men, but the Vietnamese lost over two million people, and most of those were civilians. You don't see that in the history books. And the military leaders refer to them as 'collateral losses,' people who just got in the way. This is wrong, man, dead wrong, no matter how you slice it."

"I know, most of those people never did a damn thing to anybody," Thompson agreed.

"There has got to be a better way. We just need to work harder. Killing people like this is crazy. It's insane."

"You got a point," Thompson agreed, thinking that Colburn was just about through getting these things off his chest.

But Colburn was nowhere near finished.

"I believe that as a society we are capable of overcoming war. I think we've reached the stage in history where we can evolve out of it, where we can think our way around war. No one wins, everyone loses. We know that, but we keep doing it. War can be avoided. There is a better way. There are alternatives."

"I hope you're right, 'cause there are a lot of crazy people out there with bombs," Thompson pointed out.

"And one more thing, Buck, and I'm dead serious about this: My son will never go to war as long as I'm around," Colburn added.

"Mine never went; none of 'em ever showed any inclination whatsoever to join the service. And I sure wasn't going to push 'em into it," Thompson said.

"Before I'd let my boy go off to war, I'd drive him to Canada myself," Colburn said.

"Nearly went there once myself, as you know," Thompson noted.

"Yeah, you told me."

Thompson felt good about being able to be there for Colburn. He knew that talking things out like this was good for what was ailing him. He was thinking that Colburn would now be able to settle down and get some sleep. He was mistaken.

Colburn broke down again, and Thompson decided to just leave him alone and let him cry it out.

"Larry, let's trade places," Thompson offered, and Colburn moved to the window seat. Colburn thought that he was embarrassing Thompson, but Thompson was only intending to shield his buddy from the stares of the other passengers.

Several more hours went by as the huge jet sped over the Pacific Ocean en route to the West Coast of the United States. Colburn would doze off for fifteen or twenty minutes, then wake up and look out of the window. He was mourning in silence now, and Thompson could see him wipe the tears from his face with his sleeve every so often.

Thompson had become quiet and pensive, thinking back to the reunion with the survivors. It felt wonderful seeing those people again and feeling their gratitude. He had endured much difficulty in his life as a result of what he did at My Lai in 1968, but the thought of saving even one innocent human life made the pain and the strain worth it. Even now, thirty years later, he remembered that day as if it were yesterday.

Chapter 6

The My Lai Massacre

WELL BEFORE DAWN ON THE MORNING of March 16, 1968 Hugh Thompson was up and ready for duty, as was his custom. After coffee and a light breakfast he cranked up his scout helicopter and lifted off from the base at Chu Lai, en route to join the team of fighting men who were participating in what was known as Task Force Barker. On board with him were his gunner, Larry Colburn, and his crew chief, Glenn Andreotta.

They flew over densely wooded areas and countless rice paddies and saw that farmers were already out with their crops. It was rice harvest time in Quang Ngai Province in central Vietnam. In this same region men had gone about the business of war for decades, while farmers had been engaged in the business of growing rice for centuries.

Quang Ngai Province borders the South China Sea, as do many of the provinces of Vietnam. Most of the one million or so residents of this province are rural farming people who live in small villages or hamlets, as is the case with the majority of the population of Vietnam.

Among the communities in the province is Son My Village, which is made up of four hamlets – My Lai, My Khe, Co Luy and Tu Cung. Son My Village lies between the South China Sea and Hwy. 1, the north-south artery through Vietnam, and is but a few miles from the populous provincial capital, Quang Ngai City. A rural road, Hwy. 521, connects the village to the city, and it is always filled with people going to and fro, on foot, on bikes, with carts, with cows, with huge, black water buffalo.

As Thompson and his crew flew over the area they were acutely aware that it could be swarming with the Viet Cong enemy. That's what the intelligence reports had stated, and that's why Task Force Barker had been organized – to rid the area of the Viet Cong, who had been picking off U.S. soldiers one and two at a time with land mines, booby traps and sniper fire. Thompson and his crew had a healthy respect for the elusive enemy. As aeroscouts it was their job to locate the enemy by drawing fire from them, then to get out of the way and allow the Huey gunships that accompanied them to use their awesome firepower to wipe out the VC.

At Landing Zone Dottie, about twelve miles northwest of Son My Village, the men of Charlie Company were gathering in the departure area to await the helicopters that would transport them to the target area. Most of the one hundred and five soldiers were apprehensive, nervous, as they prepared to meet the enemy head-to-head for the first time since their tour of duty had begun two months earlier. Some were concerned about the order which they received the day before to "kill everything" they would come across in the village. All were concerned, to one degree or another, with the idea that they would be fighting the more experienced 48th Battalion of Viet Cong and that they would be outnumbered two-to-one.

At a briefing the day before, their platoon leaders said all people in the village would be considered Viet Cong or Viet Cong sympathizers and that this village and the area around it was a well-known Viet Cong stronghold. They should expect to encounter no civilians, only a sizable group of Viet Cong soldiers who were experienced in the deadly art of guerrilla warfare.

The U.S. soldiers were also told that this operation would be their chance to get even with the enemy who had picked off dozens of their fellow soldiers. Adding fuel to the fire, most of the men attended a memorial service the night before for Staff Sgt. George Cox, a likable fellow who had been blown to bits by a land mine only two days earlier.

Being thus prepared psychologically, the men of Charlie Company were ready to meet the enemy, motivated not only by fear of their own demise but by the drive to avenge the deaths of their friends and comrades. They were now "fit to kill" as the first of two groups boarded the choppers and headed for Son My Village. It was 7:15 a.m.

At Son My Village well before dawn the men were in the rice paddies tending their crops. Roosters were announcing the arrival of a new day, and cows were mooing to be milked. The women had started outdoors fires for cooking and boiling water near their huts and houses. Children and old people were beginning to stir.

All but a few of the Viet Cong soldiers who spent the night in the village were up and gone, having disappeared into the darkness with their weapons and little pouches of rice. They used the cover of darkness to try to conceal the fact that this is where they lived when they could and that this is where their families lived. Some of the VC were husbands and fathers and sons of the people of Son My Village. They did not want their enemy to know this for fear that their enemy might try to harm their wives and children and parents while they were away.

Some of the people of Son My welcomed the VC. Others did not, because wherever they went they seemed to bring the war nearer to the doorsteps of those with whom they associated. The people of Son My, like so many of the people of Vietnam in general, were weary of war, tired of being awoken in the middle of the night by the sounds of bombs exploding in the distance and fearful that one day the shelling might end up in their front yards.

At 7:24 a.m. the relative peace and quiet of the village was broken as artillery fire began raining down on the western part of the community. It was here that the choppers carrying the men of Charlie Company would set down only minutes later. The shelling of this area was called "preparatory fire," designed to kill or scare away any Viet Cong who might be in the designated landing area, thus helping to secure the safety of the Ameri-

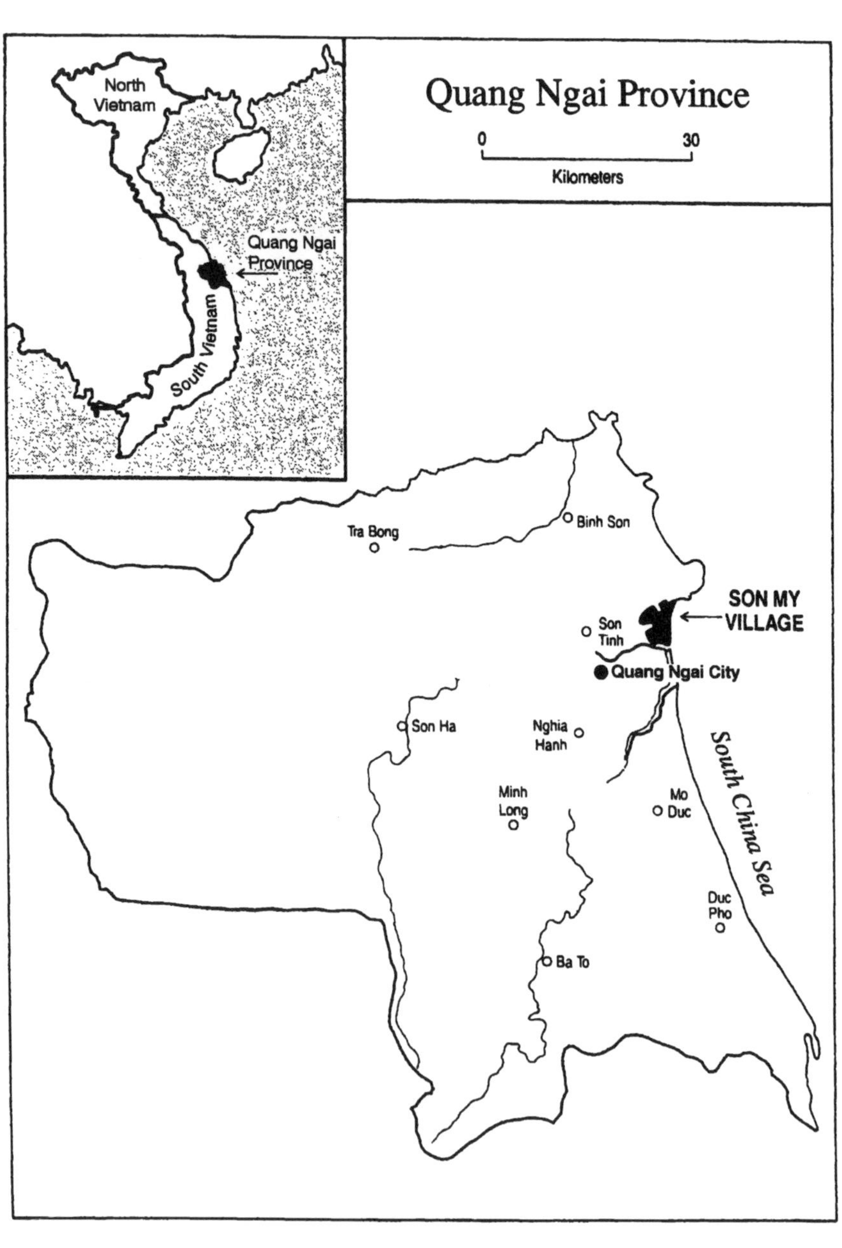
North
Vietnam
Quang Ngai
Province
South Vietnam
Quang Ngai Province
0
30
Kilometers
Tra Bong
Binh Son
SON MY
VILLAGE
Son
Tinh
Quang Ngai City
Son Ha
Nghia
Hanh
South China Sea
Minh
Long
Mo
Duc
Duc
Pho
Ba To

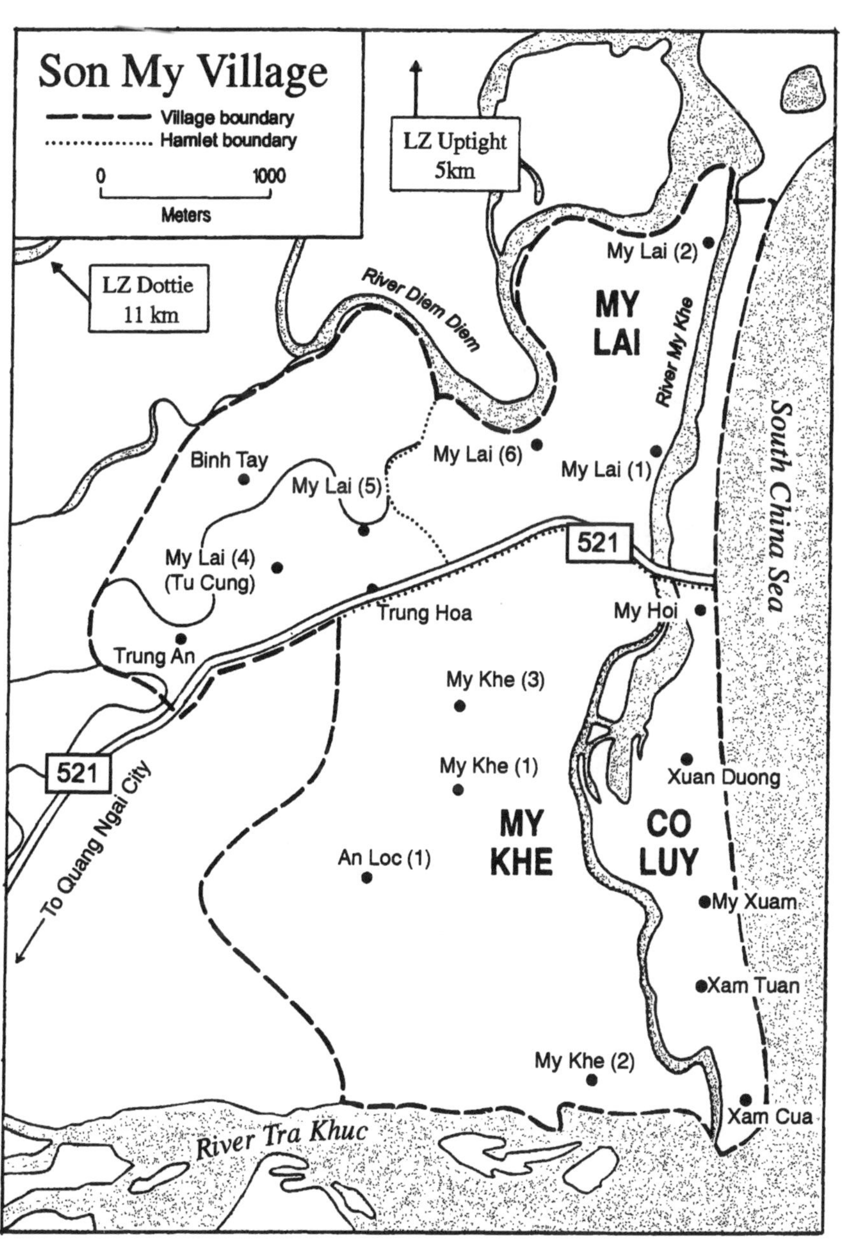

Son My Village
Village boundary
Hamlet boundary
0
1000
Meters
LZ Uptight
5km
LZ Dottie
11 km
River Diem Diem
My Lai (2)
MY
LAI
River My Khe
South China Sea
Binh Tay
My Lai (6)
My Lai (1)
My Lai (5)
521
My Lai (4)
(Tu Cung)
Trung Hoa
My Hoi
Trung An
My Khe (3)
521
To Quang Ngai City
My Khe (1)
Xuan Duong
MY
KHE
CO
LUY
An Loc (1)
My Xuam
Xam Tuan
My Khe (2)
Xam Cua
River Tra Khuc

can invaders.

The ground shook as the artillery shells struck the earth, and workers in the fields could be seen running for cover. Women dropped their cooking and cleaning chores, rounded up their children and moved quickly into the homemade bunkers under their homes. The animals panicked and scurried around nervously. Water buffalo, cows, pigs, dogs and chickens were in a state of high anxiety, as were the people of Son My Village.

The shells came down continuously for about five minutes, a hundred to a hundred and fifty rounds. A loud, piercing noise was made as each shell exploded, pounding home the message that what the villagers had feared might happen one day was finally happening. The war had been brought to their doorsteps.

A minute or two after the shelling stopped and before the dust settled two Huey gunships came screaming into the air space over the designated landing zone, firing high-powered machine guns and rockets into the hedgerows, to kill or otherwise clear out any enemy who might be lurking there. Though it was a surprise attack, the gunners and pilots anticipated that the place could be crawling with Viet Cong who would attempt to shoot or blow up the U.S. troops as they landed.

The first helicopters carrying U.S. soldiers touched down in the landing zone at 7:30 a.m., and the men scurried out quickly, expecting to be fired upon by the VC. No enemy fire was forthcoming, however.

Lt. William Calley, the leader of the 1st platoon, moved his men one hundred and fifty yards from the spot where they landed, to the western edge of My Lai, and set up a defensive position. Lt. Stephen Brooks, the leader of the 2nd platoon, moved his troops to the northwestern edge of the hamlet to secure the landing zone for the next lift of troops, who would be arriving shortly.

As Brooks' platoon moved into position they spotted several Vietnamese running away and gunned them down with bursts of fire from their automatic weapons. Whether they were unarmed civilians was irrelevant to Brooks and his men at this critical stage of the operation. If they were not armed Viet Cong they could be counted as unfortunate civilians who were caught in a crossfire between opposing forces. Or they could be listed as "enemy killed." (As the war wore on and the regard for human life – especially of the Asian variety – diminished in the minds of many soldiers and their leaders on both sides, a saying that was much used by some U.S. troops was, "If it's dead and it's Vietnamese, it's Viet Cong.")

The second lift of U.S. troops arrived at the designated landing area about twenty minutes after the first. On this lift was Lt. Geoffrey LaCross and his 3rd platoon, as well as the second part of Brooks' platoon. They were accompanied by Army reporter Jay Roberts and photographer Ron Haeberle. The media team would be covering the operation for *Stars and Stripes* and would routinely send stories and photos to hometown newspapers so the folks back home could see how the guys from their town were involved in the war. Haeberle was armed with a rifle and two cameras. One of the cameras was owned by the Army and contained standard black and white film; the other was his own and was loaded with color film, which he would use to take pictures for personal use, for unofficial purposes, in case he were to see anything out of the ordinary.

Hundreds of terrified Vietnamese women, children and old men remained in their bunkers, their huts or hiding places out in the woods, while hundreds more were making a mad dash for Hwy. 521 and hopefully to the safety of nearby Quang Ngai City. Several large groups, totaling three hundred to five hundred people, were on the road when they were spotted by members of the 2nd platoon. The soldiers opened fire, shooting indiscriminately into the crowd, as old and young alike screamed out in terror and dove into the ditches on either side of the road. They fled into the woods or otherwise managed to elude the soldiers. Ten to fifteen of the fleeing civilians were shot and killed on what they had hoped would be the road that would take them out of harm's way.

By 8 a.m. Calley's platoon of twenty-five men was moving full force through the hamlet in an eastward direction. His platoon was divided into two squads, one of which was headed by Sgt. David Mitchell. Calley and his radio operator moved through behind this squad.

Neither of Calley's squads encountered any armed enemy, nor did they receive any resistance from the civilians, who had been taken by surprise and were totally at the mercy of the U.S. troops.

As the soldiers approached, some of the civilians panicked and tried to run away, only to be mowed down with automatic weapons fire.

Once the killing started, it escalated quickly. Some of the men who were reluctant to kill unarmed, unresisting civilians became less inhibited when they saw their fellow soldiers doing it. But once first blood was drawn and the example was set their reservations were overcome by the pressure to do what their peers were doing.

Among the first people killed by Calley's group was a feeble old man with a white beard and a walking stick. A soldier knocked him down, cut his throat, and threw him down a water well. Then he dropped a hand grenade into the well, to be sure.

One of the soldiers, Varnado Simpson, spotted a woman fleeing; she was carrying something close to her chest, possibly a gun or an explosive device of some kind. He opened fire, and her lifeless body dropped to the ground. Simpson approached her cautiously, aware that she could be a Viet Cong carrying a booby trap. He rolled her over with his foot. Underneath her was a baby with half its head blown off. He had killed them both with one bullet. Simpson felt the blood drain from his head. He was light-headed, dizzy, sick, as he went down on one knee. Then something snapped in his mind.

A crazed Simpson stood up and turned his head away from

the bodies as tears rolled down his cheeks. He was not okay. He was confused and upset to the point of being deranged. There was a vacant stare in his eyes as he took his weapon off safety and headed toward a thatched hut to find other people to kill. It was as though someone else had taken over his body and mind.

The bloodbath had now begun in earnest for Simpson and others in Calley's platoon. They killed some Vietnamese by stabbing them with bayonets affixed to the muzzles of their rifles. Some villagers were instructed to come out of their huts, and they did so in hopes that their lives would be spared; instead they were shot down as they stepped into the clear. Others would not come out, and they were blown to bits by hand grenades tossed in by the soldiers.

Some of the Vietnamese who surrendered were rounded up and moved to a dirt road on the outskirts of the hamlet. They were made to sit down and be quiet as a handful of soldiers guarded them. Then, twenty to thirty minutes later, someone gave the order to get rid of them, and the soldiers poured dozens of rounds of automatic weapons fire into the women, children, babies and old men as they sat helplessly in the dirt.

Ron Haeberle, the photographer, witnessed this execution from about forty yards away. He was flabbergasted. He thought the civilians had been detained for interrogation and would be released at some point later. What would be the military rationale for killing babies and little children? he wondered, as he stood there in disbelief. When the barrage of gunfire seemed to be over Haeberle raised his camera and photographed the pitiful scene – not with the Army camera but with his own. He figured his superiors would not appreciate his bringing in photographs of this nature, as they would fall under the category of "bad press" for a military that already had a colossal public relations problem on its hands.

As he was photographing the bodies, a four-year-old boy came into his view. The boy was wounded in the foot and was limping around, crying and looking for his mother among the dead. He found her, kneeled down and took her hand in his. Haeberle was about to capture the heart-rending scene on film when he was startled by the crack of rifle fire just two feet from his ear. The fatal shot flipped the boy, knocking him into the middle of the group of bodies.

Haeberle turned and looked into the cold, dark eyes of the soldier who had just fired. He seemed to be 18 or 19 years old. Haeberle cocked his head to the side slightly in a questioning gesture, as if to ask, "Why?" The soldier looked back at him with a blank stare, with a face devoid of any thought or feeling, before turning and walking away.

A little while later, Haeberle and four other GIs were walking down a dirt road toward the hamlet when they came upon three Vietnamese people coming toward them. One was about four years old, another was eight or so, and the third was a frail old man between 70 and 80 years of age. Each was carrying his belongings in little baskets attached to either end of bamboo poles, which they supported on their shoulders.

When the Vietnamese spotted the soldiers they dropped their belongings and started crying out of fear. They stretched out their arms to the soldiers and begged for mercy.

One of the GIs got down on one knee, pointed his rifle and shot the four-year-old through the heart, dropping him where he stood. The eight-year-old dove over the younger boy to protect him from further harm and was shot in the back and killed. The soldier then shot the old man in the chest and head. Haeberle was on the verge of tears as the soldiers stepped over the bodies and continued on down the road, seemingly unaffected by what had just happened.

GIs walking on the outskirts of My Lai could hear a terrible array of sounds from the human and the animal victims of the soldiers bent on fulfilling their orders to "kill everything": the screams of teenage girls being raped, the desperate cries of the

elderly being put to death, sobbing mothers whose children had been killed, the squealing of pigs being shot, the yelping of dogs being wounded, the desperate mooing of cows and water buffalo being stabbed and slashed, the near-constant bursts of automatic weapons fire, and the intermittent blasts of hand grenades as they were tossed into huts and bunkers.

Then My Lai began to burn, and the devastation was nearly complete as the "Zippo squad" moved through, setting fire to houses, huts, animal shelters and food supplies. They threw dead animals down the community well to ruin the water supply and trampled and uprooted vegetable gardens. The orders were to kill everything and leave the Viet Cong nothing to come home to. Some of the men of Charlie Company carried out their orders seemingly with enthusiasm, in a manner that bordered on insanity; others crossed that line.

In contrast, not everyone who invaded Son My Village took part in the brutal war crimes that were committed. Among those was Harry Stanley, who found a badly wounded boy and counseled him to stay hidden until things had quieted down and all the soldiers had moved through the hamlet.

Another who refused to kill civilians was Leonard Gonzalez,

who came upon a wounded girl who was writhing in pain and sick with the fear of dying. He put his weapon down, knelt down beside the 12-year-old girl and poured water on her forehead. He tried to get her to drink from his canteen but she wouldn't. He poured more water on her forehead, stroked the hair at her temple, and looked upon her with compassion, knowing there was nothing more he could do for her. He walked away with a heavy heart.

Dennis Bunning of the 2nd platoon told his superiors simply that there was no way he would shoot civilians, no matter what the consequences. He was directed to separate from the group, to move out to the edge of the rice paddies, where he would be out of sight of the killing.

Yet another soldier who would have no part of the slaughter of women and children was Michael Bernhardt, a somewhat anti-authoritarian man of 24 who had had previous run-ins with his superiors and who was fond of writing his Congressman with complaints about what was wrong with the U.S. Army. Bernhardt knew before the massacre what was likely to happen in My Lai, and his suspicions proved out, though to a much greater degree than he imagined. The notion of killing unarmed civilians so offended his sense of morality and fair play that he decided then and there, as My Lai began to burn, that he would take the law into his own hands and would dole out the death penalty to the officers who participated and who gave the orders, and that even though the system of military justice might or might not give these guys what they deserved, he'd be damned if he was going to let these people get away with murder. Accordingly, he swore to himself that if he made it back to the States alive he'd purchase a high-powered rifle with a scope, and when these cowardly men returned home he would hunt them down like the animals that they were and would personally see to it that they were properly punished for their crimes against humanity.

As the carnage continued, Ron Haeberle came upon a group

of six soldiers guarding six women and children in the hamlet next to a hut. As he approached, one of the soldiers said, "Watch out, here comes the cameraman." The soldiers stepped back from the Vietnamese and assumed a less menacing posture.

Haeberle stepped up and focused his camera on the Vietnamese people. One of the women was holding a young boy and buttoning her shirt; one of the soldiers had partially disrobed her and had started to violate her. An older woman in a maroon-colored blouse and black pajama pants was sobbing uncontrollably, as though she were about to be killed. A girl of 10 with a terrified look on her face was huddled in close to a balding woman.

After taking the picture, Haeberle walked away, feeling there was nothing he could do for these people and hoping against hope that perhaps the adults in the group were being detained only for questioning. He had walked just a few paces when he heard a burst of gunfire. He turned and saw the six Vietnamese falling to the ground, victims of the executioners from Charlie Company.

As the systematic elimination of human life continued on the ground, Hugh Thompson and his helicopter crew began to notice from the air that there were dozens of dead or wounded Vietnamese people scattered about the area. They saw one in this rice paddy, two in that one, two on the hedgerow and a cluster of ten or fifteen on a dirt road near the woods. Thompson wondered what was going on down there, and he began discussing it with his crew.

Seeing no weapon near one of the wounded women, Thompson figured she was a civilian, so he had Andreotta drop a smoke canister near her to mark the spot so ground troops could find her and render first aid. He radioed a request for medical assistance to one of the larger gunships which accompanied his aircraft, and its pilot in turn passed the word on to the ground command unit, which was headed by Capt. Ernest Medina.

The helicopter crew remained near the wounded young woman for a few minutes before spotting a group of three or four soldiers trotting toward her. Thompson brought his aircraft down to a hover just ten yards from the woman, who was writhing in pain on the ground and holding what seemed to be a serious wound in her side. Her shirt and torso were covered with blood.

Capt. Medina walked up to her. She made a gesture with her hand summoning him forward and pointing to herself as if to say, "Help me, help me." Then her hand and arm went limp and fell to the ground; she didn't seem to have the strength to hold up her arm anymore. Medina nudged her with his foot. She looked up at him. He stepped back and shot her with his automatic weapon.

"You son of a bitch!" the three in the helicopter shouted out in unison.

"She wasn't any threat to anybody," Thompson yelled.

Meanwhile, the men of Charlie Company were completing their sweep through the hamlet and moving a group of sixty or more civilian prisoners in front of them as they emerged from the wooded area and headed for a clearing. In the clearing was a large irrigation ditch. The group being herded was made up of women in their twenties, thirties and forties, some with small children, some with toddlers, plus a dozen or more old men and old women, some of whom could barely walk and thus were causing the group to move at a snail's pace.

It was a little after 9 a.m. when they came into the clearing. Calley was talking to two of his men regarding the execution of the prisoners. Neither of the men wanted to take part in the shooting of unarmed civilians. So Calley, frustrated and irritated at the flak he was getting, gave one of the men, Paul Meadlo, a direct order to get ready to fire. As Calley and Meadlo prepared to fire the automatic weapons, some of the terrified Vietnamese began to cry and to plead for their lives and the lives of their children. The crying was hushed in a matter of a minute or two as the two Americans, standing only eight or ten feet from their victims, opened fire. The impact of the bullets knocked the Vietnamese back into the ditch. Midway through the shooting an emotionally shaken Meadlo stopped and tried to hand his weapon to another soldier who was standing nearby. The other soldier, Dennis Conti, refused to take it. As they argued, Calley was shooting the last few children still alive in the group.

Then the three men turned and walked away from the badly mangled bodies of the dead and dying, heading to another part of the village to continue their search-and-destroy mission. Meadlo's heart wasn't in it; nor was Conti enthused about slaughtering unarmed civilians.

An hour later, Calley and some of his platoon were back at the ditch. Several dozen more Vietnamese civilians had been forced into the ditch, many of them sobbing and begging for their lives, as they stood next to the piles of bodies of their families and neighbors. Others stood or squatted helplessly on the banks of the ditch, petrified with fear, horrified that their lives would soon be over.

When Calley announced it was time to get ready to shoot the people he again encountered a spirit of non-cooperation from his men. This time it was stiff resistance. He ordered Robert Maples to load up and start shooting, but Maples refused. Calley then pointed his weapon at Maples, threatening to shoot him for disobeying a direct order. Two or three other GIs stepped in and sided with Maples, and Calley lowered his gun.

Calley got into a life-threatening confrontation with Harry Stanley when he ordered Stanley to shoot the civilians. Stanley refused.

"I wasn't brought up that way, to be killing no women and children. Ain't gonna do it," Stanley stated firmly.

Calley then stuck his M-16 in Stanley's gut and threatened to kill him. Stanley responded in kind, sticking his pistol in Calley's ribs. Calley shouted at Stanley, saying he wasn't bluffing. Stanley looked Calley in the eye and said he wasn't bluffing either.

"We all going to die here anyway. I just as soon go out right here and now – but I ain't killin' no women and children," he said, even more firmly than before.

Calley saw just how resolved Stanley was, and he backed down after giving Stanley a hateful stare.

Calley then leaned on Meadlo again and together they began slaughtering the helpless people in the ditch. Amid the wailing and screaming, heads and limbs were being blown off. Blood and guts and bits of brain were everywhere. When it was over forty or fifty more Vietnamese people were dead or dying, and Meadlo was sobbing openly. Stanley, Maples and others stood there silently with their mouths open, hardly able to believe their eyes.

Shortly after Calley and Meadlo finished their dirty work, Thompson and his crew flew over the irrigation ditch and spotted the bodies. The sight stunned them. The thought crossed Thompson's mind that these people might have been killed by U.S. troops, then he quickly dismissed the thought, feeling that this sort of war crime may have been committed by Nazis, but surely not by his fellow soldiers. After all, he thought, U.S. soldiers were decent, honorable fighting men who would never stoop to mass executions of civilians. It was simply out of character for American soldiers.

So, how could those people have ended up in that ditch? he wondered.

One possibility was that when the artillery was coming in earlier in the morning they all took cover in the irrigation ditch, and they simply had the bad fortune to be in a spot that took a direct hit. That might be what happened.

Another possibility was that all these people were killed in the artillery barrage and the U.S. soldiers had rounded up their bodies and placed them in the ditch for mass burial. Maybe it happened like that, Thompson thought.

Thompson and his men pondered it and talked about it as they continued to fly around Son My Village, making only halfhearted attempts to locate an enemy who by now they knew was not going to be found in this vicinity. In the course of thirty minutes or so they received no enemy fire and saw no Viet Cong, bringing the total number of enemy seen that day to one fleeing draft-age male with a weapon, whom they had spotted and fired upon at 8 a.m. It was now 10:15 a.m.

After flying around and talking about it and trying to figure it out, they arrived at the only conclusion that made sense, the one they had been trying to avoid, the unthinkable: These people were unarmed civilians who had been systematically marched to the ditch and executed, as the Nazis had done in Europe in the 1940s and as the Russians under Stalin had done in an earlier time.

As the reality of what had happened continued to sink in, Thompson practically became sick with disgust and anger. He felt compelled to speak up, so he radioed the accompanying gunship:

"It looks to me like there's an awful lot of unnecessary killing going on down there. Something ain't right about this. There's bodies everywhere. There's a ditch full of bodies that we saw. There's something wrong here."

The pilot of the gunship heard him clearly. Thompson's complaint was then relayed to headquarters and made its way up the chain of command to those who were ultimately responsible for the assault on My Lai and Son My Village.

Even as he was taking action to try to protect the unarmed civilians, Thompson was starting to feel guilty about the death of the wounded young woman whom Medina shot. By marking her for medical assistance, Thompson had unwittingly marked her for execution. Without meaning to, he had assisted in her demise. Now guilt was beginning to flow into the dizzying confluence of emotions that raged within him.

Shortly after filing his complaint, Thompson spotted what he thought was another wounded civilian.

"We'd better get over there before someone else gets to her," he said as his little bubble helicopter zipped across the treetops and over a rice paddy en route to the woman.

She was hiding in tall grass next to a dirt road adjacent to a wooded area. Thompson brought the chopper down to a standstill hover a few feet off the ground and just about ten yards from where she was hiding. She was crouched down in a fetal position, obviously fearing for her life. She appeared to be about 70 years old.

"Stay down! Stay down!" Colburn shouted to the old woman, gesturing to her with his hands as he did. He figured that she couldn't understand English and that she couldn't hear him due to the noise of the engine, but that she could understand the gesture and would realize the chopper crew meant her no harm, but instead wanted to help her.

"Stay put for a little while, and we'll be right back to help you," Colburn continued, hoping she would understand his friendly intentions.

The helicopter crew left to continue their reconnaissance assignment, and when they returned to the scene half an hour later to check on her she was still there though bent over in an odd posture. As they looked closer the woman appeared to be dead.

"What the hell…?" Thompson said, with a puzzled and worried look on his face as he turned to Colburn.

"Damn, boss, did someone shoot her?" Colburn asked, craning his neck to try to be certain of what he thought he was seeing. "Put 'er down real close."

Thompson set the chopper down to about two feet off the ground and fixed it at a hover.

"Yep, she's gone. Someone shot her," Colburn observed in a distressed tone.

The woman's lifeless body was slumped over, her coolie hat lying beside her in the grass. The men observed that her brains had been blown out, literally.

Now, Thompson was mad. He had seen enough – more than enough. Now he was going to do something about it. He piloted the chopper back to the ditch to see if some of those who had been shot were still alive. As he began to set down he noticed that there were even more bodies than before. He saw that some of the people in the ditch were alive, though badly wounded.

Thompson got out of his aircraft and headed in the direction of a woman who was screaming in pain. As he did, he was approached by a sergeant from Charlie Company. His name was David Mitchell.

"Sergeant, I see there's some wounded in there. Those people need help. Any way y'all could help 'em out?"

"Yeah, we can help 'em out. We can help put 'em out of their misery," the sergeant said, with a cruel tone in his voice.

Thompson wasn't sure whether to take Mitchell seriously, but he gathered that he and his crew were not welcome there. A few minutes later Lt. Calley walked up to Thompson, and Thompson sensed he was talking to the man in charge.

"What's going on here, lieutenant?" Thompson asked Calley.

"This is my business," Calley answered sharply.

"What is this? Who are these people?" the angry pilot demanded, as his face grew more and more red.

"Just following orders."

"Orders? Whose orders?" Thompson asked.

"Just following…"

"But, these are human beings, unarmed civilians, sir."

"Look, Thompson, this is my show. I'm in charge here. It ain't your concern."

"Yeah, great job," Thompson said sarcastically.

"You better get back in that chopper and mind your own business."

"You ain't heard the last of this," the pilot shouted as he made his way back into his aircraft.

Colburn was all eyes. He was afraid the two were going to come to blows. As the chopper lifted off, Thompson was beet red and so angry that he couldn't talk. Colburn kept his eye on Calley and Mitchell and his finger near the trigger of his M-60, just in case.

Andreotta, too, kept a wary eye on the two men, knowing that there could be big trouble. As he was watching them, Mitchell began firing into the bodies in the ditch, finishing off some of the wounded.

"My God! They're firing into the ditch!" an incredulous Andreotta shouted.

"You've got to be kidding," Thompson responded, as he looked down and saw bodies flinching and blood spurting from the impact of the M-16 bullets.

Now even more upset than before, Thompson thought of radioing a message to the base, but he was too angry to talk straight, Thompson was totally frustrated, and he wanted to help somehow, but he wasn't sure what he should do next.

The pilot and his crew flew around for ten or fifteen minutes to cool off and collect themselves, trying to let off steam by talking it out and trying to figure out what to do, if anything. After all, what could three guys do to stop the momentum of an entire company that was on an insane, murderous rampage?

Chapter 7

A Daring Rescue

HUGH THOMPSON AND HIS CREW COULD hardly believe their eyes as they orbited the ravaged hamlet of My Lai. Bodies were everywhere. Dead people of every age were in the rice paddies, on the hedgerows, on the trails that crisscrossed My Lai, and on the main road to Quang Ngai. The bodies of water buffalo dotted the landscape.

It boggled Thompson's mind that this could be the work of U.S. soldiers. The thought of it depressed him. He felt ashamed to be associated in any way with the operation that had done this. Andreotta and Colburn felt the same, and they let their feelings be known.

As they talked and viewed the near-total devastation, Andreotta spotted a group of seven or eight GIs in hot pursuit of three Vietnamese running for their lives. Thompson and Colburn saw them a second later.

Now, Thompson knew what to do. It was crystal clear what he had to do. He was never more sure of anything in his life. And if it cost him his life, well, so be it, then he would have the satisfaction of knowing that he died while doing what a soldier is sworn to do – defending the weak, the defenseless.

"We're going in," Thompson announced with authority in his voice.

"We're with you, boss," Colburn said. "Let's do it."

All three men were in a state of high alert as their adrenalin shot up to the maximum and their hearts began to pound rapidly. They were preparing to do battle on behalf of those who could not defend themselves. They watched keenly as the American soldiers closed in on the Vietnamese, who were now scrambling into a bunker at the edge of the field.

Knowing that he was creating a confrontation that could lead to a firefight, Thompson radioed his buddies on the low gunship that he needed them to back him up.

"I'm setting down. Would appreciate some help. I'm not going to let these GIs kill any more of these people. I'm just telling you. Help if you can," Thompson shouted into the radio in a halting voice.

Thompson was precise in putting the aircraft down, far enough from the Americans so that no one would be decapitated by his rotor blades and near enough to make a statement about the seriousness of his intent.

He glanced nervously at Colburn and Andreotta.

"Y'all cover me! If these bastards open up on me or these people, you open up on them. Promise me," he said, sounding like a man who was making a last request before he was to die.

"You got it, boss," Colburn responded. "Consider it done."

Thompson got out of the chopper, taking no weapon except his sidearm, which remained in its holster. With a quick, determined step he walked up to the man at the head of the squad, Lt. Stephen Brooks. He flipped his visor up and looked Brooks in the eye.

"Hey, listen, hold your fire. I'm going to try to get these people out of the bunker," Thompson said in a take-charge tone of voice. "Just hold your men here."

Seeing that he was being given orders by a soldier of lesser rank, an annoyed Lt. Brooks responded:

"Yeah, we can help you get 'em out of that bunker – with a hand grenade!"

Thompson was not amused.

"Just hold your men here," he demanded, with a deadly serious look in his eye. "I think I can do better than that."

Not knowing Thompson, nor what this seemingly wild man

might do, Brooks told his men to stay put. He also noticed a certain determined look in the eye of Larry Colburn, who had an M-60 pointed in his direction.

The bunker in which the civilians had taken cover was an earthen mound overgrown with weeds and brush and positioned on the edge of a clearing, its back side abutting the edge of the woods. The bunker had a small opening half the width and depth of a closet door, and it was framed with dark wood.

As Thompson approached the bunker he could see three people near the opening. An elderly man with a white beard and no shirt peered out into the daylight. Seated next to him was an old woman in ordinary black pajamas with eyes that begged for mercy. A small child about six years of age clung tightly to the leg of the woman.

Colburn continued to stare at Brooks and his men, his powerful weapon pointed at their feet and his index finger twitching nervously near the trigger. The ground troops sat down or squatted, and some of them lit cigarettes or thin cigars. They figured their lives were not in danger as long as they didn't try anything aggressive. One of the ground troops kept staring at Colburn in a menacing way, and Colburn stared back, knowing that he had the upper hand.

Colburn could feel the sweat dripping down his forehead and into his eyes as the hot sun beat down upon the land. He kept a close eye on the GIs, watching their hands, looking out for any sudden moves, as he wiped the sweat off his eyebrows, one at a time. Out of the corner of his eye he could see Thompson at the

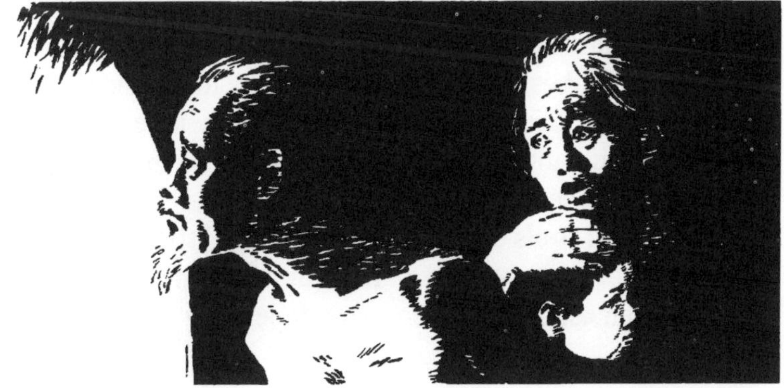

door of the bunker. Colburn's mind was racing:

Oh, no! What if the bunker is booby trapped? What if those people in there have weapons? That's just great! I'm going to stand here and watch Thompson die. What in the hell have I gotten myself into this time?

Thompson squatted down in front of the old woman sitting in the entranceway. She could see that there was something different about this soldier, as he approached her in a friendly manner. He held his hand out to her, offering to help her up.

"Y'all come with me, now. I'm going to get you out of here," he said.

The old woman hesitated for a few moments then took his hand, and he helped to ease her to her feet. The child clung to her all the tighter. The old man stepped forward, uncertain of what Thompson's intentions were, then feebly extended his arm to the tall American. Thompson took hold of the back of the old man's arm and helped him up gently. He could feel that the little man was just skin and bones.

"Just stay here close to me. No one's going to hurt you," Thompson said, as he tried to have the refugees stand where the ground troops couldn't see them.

"Anyone else in there?"

Another woman came crawling out, dressed in black pajamas and carrying a little bag of clothes and things. She was accompanied by a child of about 10 or 11.

As people continued coming out of the bunker, Thompson began to wonder what he was going to do with all of them. He couldn't evacuate them in his tiny aircraft; there was no room. He couldn't airlift them one by one, because he was low on fuel as it was. And, besides, he was sure that neither Andreotta nor Colburn would relish the idea of giving up their seats and staying behind and hanging around with Brooks' men.

Now, everyone was out of the bunker, and Thompson had nine frightened souls on his hands. He felt a little awkward, but mostly he was fiercely determined that no harm should come to these Vietnamese people who were depending on him for their very lives.

In all, there were two women, five children and two elderly men, one more feeble than the other.

Thompson talked with them as though they could understand English, and he gestured to them as he talked so they could understand his intentions. His disposition, his body language, the kind tone in his voice told them this man in U.S. Army fatigues just might be the best friend they ever had.

With all nine of the Vietnamese standing very close to him, Thompson took a few steps toward his helicopter, then stopped and looked back when he thought he heard someone else in the bunker. His newfound companions likewise took a few steps with him then stopped the instant he stopped. Thompson continued on toward the aircraft, and his entourage did as well, walking cautiously and in unison with the man who represented their best hope for life.

Thompson got back to his aircraft and found Colburn as he had left him, except that he was now soaked in sweat. Brooks and his men had all assumed non-threatening postures on the ground, their weapons lying beside them.

Thompson stood by the helicopter and radioed for help to one of the gunships that was circling overhead. His voice quivered as he spoke. He wasn't sure if he could convince his fellow pilots in the larger aircraft to land in this free-fire zone and evacuate the civilians. Such a landing would violate all protocol; it would be extremely dangerous if there were any armed Viet Cong in the area. He was hopeful but unsure as he called for help.

"Danny, Brian, I need some help down here. Can y'all come in and get these civilians out of here before someone kills them? Please, y'all. I need some help. Come pick these people up or else they're going to be dead," Thompson pleaded, realizing that what he was requesting was a radical departure from the norm. A Huey gunship just did not land in enemy territory.

Danny Millians, who was flying the lower gunship, and Brian Livingston, piloting the high gunship, were in the same unit as Thompson. They depended on one another for the success of their search-and-destroy missions, and in some situations for their very lives. They pretty much knew what the other was thinking.

Thompson and his crew risked their lives daily, buzzing around low to the ground trying to find the enemy. Millians and Livingston appreciated the risks Thompson took. They liked him as a buddy and as a fellow soldier. He always held up his end of the responsibility in combat situations. He would never ask for help unless he was in a real bind.

One of the heavily armed gunships was on the ground in minutes, while the other stayed in the air to provide cover. Colburn continued to cover Thompson and the civilians. Thompson had the old men and two of the children wait by his chopper under Andreotta's care as he escorted the women and three children to the waiting gunship. He spoke briefly with Millians about where he might take his passengers, then thanked him repeatedly for his help.

As the heavy gunship strained to get off the ground, Thompson went back to his chopper for a few minutes to check up on things and to be with the remaining refugees to provide cover. Colburn noticed that one of the old men, who was stooped over at a 45-degree angle to the ground, probably from decades of manual labor in the rice fields, was bowing to Thompson ever so slightly as Thompson approached him. It was the old man's way of showing his respect and gratitude to the soldier who had saved his life.

The big gunship lifted off and headed for the road leading to Quang Ngai. Millians felt that the Vietnamese would be safe there, out of the line of fire. The women were still somewhat apprehensive. One of them, Pham Thi Nhung, age 46, was afraid that the soldiers might fly her out over the South China Sea and drop her into the water. She had heard stories of that happening to Vietnamese people, and she became petrified with fear as she began to experience it in her mind.

Five to ten minutes after lifting off, the Huey helicopter landed in an open field adjacent to Hwy. 521, about a mile out of Quang Ngai, and two or three miles away from My Lai. The five passengers were deposited safely on the ground, and the two women, fully aware of how fortunate they were to be alive, waved goodbye as the gunship lifted off and headed back to My Lai.

Millians returned to the scene of the confrontation to pick up the remaining refugees. Thompson escorted the hobbling old men and the two wary children to the waiting helicopter. It lifted off after a brief word between Thompson and Millians.

Thompson marched back to his aircraft, casting a mean look at Brooks and his men. He lifted off quickly as Colburn and Andreotta, with their weapons at the ready, kept a close eye on the ground troops. It was time to return to Landing Zone Dottie for re-fueling, but Thompson decided instead to make one more quick pass over the irrigation ditch, to see if perhaps he and his crew might be able to help other people.

They flew over the ditch at a low altitude and got a long, hard look at the most awful scene any of them had ever witnessed. They couldn't begin to count the bodies that were in the ditch, but it seemed to be a hundred, a hundred and twenty-five, a hundred and fifty or more dead people, blown to pieces.

"Boss, something's moving down there," Andreotta said. "Can you swing back around?"

The helicopter looped around then set down quickly near the edge of the ditch. Andreotta had maintained visual contact with the spot where he saw the movement, and he darted out of the aircraft as soon as it touched the ground. Thompson got out and guarded one side of the chopper and Colburn guarded the other.

Andreotta had to walk on several badly mangled bodies to get where he was going. He lifted a corpse with several bullet holes in the torso and there, lying under it, was a child, age five or six, covered in blood and obviously in a state of shock.

As he lifted the tiny girl's head and looked into her dark eyes, she whimpered and blinked, so he knew she was alive. He picked her up and tried to climb out of the ditch but was unable to get his footing because of all the intestines, bits of flesh, blood and other body fluids. He kept slipping and became mired in the carnage. He was inching his way toward the edge of the ditch when a dying woman reached up and grasped the outside seam of his pants. She said something to him; it seemed that she was begging for help. Holding the child with his left arm, he leaned down and felt the woman's pulse with his right hand.

Observing that Andreotta was having trouble getting out of the ditch, Colburn went over to help him. He could see that Andreotta was in distress from the look on his face. Still, Andreotta was looking around to see if there was anyone else he could save. He checked the pulse of three or four people who didn't seem to be dead yet. He bent over and put his ear near the face of a woman who was desperately trying to say something to him. He held her hand as she spoke.

Colburn squatted down on the edge of the ditch, and Andreotta, holding the child by the back of the shirt, handed her up to him. Colburn held the child in his left arm then handed Andreotta the butt of his rifle, to give him something solid to hold on to. The muzzle of the gun was pointed at Colburn's stomach, and as he pulled Andreotta toward him, he realized that he had released the safety when he was standing guard. Had either of the men so much as touched that hair trigger, Colburn would have been one dead soldier. But, fortunately, neither man touched the trigger.

As Andreotta and Colburn were returning to the helicopter, Thompson got a glimpse of the child. She reminded him of the son he had back home in Georgia, about the same size. The thought that this could be his child was very disturbing to him. He lowered the visor on his helmet as he stiffened his upper lip and tried to hold back the tears. He didn't want his men to see him cry.

When Andreotta first located the child, he checked for wounds, but found none. Colburn, too, looked her over closely and found no sign of physical injury.

The three men and the child boarded the little helicopter and headed for the hospital in Quang Ngai.

Colburn held the child on his lap and again examined her for wounds and felt for broken bones, but found none. The little girl was limp, like a rag doll. Her eyes were fixed and dilated. Colburn talked to her; he snapped his fingers in front of her face, but couldn't get her to blink. She was in a state of shock, a state of altered consciousness, brought on by overwhelming psychological trauma. Colburn cried to himself.

He looked over at Thompson, who was stone silent, and he could see a stream of tears running down the side of his face.

They arrived at the hospital in Quang Ngai fifteen or twenty minutes after leaving the ditch. A Catholic nun in a white habit came out to meet them. Colburn had given the child to Thompson, who wanted to hold her for a little while.

"Sister, I don't know what you're going to do with her, but I don't believe she has any family left," Thompson said, choking back the tears.

The nun thanked the three soldiers for their kindness then took the child and cradled her as though the little girl were her own flesh and blood.

The soldiers boarded their chopper, which by now was nearly out of fuel, then stopped at a local airstrip to re-fuel. As they flew back toward Landing Zone Dottie, Thompson was quiet and pensive. The more he thought about what had happened that day the angrier he became, and at some point the anger again turned to rage.

He was going to march right up to his commanding officer

and report what he had seen at My Lai. And, no, he would not settle down. He would not mince his words when he reported what he considered to be war crimes. The men of Charlie Company had slaughtered hundreds of unarmed, unresisting civilians, and their behavior was a stain on the uniform of every American soldier who had fought honorably in this grueling war. He would make an official complaint; he would tell the truth about what he had witnessed, no matter what the consequences.

The little bubble helicopter set down at LZ Dottie at about 11 a.m. Thompson shut down the engine, flipped up the visor on his helmet, and stormed up to his platoon leader, Barry Lloyd, to report what he had seen. Throwing his helmet on the ground, Thompson talked and shouted angrily about U.S. troops behaving like Nazi executioners.

"There's a ditch full of dead women and children over there. We saw one armed VC all day. We never captured one damned weapon. They're killing the women and children!" he related.

Lloyd could hardly get a word in edgewise. He stood there wide-eyed and listened as the pilot vented his anger and outrage.

"You see these wings?" Thompson said, pointing to the aviator wings sewn on to his fatigues just above his left pocket. "These wings are sewn on with thread, and I'll rip them off and stay on the ground before I'll ever take part in anything like that. I don't want to have anything to do with an operation like that – ever!"

Lloyd read him loud and clear. There was no mistaking Thompson's meaning.

The next man to get an earful was the operations officer for the aviation section. As Thompson continued his report of what he had seen, his commanding officer, Major Fred Watke, came up to the operations van and tried to calm him down. Watke listened and understood enough of what Thompson was saying to realize that there was a major problem with the My Lai operation. He walked directly over to report the massacre of civilians to Lt. Col. Frank Barker, who, in turn, relayed orders to Capt. Medina that Charlie Company was to cease firing immediately.

Thompson received some degree of relief and satisfaction from having reported the massacre and knowing that a cease-fire had been ordered. But his outrage had not been totally defused. He was nowhere near finished with getting this off his chest.

Accordingly, after lifting off from LZ Dottie around noon, he headed back to My Lai. The hamlet was still smoldering, and the bodies of women, children, babies and old men were strewn about the fields and stacked five and six deep in the irrigation ditch.

As the scout helicopter approached the ditch, eagle-eye Andreotta spotted a small group of GIs sitting in the shade relaxing, taking a smoke break, not at all looking like men who were concerned about the enemy being anywhere near.

"Well, well, well, what we have here?" Thompson said with mischief in his voice.

Colburn had a feeling Thompson might try to give the ground troops some grief.

"Hang on, boys," the pilot said as he put the helicopter into a 45-degree dive. "Let's see if we can scare the hell out of them."

The men on the ground heard and then saw the chopper heading straight for them. It was coming in at eighty or ninety miles per hour and it looked as though it were going to crash into them. They dove for cover as the chopper pulled up, within ten or fifteen feet of where they were lounging. Thompson pulled out of the dive, and on the way back up the rotor blade clipped a tree, and a piece of the blade broke off. He hadn't pulled up quite soon enough.

If the daredevil pilot had succeeded in his mission of scaring the daylights out of the ground troops, he also nearly managed to get himself and his crew killed – and to give Colburn and Andreotta heart attacks.

Though he derived a measure of satisfaction from terrorizing the troops, Thompson was still very angry, still beside himself with rage, as he made his way back to his base at Chu Lai that afternoon to try to unwind and to talk with his chaplain about what he had seen.

Chaplain Carl Creswell, an Episcopalian priest, was shocked

by what Thompson was telling him and, as Thompson had done, was determined to report the incident to his superiors. He would not look the other way, nor dismiss it merely as one of those things that happens in war.

Knowing the chaplain was with him on this gave Thompson a degree of solace. They had known one another for only three months, but each considered the other to be a friend. Thompson was taking Confirmation lessons from Fr. Creswell.

That night they went to the officer's club and drank and talked at length. It was well after midnight when they said good night, and Thompson headed for his room to try to get some sleep. A warm spring breeze blew through the base, and Thompson could hear the crackling of palm branches as they swayed in the breeze. He envisioned the faces of the dead in the irrigation ditch that he had witnessed that morning, but the image was overwhelming, and he pushed it out of his mind. He thought back to the bunker and remembered the faces of those he had saved: the wary old man with the white beard and bony arms, the old woman with the eyes that begged for mercy, the beautiful, vulnerable, little children whose lives he had held in the palm of his hand.

He thanked God that he was able to help them, and at the same time he was experiencing a growing sense of remorse that he hadn't done more.

Had I figured out right away that a massacre was occurring, had I not spent time denying that our soldiers could have done this, had I moved in on first impulse, then more lives could have been saved. I'm sorry I didn't do more. O my God, I am heartily sorry that I failed to do more than I did...and I firmly resolve with the help of thy grace that the next time something like this happens I will move quicker and do better to protect those who cannot protect themselves. Amen.

It was a prayer he would pray a thousand times in the years to come, and with the prayer would come the haunting thought that he could have done more.

Drifting in and out of sleep until nearly dawn, Hugh Thompson lay in his bunk, listening to the muffled sounds of artillery in the distance, half mourning and half praying for the people of My Lai.

Chapter 8

Hazardous Duty

WHILE THE MY LAI MASSACRE WAS THE most disturbing thing he had ever witnessed, Thompson felt he had no choice but to go on fighting the war. Distracted and somewhat depressed, he would get up every morning and put one foot in front of the other, hoping he could remain alive until his tour of duty was over.

Among his first duties after the massacre was to report to his superiors and describe again, calmly and carefully, what he saw and did at My Lai. He first reported to Major Fred Watke, his commanding officer, a kind and understanding fellow who was more like a father to him than a military superior. Next he told his story to Colonel Oran Henderson, Commander of the 11th Infantry Brigade.

Having reported to the proper authorities in a calm and rational manner, Thompson felt a little better about things. He felt he had done his duty as a soldier. The ball was in the court of his superiors, and he assumed they would take the necessary steps to investigate the massacre and to see to it that the guilty parties were punished.

Though reporting in had taken some of the load off his mind, he was still heavily burdened. By day, he did his job and tried to concentrate on the tasks at hand. By night, he was awoken by nightmares which centered on the ghastly sight he had witnessed at the irrigation ditch. He wasn't getting much sleep.

Thompson continued to benefit from the counsel and camaraderie of Fr. Creswell, the chaplain, sometimes over drinks at the officers club and sometimes in the make-shift chapel which overlooked the South China Sea. The friendship of this Episcopal priest helped to ease his mind, though a feeling of impending doom was beginning to creep up on him. He was starting to fear for his life. He could be killed in a helicopter crash. The higher-ups might mark him for assassination because he could implicate them in the murders of Vietnamese civilians. They could send him into combat much more than usual, thus doubling or tripling his already-high chances of getting shot down by the enemy.

Practically every day now he would rise before dawn, and shortly after first light he was lifting off from the base at Chu Lai to go out and fight the war. The missions seemed to be getting more frequent.

The fair-haired boy from Georgia was beginning to worry about whether he would ever see his wife and children again. He was growing more and more concerned for his safety and that of his crew. For a brief moment he even questioned whether he had done the right thing by saving the civilians at My Lai, but he ran that thought out of his mind as quickly as it entered.

The recurring nightmares, the lack of sleep, the concern for his safety were turning Hugh Thompson into a bundle of nerves. He was smoking heavily, eating poorly, drinking himself to sleep, spending more and more time with the chaplain, and looking nervous, out of sorts, worn down by the war.

It was past time to unwind, so two weeks after the massacre Major Watke called him in, offered him a smoke, put his arm over his shoulders, and told him it was time to take a week of R & R. Thompson objected halfheartedly that he had been in-country only three months, but Watke told him the subject was not open for discussion. Case closed, call your wife, get a ticket for Hawaii, the CO ordered in a kind voice.

A few days later, as Easter weekend was beginning, Thompson was flying out of Da Nang on a military-chartered plane en route to Hawaii. There he would meet his wife of five years, Palma, a pretty blue-eyed blonde in her early twenties. The plane touched down on Good Friday, and she was waiting for him at the Reef Hotel on Waikiki Beach in Honolulu.

It was a *rendezvous* frequented by military men coming in from Southeast Asia and their wives flying in from the U.S. mainland. There were sandy beaches, palm trees, warm spring breezes, romantic suppers, good hotel rooms, the kind of place where a young couple in love could enjoy one another's company, free from the distractions of the outside world.

The time together was like a second honeymoon, though Palma was noticing that she didn't seem to have her husband's undivided attention. He was in Hawaii, yes, but his mind seemed to keep drifting back to Vietnam. On the third day she spoke up.

"What is it, baby? What's wrong?" she asked.

"Oh, nothing," he responded.

"Something's wrong. I can see it in your face. Talk to me. I'll understand."

"Everything is alright, okay?"

"No, it's not okay, Buck. Don't shut me out. Now, talk to me," she said firmly.

"Okay, okay. Something happened over there. Something big."

"Yes, go on. What was it?"

"Well, I can't really say, but I'll tell you one thing: Heads are going to roll."

"Whose heads? Not yours?"

"No, it's people at the top."

"Whose heads? What are you talking about?" she asked, raising her voice.

She was getting frustrated and more than a little annoyed. She didn't know it, but her husband was purposefully being vague in an effort to protect her. He had come to believe that his own life might be in danger, on and off the battlefield, because of what he knew, what he had witnessed at My Lai. And he figured that, by extension, if his wife didn't know anything about it then no one would have a reason to harm her.

"Buck, whose heads?" she repeated.

"Look, never mind. Just drop it. I can't tell you any more than that. What time do you want to go to supper?"

"Oh, I don't care. Let's go at 7:30 or 8. I don't care," she said, exasperated that he wouldn't tell her what was on his mind.

Other than that little spat, they continued to enjoy one another's company, sun-bathing on the beach, swimming in the ocean, eating, drinking, dancing, sleeping late, attending Easter Sunday church services, talking about things back home, pretending that a war was not occurring, and imagining that this was where they lived, in Hawaii, in paradise.

Being able to get his conscious mind off the war was doing Hugh Thompson a lot of good, but he would frequently wake up with nightmares about My Lai, usually between 3 and 4 a.m. It happened again in the wee hours of the morning in which he was to return to Vietnam.

He sees the dead piled one on top of the other in the ditch, mangled and bleeding, then he hears the moans and groans of people in unbearable pain, begging for mercy, for someone to help them, but there's no one there to help except him, and he wants to help but he can't because he can't move, he's paralyzed. Then Lt. Calley appears and tells him to get out of there and mind his own business, and he's thinking that this is his business because he is a soldier and so his business is to protect people just like these. And now he's mad as hell and wants to fight Calley and save the people but he can't because he can't move. He feels helpless and powerless, he's breathing heavily, his heart is pounding so hard that it wakes him up, and for a few seconds he doesn't know where he is. Everything is dark.

Trembling and mumbling, Thompson got out of bed and felt his way toward the bathroom for water.

"Buck, you okay, baby?" Palma asked him.

"Uh huh."

"You have another bad dream?"

"Uh huh."

"You want to talk about it?"

"Nope."

"Buck, you're going back today. I won't see you again for eight or nine months..."

Thompson's fear of the unknown was finally giving way to his wife's plea to let her into his life.

"Okay, okay. Something did happen over there. Something terrible. Lots of people got killed in this little village, women, children, old men. They wiped out the whole village."

"Who did?"

"One of the ground units."

"Our guys?"

"Yep, our guys."

"When?"

"Oh, about three weeks ago. But I can't say any more."

He came out of the bathroom and lit a cigarette. He looked out of the window toward the ocean.

Palma sensed that he wanted to say more, that he needed to talk this out.

"How many people got killed?"

"Plenty."

"But, how many, Buck?"

"Maybe two, three hundred."

"They killed children?"

Thompson didn't answer.

"Buck, did you say they killed children, too?"

He didn't answer. She could see that he had buried his face in one of his hands and was crying.

"Yes, baby, they killed kids just the same age as Bucky and Brian," he said, referring to their children, ages four and two.

Now, Palma was silent, shocked by what she was hearing.

"I can't say anything more about it," Thompson said, still looking out the window toward the ocean.

Palma wasn't sure if he couldn't talk about it anymore because it was too hard on him emotionally or because his superiors had forbidden him to discuss it.

"I understand if you don't want to talk about..."

"One more thing I've got to tell you is about this little kid in the ditch."

"A little kid?"

"Yeah, same size as Bucky."

"Oh, Buck. This is one of the kids they killed?"

"No, this kid was alive. She was buried under a whole stack of bodies, and we set the chopper down and got her out of there. Same size as Bucky. I was thinking, 'What if that was our kid?'"

Palma sat quietly reflecting on the question her husband had posed. He lit a cigarette. It seemed that the conversation was over. But he wasn't finished.

"I got to hold the baby for a little while..."

"What baby?"

"I mean, the little kid. We brought her to the orphanage a few miles away, and I got to hold her. She was limp, like a little rag doll. She was in shock. I gave her to a nun and told her to take care of the baby because I thought her parents were probably dead."

Sitting up in the bed, Palma felt sad and vaguely ill. She was glad to have been there for her husband, to provide a sympathetic ear. She felt sorry for the child, for the child's parents, and for her tortured husband.

The time together did both of them a great deal of good, though Palma was very concerned about the man she loved. Saying good-bye at the airport was a tearful, emotionally difficult time, as it almost always is between husbands and wives who realize they may never see one another again.

Thompson was in good spirits when he returned to Chu Lai, calm, rested, more optimistic about life than when he left. However, shortly after his arrival he was told that his commanding officer, Major Watke, had been seriously injured in a helicopter crash. He was in the hospital, he may or may not make it, but either way he was finished as the CO of Thompson's unit.

And there was more bad news: Glenn Andreotta, the crew chief on Thompson's aircraft, was dead; he had been killed just a few days earlier while working as a gunner on a chopper that was shot down.

Shocked and depressed over the news, Thompson sought out his friend, the chaplain. Together they fretted over Watke's chances for survival and mourned the death of Andreotta, who was barely out of his teens.

They talked late into the night, over drinks, and the chaplain said it was his understanding that Andreotta's helicopter was struck by enemy fire and burst into flames when it hit the ground. He had heard that when the 'copter was going down Andreotta was still firing his M-60 at the enemy position so that the pilot of the helicopter accompanying his would know where the shooting had come from and could avoid being ambushed. Thompson was thinking that this sounded just like something Andreotta would do, always trying to help someone else, unselfish till the end. The chaplain also related that as the aircraft was going down Andreotta was struck by a bullet and was probably dead before he hit the ground.

There were two other soldiers on the aircraft that day. One survived, but the other, Charles Dutton, didn't. Dutton was severely injured in the crash. His clothes were on fire and he was rolling around on the ground, screaming in pain, and trying to put out the fire. An enemy soldier ran up to him and shot and killed him instantly. The soldier then turned to Barry Lloyd, the pilot, who was also rolling around on the ground, writhing in pain as a result of injuries he sustained in the crash, including crushed ankles. The soldier rolled Lloyd over with his foot. Lloyd was gritting his teeth and clutching his crucifix, apparently thinking that his time had come. Then, surprisingly, rather than shooting Lloyd, the enemy soldier turned and jogged away. Whether this had something to do with the crucifix or whether he may have heard a U.S. gunship rolling in was not clear. The answer to this question disappeared into the jungle with the soldier.

Within a few days of his return from R & R, Thompson was back in the swing of things, buzzing around in his little bubble helicopter, searching out the enemy. He was accompanied by Larry Colburn and a new crew chief.

One of the areas they worked regularly was Quang Ngai Province, where My Lai is located, and as they flew past a certain mountain every day they would get shot at by a fellow they started to call "One Shot Charlie." The guy would get off one round only, with a rifle. Each time, the shot came from the same place, give or take a few yards. More than anything, Thompson and his crew were amused by this never-say-die warrior who couldn't seem to hit the broad side of a barn from fifty paces, until one day "One Shot Charlie" got lucky.

"We're hit!" a surprised Thompson shouted.

"Where?" Colburn asked.

"I don't know."

"You want to set down here and call in the blues?" Colburn asked, referring to the ground troops whose job included rescuing the crews of downed helicopters.

"Hell no! This ain't our real estate," Thompson shouted.

The bullet had hit the engine's cooling fan, so the air that circulates to cool the engine quit circulating. The engine was overheating.

Thompson turned the helicopter around immediately and headed for the safety of Landing Zone Dottie. On his final approach to the airfield, the pilot of the gunship trailing Thompson's aircraft radioed a message:

"You'd better land that thing!"

"Why's that?" Thompson asked.

"Because your aircraft is on fire!"

He didn't have to be told twice. He landed the helicopter immediately, and all three aboard dove out as it touched down. The larger gunship landed only seconds later and lifted off with its three extra passengers as soon as they were aboard. The helicopter lay smoldering on the ground, its engine ruined, its body going up in flames.

Spring turned to summer in central Vietnam, and the tropical heat sapped the energy out of the men. The war wore on and the death toll on both sides mounted. For every U.S. military man killed in action, twenty, thirty, forty or more Vietnamese died, mostly civilians. The July heat was nearly unbearable, and the pace of combat was at a high pitch.

Among the Americans killed was Lt. Stephen Brooks, the platoon leader who was hot on the trail of the fleeing Vietnamese when Thompson interceded. Also killed was Lt. Col. Frank Barker, who had organized the task force which wiped out My Lai and its people; he died in a mid-air collision between a U.S. Army helicopter in which he was a passenger and a fixed-wing spotter plane. Among the other casualties of war, and particularly of the My Lai massacre, were men like Varnado Simpson, who were being eaten alive with guilt or scared out of their wits over the thought of being found out and hung for murder.

In addition to the human casualties, the truth about the massacre was well on its way to an early grave. Officers in the chain of command made a concerted effort to unceremoniously bury the truth – thus helping to prove the old adage, "The first casualty of war is the truth." Brigade Commander Col. Oran Henderson's report to Maj. Gen. Samuel Koster, Commanding General of the Americal Division, was nothing short of incredible. In the report, filed a month after the massacre, he denied that civilians were gathered together and shot. He attributed this conclusion to interviews with Capt. Ernest Medina, Commanding Officer of Charlie Company, and others with command responsibility. It stated, in part:

> It is concluded that 20 noncombatants were inadvertently killed when caught in the area of preparatory fires and in the crossfires of the U.S. and Viet Cong forces on 16 March, 1968. It is further concluded that no civilians were gathered together and shot by U.S. soldiers. The allegation that U.S. Forces shot and killed 450 to 500 civilians is obviously a Viet Cong propaganda move to discredit the United States in the eyes of the Vietnamese people.... It is recommended that a counter-propaganda campaign be waged against the VC....

Word of the massacre was getting around Vietnam to U.S. troops, even though the superiors of the men in Charlie Company had ordered them to be quiet about what happened there. One of the soldiers who got wind of the massacre was Ron Ridenhour, an infantryman who ended up in the same unit as some of the men who participated in the massacre. He heard the story from them, firsthand and in considerable detail. A patriot who believed what Charlie Company did at My Lai was a despicable crime, Ridenhour vowed to find out the truth of what happened and to report it when he got back to the States. He had a strong feeling that the military leaders in Vietnam who were responsible would attempt to cover up the tragic events of March 16.

Ridenhour formed an alliance with Michael Bernhardt, one of the members of Charlie Company who saw firsthand what happened at My Lai, and who refused to participate in it. They promised to support one another in their efforts to let the story be known in the U.S. so that the killing of the Vietnamese civilians would not go unpunished.

Meanwhile, however, Bernhardt was being punished for having refused to participate in the massacre. He was being kept out in the field for long stretches of time, given the most hazardous duties, and denied proper medical treatment for an intestinal disorder and "jungle rot" that was devouring the skin on his feet, calves and thighs. More often than not, he was made to walk point, in front of his squad, thus increasing his chances of being killed by a booby trap or taking the first bullet in a frontal ambush.

Mental anguish, physical illness and constant sweating from the oppressive heat caused Bernhardt's weight to drop from 145 to 105. He was very weak and beginning to hallucinate, seeing people and things that were not there in reality. Two days before his duty in the field was to end, he set his weapon down and as a supply helicopter was about to lift off he dove into its cargo area and was transported back to base. The doctor at the base hospital got an IV into his arm right away and declared he should have been brought in for medical treatment two months earlier.

As Bernhardt struggled to stay alive until his tour of duty was over, Hugh Thompson was engaged in especially hazardous duty of his own. By July he had been re-assigned from the base at Chu Lai to one at Da Nang and attached to a division of the Marines. Da Nang was being bombarded by rocket fire coming from several points around the city. It became Thompson's job to fly search-and-destroy missions over the so-called "rocket belt," to locate the people who were launching the rockets, and, working with a second scout helicopter, to take out the enemy and their weapons, permanently.

On one such mission, Thompson's helicopter came upon a Viet Cong rocket squad who were having chow. None of them was standing guard. Their weapons were stacked ten or fifteen feet from where they were sitting, so they didn't have time to grab their guns to defend themselves when the chopper appeared. The gunner on the chopper opened fire on the men, and they all ran into their bunker, without weapons.

Thompson called in the second helicopter. He put his chopper down to a hover at ten or twenty feet from the bunker's entrance, to keep them from escaping. He then radioed a ground unit of Marines who were in the immediate area. They arrived within ten minutes and blasted the bunker with automatic weapons fire, killing everyone inside. One of the bullets ricocheted and hit Thompson's fuel tank. The fuel gushed out, and Thompson had to land the chopper then and there. He radioed the other pilot to set down and give him and his gunner a ride. Thompson jumped on one skid and his gunner got on the other. A third man on the chopper with them, a Marine, asked, "Hey, what about me?" Thompson responded, "Sorry, no room; we'll send someone back for you." The helicopter lifted off to return to base, leaving the Marine stranded. His anxiety was short-lived, however, as another chopper came a few minutes later to evacuate him to friendly ground.

A few days later, another Viet Cong rocket squad came out on the losing end of one of Thompson's search-and-destroy missions. Thompson's chopper and the one flying with his wiped out ten of the enemy, and Thompson radioed for the nearest ground unit to come in and collect the weapons captured in the raid. A small infantry squad was sent in that direction. They came upon a large, open field, which gave them no place to hide in the event they were fired upon, so the leader of the squad radioed a request to Thompson to provide air cover for them as they crossed the field. Thompson did as he was asked.

As the Marines got into the field a little way, automatic weapons fire opened up on them. They hit the dirt, and Thompson's 'copter made a run on the position where the fire was coming from. The ground troops were pinned down. The 'copter made a second run on the enemy position, and the firing ceased. Before it did, though, Thompson's aircraft took a bullet, knocking out the radio. He landed to survey the damage, something he seldom would do in hostile territory. He felt relatively safe this time, though, since the enemy had apparently been killed or had withdrawn into the jungle.

He asked to use the ground unit's radio so he could let the pilot he was working with know that he had been hit and that his radio was knocked out. While on the ground, he noticed the smell of fuel coming from his aircraft, and he began to worry that the round he took might have punctured his tank. But seeing no puncture mark, he lifted off and continued providing cover for the ground unit as they hustled across the field.

The bullet that hit the chopper had indeed punctured the tank in a place that was not readily detectable. As a result, just as they entered the airspace over the landing area in Da Nang the engine stopped. It was out of fuel. Fortunately, they were flying high enough that they were able to avoid crashing by utilizing the 'copter's auto-rotation feature. Were it not for this emergency feature – which allows the blades to continue to rotate and function though the engine is not running – the chopper would have fallen from the air like a wounded bird and the crew more than likely would not have been able to survive the crash.

In all, the choppers Thompson flew were hit by enemy fire eight times during his tour of duty. In four of those instances the aircraft were lost to the Army, casualties of war. If his helicopter were hit while flying over hostile territory, he would not, as a rule, land it there, but rather would try to make it back to the base. He had developed a simple philosophy about the value of a helicopter as compared with the value of human life: He would readily run the risk of ruining the 'copter before taking even the slightest unnecessary chance with his life or that of his crew.

He assured his crew on more than one occasion: "As long as this engine is running and these blades are turning, we're going home."

To do otherwise, to set down in enemy territory, would make his chopper a sitting duck, as it were. The enemy spent a lot of time and energy trying to shoot down these elusive birds of war, so every U.S. pilot knew that landing his aircraft in hostile territory was, in most cases, flirting with death. It would give the hunted a rare opportunity to become the hunter, and these skilled guerrilla warriors were not likely to let such an opportunity go by without trying to take advantage of it.

On the morning of August 21 Thompson left the military base at Da Nang at first light and was headed for the base at Chu Lai to have routine maintenance done on his aircraft. He was alone in the little bubble helicopter, and had begun his descent into Chu Lai, taking an approach to the airfield that 'copter pilots used frequently.

The Viet Cong were waiting, listening, hoping for a clear shot at a low-flying 'copter that would come into the range of their machine guns. They opened fire when the aircraft was at an altitude of approximately six hundred feet, striking and shattering the Plexiglas bubble which surrounded the cockpit. Thompson was hit and wounded in the calves and thighs by flying glass. The engine was also hit, and it shut down that instant; the tail rotor was damaged as well. The aircraft, flying at approximately 60 m.p.h., began an immediate and rapid descent. The pilot tried to break the fall by utilizing the auto-rotation maneuver, but that worked only to a degree, and the 'copter hit the ground hard.

The impact of the crash injured Thompson's back severely, and he grimaced in pain as he unlocked his seat belt and started to crawl out of the wreckage. As he did he noticed his legs felt numb, like they were asleep. They were also bleeding heavily from the wounds caused by the flying glass, and his fatigues from mid-thigh on down were soaked in blood. He tried to get out of his seat using his legs to push himself up, but his legs seemed to be paralyzed.

He managed to crawl out of the mangled 'copter, which was lying on its side, fearing that it might burst into flames at any second. Using his arms and elbows, he dragged his body away from the aircraft, cringing in pain all the while. He had covered only ten or twelve yards when he heard voices in a language other than his own. The frightened soldier looked back over his shoulder and saw a group of six or seven Vietnamese, dressed in black pajamas, some of them with weapons, emerging from a tree line forty or fifty yards on the other side of his helicopter. Realizing he had forgotten his automatic weapon, a car-15, in the 'copter, he turned around and crawled back to get it. He knew that the .38-calibre pistol strapped to his belt would be no match for the people coming his way, if they were who he thought they were.

He held the car-15 with both hands, keeping it off the ground, away from the dirt and sand, as he crawled on his elbows toward a sand dune to take cover. He had gone down very near the beach of the South China Sea, just a mile north of the base at Chu Lai. The pain in his lower back was excruciating, but the instinct for self-preservation was even stronger as he scrambled for dear life.

The injured pilot took cover behind the dune and pointed his weapon in the direction of the Vietnamese. He could see that he left a line in the sand, so he knew they could track him down easily. But at least he had a chance now that he was adequately armed.

He nearly passed out a couple of times from the pain but fought through it to remain conscious. He knew that he needed to maintain consciousness or he would be a dead man. He stayed low behind the dune and watched the Vietnamese as they cautiously approached the 'copter.

Meanwhile, a handful of U.S. soldiers, who happened to be in the area, were double-timing it along the edge of the beach and headed for the spot where some of them had seen the chopper go down. The Vietnamese heard them coming and faded back into the nearby wooded area, then quietly disappeared from the scene altogether.

The U.S. soldiers secured the crash site then hurriedly searched the helicopter for its pilot and crew. Finding no one, they looked around the immediate area and located the injured pilot. He was unconscious, in shock.

Not knowing how seriously wounded he was, they loaded him onto a stretcher and carried him to their outpost for first aid. He was then flown by helicopter to the 27th Surgical Hospital at Chu Lai for immediate care and further examination. He regained consciousness while in the hospital, five or six hours after the crash, and began complaining of severe pain in his back and numbness in his legs. He asked for something to stop the pain, but the doctor would not give him anything until he was finished testing and trying to determine the extent of the injuries.

Finally, the doctor ordered a shot to stop the pain, and Thompson floated off into another world, free from pain and worry. Soon thereafter he was again loaded onto a medical evacuation helicopter and flown from Chu Lai southward to Saigon for further medical treatment. After numerous X-rays and extensive examination the doctors declared that Thompson had sustained a serious compression fracture of the spine. His back was broken. The war was over for this soldier.

The patient was then flown to the 106th General Army Hospital in Tokyo, Japan, and put into traction in hopes of preventing any number of complications, not the least of which could be permanent paralysis of his legs.

He was rigged up in what is called a Stryker frame, a contraption designed to relieve the pressure on broken bones or to uncompress a spine which has been traumatized.

Now, in addition to the extreme pain in his back, Thompson was completely immobilized and uncomfortable. He was facing a long period of recovery and rehabilitation that would have tried the patience of a patient person. And patience was not one of his virtues.

There he was, stuck in an Army hospital halfway around the world, staring at the walls, waiting for time to heal him, sometimes watching television, occasionally making small talk with other wounded soldiers, understanding there was a chance he would never walk again, glad to be alive and at the same time not so glad to be alive, feeling alone and forgotten though he was in the middle of a busy ward, having a lot of time on his hands to drift from thought to thought. He wondered how the little Vietnamese kid from the ditch was doing. He wondered how the Army was coming with its investigation into the massacre.

The days went by slowly, as they would for any bed-ridden person in a hospital, and even more so since he was immobilized and in traction. It was like being chained down. One day dragged into another, then another, then another. A week passed, then ten days, then eleven. Thompson enjoyed looking at the nurses, and talking to them. They all seemed pretty to him. He convinced one of them to smuggle in a beer one night, then the next, until it became a little ritual, one of the highlights of his day.

Two weeks in the hospital gave way to three and finally it was time to go home. The patient had reached a stage in his recovery where it was reasonably safe to move him.

Still in traction and unable to walk, he left Japan on a medical evacuation plane in mid-September. When he reached the States, he spent a day or two in the hospital at Andrews Air Force Base in Virginia before being flown to Martin Army Hospital at Ft. Benning, Georgia, where he remained in traction for another week.

Then he started a regimen of physical therapy and slowly regained his ability to walk. In the first few weeks he resembled a 90-year-old carefully sliding his feet forward on an uneven floor, taking great care not to fall and break something. After a couple of weeks of therapy he was standing up relatively straight again, with the help of a back brace, and walking as normally as could be expected for a guy with a broken back.

If the Army provided first-rate medical care to help him get past the physical trauma of war, it did little or nothing to prepare him for the real and major psychological adjustments that any combat soldier needs to make when he returns from armed conflict. There was no de-briefing, no readjustment counseling, no advice on dealing with the growing number of his own countrymen who were adamantly opposed to any U.S. involvement in the Vietnam War. Nor was there anyone there to point out that when a soldier comes home and is off duty, spending time with his "significant other" means being with and communicating not with his Army buddies and comrades, but rather with his wife or girlfriend.

Failure to make these adjustments would strain Thompson's marriage and bring discord into his home within weeks of his release from the hospital.

Now that he was up and about in something of a normal fashion, it was time for Thompson to get back to work. He reported for duty at Ft. Rucker, Alabama, in January of '69. His job was teaching soldiers to become helicopter pilots.

When the work day ended, he felt a calling to go to the officers club for a few beers and some conversation with the boys.

They would drink and smoke and talk about aviation, about the Army, about the war. Men who have been in combat seem to have a need to talk about it a lot or to not talk about it at all. Talking about it with their own kind, with other men who have experienced it, seems to heal something in their psyches that has been injured as a result of having been engaged in mortal combat. Discussing it with wives or mothers or sisters just isn't effective in treating the wound. Just as there are certain needs a woman has that a man will never be able to meet, so, too, are there certain things a woman will never be able to do for a man, and understanding what he went through in combat is one of them. So, men who have been to war will gather at the officers clubs to seek a certain understanding, to try to have a certain emptiness filled. It is a form of therapy, albeit ill-defined and unpolished.

In a real way, Thompson had a new lease on life, having survived the crash that could have killed him. He was back home, out of harm's way, living in the same place as his family, and teaching a subject he knew quite a bit about, through previous study and experience.

But after just a few months of being back in the States he was becoming restless. Teaching aspiring pilots to fly helicopters was getting to be routine, as were his frequent and sometimes prolonged visits to the officers club. He would get home late and find the supper cold, the children in bed asleep, and his wife, Palma, feeling neglected and angry over the direction in which things seemed to be headed.

By March of '69, they were both questioning whether he was cut out to be a "family man." One argument led to another, and by April they were separated. Divorce would follow some months later.

Through all of this, Thompson was finding it odd that he had heard nothing about the My Lai massacre since his return home. There was nothing in the press, nothing in the rumor mill at the officers club. Nor was he hearing anything about any soldiers being court-martialed for what happened there. He found the silence on this subject to be bothersome.

So did Ron Ridenhour. Now out of the Army and living in Phoenix, Arizona, Ridenhour kept hoping that the story would somehow, finally, make its way back to the U.S. He suspected now, as he did while he was in Vietnam, that the Army brass who were involved would keep the story under wraps and never let it be known in the U.S., if they had anything to say about it. With this as a given, he had been wrestling with his conscience over whether he should be the one to blow the lid off the coverup. Surely, there would be unpleasant consequences which he personally would have to endure if he spoke up. But he knew also that if he didn't say anything, and no one else did either, then perhaps no one would be brought to justice for these crimes and, possibly more importantly, if unchecked this type of behavior could be repeated and hundreds or even thousands of innocent civilians could continue to be murdered in other wartime situations similar to the one at My Lai.

In the end, Ridenhour's habit of doing the right thing won out. As Thompson had done at My Lai, Ridenhour made a firm decision to do what he knew was right, regardless of the consequences. His hunger for justice, his reverence for human life and human rights, his anger and rage over the murder of unarmed civilians, all of these things played a part in his decision to speak up.

Accordingly, he sat down and wrote a letter describing his understanding of what happened at My Lai – nicknamed "Pinkville" – and urging that the massacre be investigated thoroughly. It was dated March 29, 1969 and mailed to a number of people in positions of power and authority, in the legislative and executive branches of government and in the military. By spreading it around to key people in all these areas Ridenhour was trying to assure that someone who saw it would act upon it, even though others might dismiss it as a ridiculous claim, allow it to get lost in channels, or set it aside and forget about it. He sent the letter to President Nixon, the Secretary of the Army, the Chairman of the Joint Chiefs of Staff, and about two dozen congressmen and senators.

> Gentlemen:
>
> It was late in April, 1968 that I first heard of "Pinkville" and what allegedly happened there. I received that first report with some skepticism, but in the following months I was to hear similar stories from such a wide variety of people that it became impossible for me to disbelieve that some-

thing rather dark and bloody did indeed occur sometime in March, 1968 in a village called "Pinkville" in the Republic of Vietnam....

Pfc. "Butch" Gruver, whom I had known in Hawaii (and who later became a member of "Charlie" Company),... told me the first of many reports I was to hear.... He recalled seeing a small boy, about three or four years old, standing by the trail with a gunshot wound in one arm. The boy was clutching his wounded arm with his other hand, while blood trickled between his fingers. He was staring around himself in shock and disbelief at what he saw.

"He just stood there with big eyes staring around like he didn't understand; he didn't believe what was happening. Then the captain's RTO (radio operator) put a burst of M-16 rifle fire into him."

...Although he had not seen it, Gruver had been told by people he considered trustworthy that one of the company's officers, 2nd Lt. Calley, had rounded up several groups of villagers (each group consisting of a minimum of 20 persons of both sexes and all ages)... then machine-gunned each group....

Somehow I just couldn't believe that not only had so many young American men participated in such an act of barbarism, but that their officers had ordered it....

Pfcs. Michael Terry and William Doherty...were veterans of "Charlie" Company.... Around noon the two soldiers' squad stopped to eat.

"Billy and I started to get out our chow," Terry said, "but close to us was a bunch of Vietnamese in a heap, and some of them were moaning. Calley...had been through before us and all of them had been shot, but many weren't dead. It was obvious that they weren't going to get any medical attention so Billy and I got up and went over to where they were. I guess we sort of finished them off."

Terry went on to say that he and Doherty then returned to where their packs were and ate lunch....

If Terry, Doherty and Gruver could be believed, then not only had "Charlie" Company received orders to slaughter all the inhabitants of the village, but those orders had come from the commanding officer of Task Force Barker, or pos-

> sibly even higher in the chain of command....
>
> I remain irrevocably persuaded that if you and I do truly believe in the principles of justice and the equality of every man, however humble, before the law, that form the very backbone that this country is founded on, then we must press forward a widespread and public investigation of this matter with all our combined efforts. I think it was Winston Churchill who once said:
>
> "A country without a conscience is a country without a soul, and a country without a soul is a country that cannot survive."
>
> ...I have considered sending this to newspapers, magazines and broadcasting companies, but I somehow feel that investigation and action by the Congress of the United States is the appropriate procedure....
>
> – *Ron Ridenhour*

Ridenhour's letter hit Washington like a bombshell. Those in the military hierarchy, as well as their Commander-in-Chief, were already aware, to some degree, of what they referred to as "the My Lai incident." But the report from the ex-soldier was a complete shock to most of the congressmen and senators. Some absolutely refused to believe it. Others didn't want to believe this about men who wore the military uniform of the United States. Some viewed it as a sort of un-American attempt to besmirch the name of the U.S. military and undermine the war effort.

In a matter of days after receiving the letter, in the first week of April, the Army started a preliminary investigation into the massacre and into the possibly fraudulent manner in which it was originally reported by those with command responsibilities.

Two months later, in the first week of June, the Army ordered Lt. William Calley to leave Vietnam and return to the United States.

That same week Hugh Thompson was called into his superior's office at Ft. Rucker and given orders to report to the Office of the Inspector General of the Army, in Washington, D.C. He was not told why he was being summoned.

Chapter 9

The Pursuit Of Truth And Justice

HUGH THOMPSON ARRIVED IN WASHINGTON, D.C., on June 10, 1969, the day before he was to report to the Inspector General's Office. With a little time on his hands, he took a cab to Col. William Wilson's office in hopes of visiting with him informally, to find out why he had been summoned. He envisioned them chatting over coffee.

Instead, when he arrived he was greeted coldly, if not rudely, and told to return at the appointed hour on the designated day. The staff officer who stood between Thompson and Col. Wilson was not given to Southern hospitality, as was the soldier from Stone Mountain, Georgia.

Thompson summoned a cab, lit a cigarette, and waited for his ride back to the Holiday Inn in Arlington, Virginia, where he would nurse his stiff, aching back and kill time by chatting with other soldiers who were staying at the same hotel. The men with whom he drank and talked had no idea who Hugh Thompson was, except that he was a Southerner who had flown a scout helicopter in Vietnam and lived to tell about it.

The following morning, Thompson and Col. Wilson got down to business. With his back brace helping him to sit up straight, almost at attention, Thompson listened intently as the inspector began his inquiry.

"Where were you on March 16, 1968?" Wilson asked in a gruff tone.

"I'm not sure. I think I was in Vietnam, sir. Or I might have been in Hawaii on R & R," Thompson answered in a halting voice.

"Weren't you at My Lai, South Vietnam?"

"No, sir, I've never heard of My Lai," Thompson answered.

The inspector stopped cold and scowled at Thompson. He thought Thompson was lying to him. They were off to a bad start.

"You've never heard of My Lai?" he asked, raising his voice.

"No, sir."

"Do you recall an incident wherein you hit a tree with your helicopter and broke your rotor blade?"

"Oh, yes, sir."

"That happened in My Lai on the date in question," the inspector stated.

"Okay, yes, now I remember. That was Pinkville. We called it Pinkville. I didn't know it as My Lai."

Col. Wilson continued to question the former scout helicopter pilot, as staff members took notes and tape-recorded what was being said. For more than five hours, an animated Hugh Thompson readily recounted what he saw and did on that day when five hundred and four Vietnamese civilians were slaughtered and ten were air-lifted to safety.

What the inspector was hearing corroborated what was contained in the letter from Ronald Ridenhour. He knew then and there, without a shadow of a doubt, that something dark and evil had occurred at My Lai, just as Ridenhour had written. He likewise figured with certainty that the Army's first investigation of the incident was no investigation at all, but rather part of a sinister plot to cover up war crimes committed against the very people whom American soldiers were in Vietnam to protect.

Wilson was glad that Thompson had come. Thompson's visit was a turning point in his – and the U.S. Army's – efforts to get at the truth about what happened at My Lai. Heretofore, the allegations in Ridenhour's letter were merely hearsay, rumors, unsubstantiated charges by someone who wasn't there when the crimes occurred. But now, all of a sudden, in just a matter of hours, in a meeting that did not have the trappings of an historic event, Thompson had provided the eyewitness account that gave weight and substance to the allegations of possibly the most extensive war crime in U.S. military history.

The inspector kept Thompson in Washington for two days after their initial meeting. He wanted Thompson to positively identify Calley as the lieutenant he confronted and argued with at the irrigation ditch. Accordingly, Col. Wilson ordered Calley to come in on June 13 and to stand with other men in a lineup. Thompson looked closely at each of the half dozen men who were presented. He picked Calley without hesitation. He was positive.

Col. Wilson reported his findings to the Secretary of the Army, Stanley Resor, who was greatly disturbed to learn with certainty that not only were the crimes committed by U.S. soldiers but that they were apparently covered up by the superior officers whom he had trusted to report truthfully. The original investigation by the Army had been worse than a watered down version of the truth; it had been a deliberate misstatement of the facts, a lie.

Additional witnesses to the massacre were interviewed by the Inspector General's Office, some in Washington and some in their own cities, and a flood of information was forthcoming. Many of them were anxious to talk and seemed relieved to get their stories off their chests, to clear their consciences. Others were frightened and evasive. By the end of June, the Inspector General's Office was recommending that a criminal investigation into the My Lai incident be launched forthwith.

Two months later, on September 6, Lt. William Calley was charged with the murder of one hundred and nine Vietnamese civilians. The following month, Sgt. David Mitchell was charged with assault with intent to murder thirty Vietnamese civilians. In the months to come, more than twenty others would be charged.

In November, the Secretary of the Army announced that he was appointing Lt. Gen. William Peers to head up a second investigation of the My Lai incident, with emphasis to be placed on studying the veracity of the Army's first investigation, which appeared to be a whitewash.

Meanwhile, the Armed Services Committee of the U.S. House of Representatives was taking a keen interest in the events at My Lai. The committee was chaired by L. Mendel Rivers, a conservative Democrat from South Carolina. In November he asked the Department of the Army to furnish his committee with any and all information it had on the My Lai incident. The Army complied with the request, but not fully.

The following month the Investigating Subcommittee of the House Armed Services Committee heard secret testimony from Secretary Resor regarding the massacre and its coverup. The subcommittee also called three others to speak with them privately – Hugh Thompson, Lt. Gen. Peers and Capt. Ernest Medina. After hearing what they had to say on the subject, Rivers decided that his committee should make an independent, in-depth study of the My Lai incident. To achieve this goal, he appointed a special subcommittee, to be chaired by F. Edward Hebert (D-La.). Other members would be Samuel S. Stratton (D-N.Y.), Charles S. Gubser (R-Calif.) and William L. Dickinson (R-Ala.).

Rivers, Hebert and others were in agreement that the Army's ability to investigate itself had thus far proven to be suspect. They figured that an inquiry by an independent entity, such as their Congressional subcommittee, would be more impartial and would dig harder for the truth, no matter what it might prove to be – or so they said. They knew that their ability to subpoena witnesses was a powerful tool, one that would assure them that they would have a significant role in determining the outcome of this whole sordid mess. In short, they seemed to be saying, at least in public, that their subcommittee would be an instrument to assure that the truth would come out and, by inference, that justice would subsequently be served.

On the surface, it seemed like a good idea, but there was a problem. Secretary Resor felt that this was the Army's business and that it could best be handled without interference from Congress. He urged Rivers and Hebert to stand back and allow the

Army to do the investigating and thus permit the system of military justice to run its course unimpeded. He argued that the very process of the subcommittee's subpoenaing witnesses and taking their testimony could have the effect of preventing the successful prosecution of the guilty parties.

Resor wrote to Hebert on the subject:

> Dear Mr. Chairman:
>
> I am deeply concerned to learn of your Subcommittee's plan to call potential witnesses in presently scheduled or potential military justice proceedings during your formal Executive Hearings, commencing on April 15, 1970, regarding the alleged suppression of information pertaining to the Son My incident.
>
> As I have emphasized on previous occasions, we fully appreciate your interest in obtaining sufficient information to discharge your constitutional responsibilities. At the same time, however, I have attempted...to convey my belief that discharge of our own responsibility to execute the laws will be *imperiled* by such actions as your Subcommittee now contemplates.
>
> ...I am compelled to urge once again that the discharge of our respective responsibilities can be reconciled only if interviews by the Congress of witnesses in pending court-martial cases are *deferred until they can be conducted without prejudice to the defendants.* In the meantime, I have already furnished you with the findings and recommendations of the Peers-MacCrate Inquiry. The record of the testimony which you have requested is being provided to you as rapidly as it becomes available and should constitute an adequate basis for your independent review of these conclusions.
>
> ...I have carefully considered your request...that the Army arrange for the appearance before your Subcommittee of some 39 civilian and military personnel. The vast majority – if not all – of these individuals are material witnesses to offenses under the Uniform Code of Military Justice alleged to have been committed at Son My or during the course of the subsequent inquiry conducted within the Americal Division. Thirteen of these men, furthermore, have been formally charged and may ultimately be tried by courts-martial.

> I have concluded, therefore, ...that it would be inappropriate for the Army to voluntarily make available the witnesses requested by Mr. Reddan (the committee's attorney). As I stated in that earlier letter, furthermore, I would hope that you would carefully consider the matters I have raised before you pursue further a form of investigation which involves compelling the attendance of potential witnesses and defendants in military justice proceedings....
>
> Sincerely,
> *Stanley R. Resor,*
> Secretary of the Army

Hebert may have considered Resor's request, but he went against his wishes nonetheless.

The idea that the Congressional hearings could have the effect of wrecking the Army's chances to successfully prosecute the guilty parties was not news to Mendel Rivers, nor to Hebert. Rivers was keenly aware of what he and Hebert were doing and, in fact, Rivers was on record as saying publicly that he did not want U.S. servicemen court-martialed for what happened at My Lai and would do everything he could to try to prevent them from going to trial. He stated as much in April of 1970 when he addressed the Chamber of Commerce in Altus, Oklahoma, the home of Altus Air Force Base.

"We bring them home from the Army and let some idiots try them like this.... I will have something to do in this (matter). You just wait and see. They're not going to get away with this," he said, sounding like a man determined to have his way.

He did not say specifically how he planned to interfere with the trials. However, when he returned to Washington he told an anonymous Congressional source that he was banking on the investigating subcommittee, whose hearings were just getting under way, to somehow help him achieve his goal. He said he hoped the subcommittee would "come up with something that (we) can use as a lever."

In early December of 1969, before the controversy between the Army and the Congressional committee erupted full force,

Thompson told his story in executive session to the full House Armed Services Committee. The majority of those in attendance seemed to feel that Thompson had provided solid evidence that indeed an awful massacre had occurred at My Lai and that those responsible needed to be brought to justice.

Rivers, a strong-willed man with a mind of his own, did not seem to hear what the other congressmen in the room heard. Though he had admonished them not to speak to the press about what was said in these executive sessions, he apparently exempted himself and spoke pointedly to the reporters who were standing by hoping that someone would make a statement.

"Thompson gave us no information to lead us to believe that anyone committed a massacre at My Lai," Rivers stated, much to the amazement of others who were in the same room and heard the same story from Thompson.

"We haven't found anybody whose testimony would convict anybody of anything.... We haven't found any evidence of a massacre. But we haven't gotten as far along as the Army has. We're perfectly wide open. I'm being fair-minded," he added.

Rivers couldn't stand the thought that U.S. soldiers would have disgraced the uniform that he so revered. If it were true, if there had been a massacre and a coverup, it would be an awful blow to the honor and integrity of the U.S. Armed Forces, which he fiercely defended and promoted in his role as chairman of the House Armed Services Committee. Rivers may have tried to pass himself off as an objective, open-minded chairman, but in fact he was simply a tough advocate of the military. His disposition was one of blind patriotism, and his colors had been showing for years.

If Rivers' objectivity was open to debate, the impartiality of the men on his committee was called into question, as well, by newspaper reports that the "entire subcommittee broke out in unanimous applause" when Capt. Ernest Medina tried to clear the name of one of the officers who was responsible for the massacre.

Referring to the late Lt. Col. Frank Barker, commander of Task Force Barker, the unit which annihilated the hamlet and nearly every living thing in it, Medina had this to say:

"Lt. Col. Barker was an outstanding task force commander, an outstanding soldier. I'm sure he believed that there was no incident of war crimes or atrocities committed at My Lai-4. And I asked to make this statement on behalf of Mrs. Barker because Col. Barker is dead."

Medina's statement seemed to touch the hearts of the congressmen. However, the part about "no incident of war crimes or atrocities" did not come close to touching the truth. Just how far Medina was from the truth began to come clear only a month later as war crimes indictments were handed down and stories about them began hitting the media with regularity.

In the months to come, the list of those charged with war crimes and crimes against humanity, which already bore the names of Lt. Calley and Sgt. Mitchell, would grow by eleven. Most prominent among them would be the name of Capt. Ernest Medina, who was the immediate superior over Calley and two other platoon leaders whose men slaughtered the civilians of Son My Village; he was charged with the murders of one hundred and seventy-five civilians, primarily because he failed to stop what was going on all around him. Other ground troops charged with crimes ranging from assault to rape to murder were: Pfc. Gerald Smith, Sgt. Charles Hutto, Capt. Eugene Kotouc, Lt. Thomas Willingham, Sgt. Kenneth Hodges, Sgt. Escquiel Torres, Pfc. Max Hutson, S-4 William Doherty, Cpl. Kenneth Schiel and S-4 Robert T'Souvas.

Others against whom charges would be prepared involved men with command responsibility. They were accused of actions or inactions such as dereliction of duty, failure to report a war crime, cover-up and the like. Included were: Maj. Gen. Samuel Koster, Brig. Gen. George Young, Col. Oran Henderson, Col. Nels Parson, Lt. Col. Robert Luper, Maj. Charles Calhoun, Maj. David Gavin, Maj. William Guinn, Maj. Robert McKnight, Maj. Frederic Watke, Lt. Kenneth Boatman and Lt. Dennis Johnson.

More criminal charges would have been filed against the men on the ground that day, but three-fourths of the one hundred and four who were in Charlie Company were now out of the service

– and therefore immune from prosecution by the Army. The Army no longer had jurisdiction over them. Nor did any U.S. civilian court, since the crimes had not occurred on U.S. soil. Nor did any Vietnamese court, since the men were no longer in Vietnam, and there was no extradition treaty between the two nations.

The remaining and perhaps most appropriate forum for trying these men would be a military commission – which did not exist and therefore would have to be assembled – but President Nixon gave no support to this remedy whatsoever. To convene a military commission, then indict and try the suspects, would be to hold war crimes trials on U.S. soil – a shameful spectacle which would imply that American soldiers were at least suspected of some of the same sort of atrocities committed by the Nazis in World War II. President Nixon feared this would disgrace the country, undermine the war effort, and fuel the antiwar movement in a manner that was unprecedented. The courts-martial which would be starting soon – involving Calley, Medina, Mitchell and others – would generate more than enough bad publicity about the Armed Forces. To allow additional trials through a military commission would be to invite a public relations nightmare.

In dismissing the suggestion for a military commission, Nixon put an end to any chance that justice would be served during his administration, where the ex-servicemen were concerned. And in doing so, he violated the Geneva Conventions. As a signatory to the Conventions of 1949, the U.S. had given its word of honor that it would prosecute its own war criminals, just as other nations had given their word to try their own. Nixon left the issue to be resolved by the next President, or the next, or possibly the one after that.

President Nixon felt it would be a damaging blow to the honor of the United States if any of the ground troops were convicted of war crimes, but it would be even worse if any of the high-ranking officers were implicated. Accordingly, in an effort to minimize the public relations damage which the massacre would do to the Armed Forces, Nixon made an effort to head off the indictments of any of the officers with command responsibility at the time in question. He sent word to Gen. William Westmoreland, the Commander of U.S. Forces in Vietnam, through an intermediary, that he was to cooperate with whitewashing the chain of command in Vietnam. But the general would have no part of it. He stood up to the Commander-in-Chief and refused to be a party to what he considered obstruction of justice. Westmoreland, like Gen. Peers and Secretary of the Army Resor, was committed to bringing to justice all the guilty parties who had sullied the uniform of the American soldier.

Meanwhile, F. Edward Hebert and L. Mendel Rivers – whom Nixon relied on to support his programs and espouse his philosophies in the House of Representatives – were working on a plan to prevent the conviction of any of the ground troops who took part in the massacre.

Thompson testified before the Army's board of inquiry on several occasions during his months in Washington, which began in June of 1969. In the earliest sessions he would tell his story without the benefit of having an attorney. He felt no need to be represented by counsel, since he was a witness for the government, for the prosecution. He would simply tell the truth in his own words, relating what he saw and did that day at My Lai. He hadn't done anything wrong, so he didn't have anything to hide. He wasn't one of the soldiers who would be on trial.

But something happened to change his mind about needing a lawyer. As he was relating how he landed his chopper to rescue the civilians and told his men to cover him, some of the members of the board began pressing him on that point. Who was he having his men cover him against? Who might pose a threat to his and the civilians' safety? The American troops who were pursuing the Vietnamese? Did he tell his men to point their weapons at American soldiers?

Thompson started to get nervous. He was getting uncomfortable with this line of questioning, very uncomfortable. Were they trying to set him up for court-martial? He sensed that this was the case, so he started to mince his words. Then he asked for a lawyer. He would encounter nearly identical questions from the full House Armed Services Committee and later from the Investigating Subcommittee.

One of those who gave him a hard time on this issue was Mendel Rivers. It was obvious from the questions Rivers asked and the manner in which he talked to him that Thompson wasn't Rivers' kind of soldier. The idea of an American soldier having his men point their weapons at their comrades – no matter what the reason – just didn't set right with Rivers. And the idea that Lt. Calley and others would be court-martialed for carrying out orders didn't set well with him either. The thought that Americans may look upon Thompson's actions as good and Calley's as evil seemed all turned around to Rivers. Thompson is the one who should be punished and Calley should be praised for doing the tough work that infantrymen are called upon to do, Rivers figured at the time.

One evening following a meeting of the full committee in which Thompson was present, Rivers took Thompson to the steps of the Capitol and initiated something of a news conference. TV network news cameras were there and rolling as Rivers proceeded to dominate the discussion, praising the U.S. troops in Vietnam, talking about the need for further study of the alleged My Lai incident, and promising to take a closer look at the report that Thompson had ordered his men to point their weapons at fellow soldiers. Thompson, who could hardly get a word in edgewise, felt embarrassed and somewhat intimidated by the aggressive, articulate congressman who knew how to play to the news cameras.

Thompson had sensed Rivers' hostility previously and now he was reading it loud and clear. Rivers apparently felt that Thompson had acted improperly at My Lai, that he had conducted himself in an unmilitary-like manner. Thompson was becoming convinced that Rivers was setting him up to be court-martialed.

He was getting worried. First came the aggressive questioning from the Army's board of inquiry, and now Rivers seemed to be trying to move in for the kill.

Frightened and disheartened, Thompson stopped at a liquor store for a bottle of whiskey on the way back to his hotel in Arlington. He would try to drown his fear and his growing sense of alienation. He felt alone and very much unappreciated.

I risk my neck to save these defenseless people from being murdered, and this is the thanks I get. Now, they want to court-martial me. Oh, no, I'm not going to jail. I'm going to Canada. I'll desert the Army before I let them send me to Ft. Leavenworth.

The soldier poured himself a Seagrams and water, picked up the phone, and started calling for the departure schedules of the major airlines with flights from Washington to Canada. He had just about convinced himself that deserting the Army would be the one sure way to avoid the depressing fate that was looming.

As the evening wore on his thinking vacillated. He wondered what his life would be like in Canada, what it would feel like to be free and out from under all this pressure. Then he considered his parents, who had reared him to do the right thing, to be brave and upstanding, to take his punishment like a man when he did something wrong.

If I run away from this, they'll be so ashamed of me, and I'll be ashamed of myself. I can see the headline in the newspaper in Stone Mountain now: "Son of Mr. and Mrs. Hugh Thompson Sr. deserts the Army and flees to Canada." And the subhead: "Big Vietnam war hero turns out to be not so brave after all."

Through the night he tossed and turned and fretted over which way to go. His subconscious mind finally worked it out for him: He would act in a manner consistent with his idea of what it meant to be a man and a soldier.

Thompson was up before dawn, and after a quick shower and shave he was buttoning his uniform. He looked in the mirror and briefly studied his face and his uniform.

This is who I am. Lt. Hugh C. Thompson Jr., U.S. Army, Vietnam veteran. Welcome home, soldier. Reporting for duty, sir... Your assignment: March up there and tell the truth. Keep telling the truth, and don't let those silver-tongued devils back you into a corner... Ye shall know the truth, and the truth shall set you free... Truth is, I am proud to be an American soldier, glad I did what I did at My Lai, and I'm not going to let any gray-haired s.o.b. turn this around on me... Ain't gonna let nobody turn me 'round, turn me 'round, turn me 'round...

Thompson spent the better part of a year in and out of Washington, doing his part to help the Army understand what happened at My Lai and testifying before various boards and committees. He was, in a way, a professional witness. He cooperated with the official, full-scale inquiry headed up by Gen. Peers, providing details that helped him piece together much of what happened on the day in question. He even returned to Vietnam with Gen. Peers to walk him through the events of the day as he knew them and to point out where he had spotted the bodies of the civilians. Thompson would give testimony in fifteen or twenty Article 32 hearings (similar to grand juries) which targeted the twenty-five men who were recommended for court-martial. Later, he would serve as a chief witness for the prosecution, telling his story over and over and over again, with a high degree of consistency all the while. His testimony would be damaging to the defense; his observations would help to form the superstructure, the backbone of the cases against several men accused of murder or coverup.

Thompson was called to testify before the House Armed Services Subcommittee on April 17, 1970. He was represented by counsel, Capt. Kenneth Johnson, whom the Army had assigned upon Thompson's request a few months earlier when it became apparent to him that he may have a real need to protect himself.

After hearing Thompson's story of what he had witnessed from the air at My Lai, committee members and their attorneys, John T. M. Reddan and John F. Lally, began trying to pin him down on what would be an offense that could get him court-martialed, i.e., the question of whether he threatened the lives of other U.S. soldiers.

"Did you expect American troops to fire on you?" Reddan asked.

"I didn't," Thompson answered.

"Did you consider it a possibility?" Reddan asked.

"Why would they want to fire on you? You wore their uniform," Hebert chimed in.

"Did you have any reason to fear the American troops?" Reddan asked.

Then committee member Charles Gubser joined in:

"You did not order your crew to cover you against Americans?"

"To the best of my knowledge, I did not," Thompson answered.

Hebert was getting frustrated. It was sounding as though Thompson was changing his story to protect himself.

"Members of this committee have been challenged about a statement that you allegedly made to the full committee. Let's get the cards on the table. I was the one individual that examined you on your appearance before that committee...to get an answer from you as to whether you had pointed your guns at American troops," Hebert said.

Thompson responded:

"Guns were pointed that way, and a gun was also pointed the other way, sir."

Now Hebert was angry.

"Don't let's kid. We know what we are talking about. But the image has been given, by individuals who have written stories about this...and the impression went out that you had told your people to train their guns, and rescued these people at gun point, because you were covering the Americans...."

Then, dropping any pretense of objectivity, Hebert continued:

"I can't conceive under any condition that I would order my people, wearing the same uniform that my brothers and colleagues in arms are wearing, to say, 'Shoot them.' I can tell you that definitely, with finality. No hesitance on my part."

After Hebert finished, Gubser jumped in again and asked Thompson three more times if he gave an order to his men to cover him against U.S. troops. Thompson kept saying no, that he only told his men to cover him in general, not specifically against U.S. troops, since the Viet Cong could have been lurking in the woods behind the bunker.

Hebert got back in the act:

"What has blunted your memory so dramatically between December and April? At that time you were vocal and articulate.... In December you were positive, you were definite. You didn't rely on 'I don't remember' this and that.... You were certainly a definite and very positive witness. You even admitted that you were the one that blew the whistle on the whole thing....

"Your presence impressed me a great deal. Your full knowledge and comprehension and ability to be articulate impressed me a great deal, because you carried great weight with your testimony. It has been the backbone of books and articles and everything as a result of your positiveness.

"And now we come to the end of April...and I find a different man on the stand. The man I find on the stand today just has a hard time remembering. He is not positive. He halts."

Hebert indeed had a different man on the stand, a soldier who wanted to tell the truth as he had seen it, but at the same time felt a real need to protect himself legally lest he end up at Ft. Leavenworth prison for many, many years for doing something which – taken out of context – could be grounds for a court-martial.

As part of his strategy of self-defense, Thompson took the Fifth Amendment on a few occasions, refusing to answer questions on the grounds that he might incriminate himself. Hebert and Reddan were irritated by this tactic.

Thompson wanted the committee to get off his back about the issue of what he ordered his men to do when he set down to rescue the people in the bunker. The more he tried to move them along to what he considered more important issues, the more frustrated and aggressive they became in their line of questioning.

"Did you have any reason to believe they were there?" Reddan asked, referring to the idea that there may have been Viet Cong near the bunker where the refugees had taken cover.

"Yes, sir."

"What was your reason for that?"

"It was in Vietnam, sir."

"...This is a serious matter, lieutenant, and I would appreciate an answer which is not facetious...."

"Sir, I was not trying to be facetious or anything. I feel that the enemy was there, but I didn't see them," Thompson explained.

Shortly after this exchange, the other attorney, John Lally, moved on to what Thompson first told his superiors when he was reporting evidence of a massacre.

"Did you complain of indiscriminate firing? Did you use those words?" Lally asked.

"No, sir, I didn't use those words, because I stay away from big words," Thompson answered in his usual Southern drawl.

Some of the members of the subcommittee were starting to get the idea that Thompson was a wise guy. They knew by now that he had developed some savvy as a witness who would consistently tell the story of what he had seen, while at the same time resisting being drawn into self-incriminating statements.

Thompson turned out not to be one of the subcommittee's favorite witnesses, and that was fine with him. This wasn't a popularity contest; it was serious business. He had a position to protect. The subcommittee chairman had his own agenda – plus a hidden agenda – and Thompson had his. And if the agendas weren't in perfect harmony, then that was just too bad.

Thompson was distracted by the stress of the subcommittee hearings and fearful that Hebert or one of the lawyers he worked with might try to have charges brought against him for his role in stopping the My Lai massacre. Though he was afraid of what might happen to him, he did not allow the fear to paralyze him, and he continued to get up every morning and report for duty. His main role in the service now was to work with the Army's legal corps in their effort to prosecute those who committed crimes at My Lai.

He testified for the prosecution in the courts-martial of Lt. William Calley at Ft. Benning, Georgia; Capt. Ernest Medina and Sgt. Charles Hutto at Ft. McPherson, in Atlanta, Georgia; and Col. Oran Henderson at Ft. Meade, Maryland.

He was preparing to testify in the case of Sgt. David Mitchell at Ft. Hood, Texas, but the case collapsed when his testimony and that of three other witnesses was disallowed by the judge for technical reasons. These reasons had to do with the fact that Thompson and the others had testified before the Congressional subcommittee and that the subcommittee, under Hebert's leadership, had classified the testimony. In doing so, Hebert was preventing its release to anyone – including the courts and the defense attorneys – until some time in the future when all the trials were over and the appeals process was exhausted.

This scuttling of the prosecution's efforts is exactly what Secretary of the Army Stanley Resor was afraid of when in the winter of 1969 he began pleading with Congressmen Rivers and Hebert to hold off on taking testimony until after the military justice process had run its course. He tried to tell them that their taking testimony – and then classifying it until they were ready to release it– might wreck the Army's efforts to prosecute the guilty parties. But they ignored him and proceeded with their hearings because, ostensibly, they wanted to discharge their Congressional responsibilities to find the truth and help to assure that justice was done. But, in actuality, they knew that by taking testimony and retaining the option of releasing it when they wanted to that they would become significant players in the process of determining who, if anyone, would be convicted in the My Lai trials. And being staunch advocates of the U.S. military and its image, they, like President Nixon, were very displeased with the spectre of U.S. servicemen being convicted of war crimes. It wouldn't be good for the Army, for the country in general, nor for the war effort, they felt.

By refusing to release the testimony – which involved statements from more than one hundred men – they were providing grounds for the dismissal of all charges against all five men who were court-martialed. The defense is entitled to all testimony and evidence which the government has in its possession, according to the Jencks Act, which is designed to prevent what attorneys and judges refer to as "trial by ambush." That is, in the interest of fairness to the defendant, the defense must have access to the same information as the prosecution, lest the prosecution surprise the defense with damaging evidence which the defense is unable and unprepared to refute.

In all five of the cases that went to trial the defending attorneys tried to get their clients off by using the Jencks Act to their advantage. All of the five judges heard arguments relative to the defendants' Constitutional rights under this tenet of law, and four of them ruled essentially that any material fact dealing with the cases at hand could be derived from testimony that could be obtained in their courtrooms; therefore, fair, even-handed trials could be held even if Hebert continued to refuse to turn over the testimony he had obtained in his hearings.

The one judge who ruled that the Jencks Act did apply in his case was Col. George R. Robinson, who presided over the Mitchell trial. Hebert repeatedly refused to turn over his records that pertained to Mitchell's activities on the day in question. As a result, the government was in possession of testimony to which the defense was being refused access. Consequently, Thompson and three others who testified before Hebert's subcommittee were essentially disqualified as witnesses for the prosecution. Without its star witnesses testifying, the prosecution's case was weakened to the point of being unwinnable. So the case collapsed, and Mitchell walked out scot-free.

William Eckhardt, prosecutor in the Medina case and two others, would state later that Hebert and Rivers, through the use of their investigating subcommittee, had deliberately attempted to sabotage the prosecution of those responsible for the My Lai massacre.

"Hebert and Rivers decided that these trials were detrimental to the interests of the United States of America and they tried, calculatingly and technically using the Jencks Act, to sabotage them," Eckhardt charged.

Moreover, Eckhardt added, besides trying to get Calley and the others off the hook, they tried to turn the table on Thompson and set him up to be court-martialed for threatening the lives of fellow soldiers.

"Another key to sabotaging the prosecution was to get Hugh Thompson," Eckhardt observed, explaining that if Thompson were to be successfully discredited then one of the pillars of the prosecution's cases would collapse.

So, it was not paranoia, but perceptiveness on Thompson's part when he sensed that Hebert and Rivers were out to get him, that they were attempting to portray him as a soldier who had committed unlawful acts during the My Lai incident.

Eckhardt was not alone in his observation that Hebert and Rivers tried to sabotage the My Lai trials. In November of 1970, just a few days after the collapse of the prosecution's case against Sgt. David Mitchell – thanks in large part to Hebert's and Rivers' shenanigans – seventeen Congressmen sent a letter to Hebert pleading with him to release the testimony which he was withholding. Edward I. Koch, Donald M. Fraser, John Conyers Jr., and William F. Ryan were among those signing the letter. They were concerned that the prosecution's case against Lt. Calley was in imminent danger of collapsing in the same manner and for the same technical reasons that the case against Mitchell had caved in. The letter stated, in part:

> ...Judge George Robinson, the presiding judge at the Mitchell trial, ruled that prosecution witnesses who testified before your Committee could not be called to testify at the trial unless their prior testimony before your committee is made available to the defense for the purposes of cross-examination; those witnesses therefore were not available for that trial.
>
> Colonel Reid W. Kennedy, the presiding judge at the Calley trial, has requested that the transcript of your Committee's hearings be released. We believe that such requests – particularly since they came from the presiding judges who are in the best position to know what is needed for a fair trial – should not be denied.
>
> ...Congress, not being subject to court subpoena, should provide the evidence willingly as a matter of national honor.
>
> Therefore, we respectfully urge that your committee release the transcript from the hearings on the My Lai incident....
>
> ...Release of the hearing transcripts is a major factor in allowing the trial of Lt. Calley to proceed fairly, and at the same time ascertain what really happened at My Lai.

The following month, Illinois Congressman Abner J. Mikva, a

member of the House Judiciary Committee, wrote to Rivers pointing out that what he and Hebert were doing looked very much like obstruction of justice:

> The Jencks rule...holds that if the Government, including Congress, does not wish to produce documents which fall within the scope of the rule, the testimony of the witness involved is inadmissible. Thus (what) compels congressional action in this case (is) the dictates of fairness and the desire to avoid obstructing the administration of justice.
>
> ...My review of the relevant cases and statutory provisions leave me more convinced than before that the Committee's decision to withhold from a defendant...evidence which may be necessary to his defense, and simultaneously deny to the prosecution testimony of important witnesses, is a decision that can reflect credit on neither the Committee nor the Congress. It must seem a sorry spectacle to the citizens of this nation to see the foremost lawmaking body in the land obstructing administration of the very laws it writes.

The arguments being made by Mikva, Koch and the others were nearly identical to those spelled out in a series of letters Hebert received earlier from Secretary of the Army Stanley Resor, who also felt that Hebert and Rivers were engaged in a conspiracy to sabotage the trials. Again, Hebert's and Rivers' motive was to exonerate the U.S. Army and protect the image and reputation of the American soldier as a man who served his country with honor, period. And the charges being brought against U.S. soldiers ran counter to this ideal. So, if the charges were dismissed, or the accused could otherwise avoid being found guilty, then the image could be preserved, at least for the most part. Consequently, history would never record that American soldiers were convicted of war crimes at My Lai.

Hebert's and Rivers' seeming obsession with guarding the image of the U.S. Army was confirmed by Robert MacCrate, the civilian attorney who worked closely with Gen. Peers to investigate the cover-up of the My Lai massacre. MacCrate, who would later serve as the president of the American Bar Association, stated that not only did they attempt to sabotage the courts-martial of Calley and the others, but they also tried to discredit The Peers Inquiry. After four months of investigation, including a return trip to the scene of the crime, Peers concluded that extensive war crimes had been committed and that officers in the chain of command in Vietnam had conspired to cover up the crimes.

"After Gen. Peers and I returned from Vietnam we appeared before the House Armed Services Committee to confirm the truth of the allegations of the massacre. But they didn't want to hear it. 'It's true; it's true,' we kept telling them," MacCrate related.

Angry and upset over what they were hearing, Hebert and Rivers regarded Gen. Peers' report as "antiwar propaganda" that assaulted the honor of America's Armed Forces and "put a cloud over the Army," according to MacCrate.

"Members of the House Armed Services Committee were throwing every question in the book at us (to try to discredit our report)," MacCrate revealed. "They were doing their best to sabotage our investigation. They just couldn't accept the idea of anyone accusing the U.S. military of a massacre. It was just unacceptable in their minds."

Rather than accepting the well-documented fact that many U.S. soldiers had behaved dishonorably at My Lai, Rivers and Hebert figured if someone needed to be singled out for his misdeeds at My Lai it should be the rogue helicopter pilot who interfered in the ground operation, ordered his men to turn their weapons on fellow soldiers, and countermanded the orders of superior officers. This was their game plan – to exonerate Calley and his men and to send Thompson to prison – and it was obvious to prosecutor Bill Eckhardt, Gen. Peers and others.

Gen. Peers questioned Hebert's and Rivers' motives and was

more than a little suspicious of their definition of "justice." In his book, *The My Lai Inquiry*, which would be published some years after all the investigations, hearings and trials were over, he would write:

> One part of the (Hebert) subcommittee report I fail to understand is why it made such an issue of Warrant Officer Thompson's confrontation with ground troops at My Lai and his subsequent awards and decorations. Approximately one-fourth of the report is devoted to Thompson's verbatim testimony. In reading the quotes from his testimony, it appears to be more of an inquisition than an investigation; they had him so confused he did not know which way to turn. The only plausible reason I can offer is that they were misdirected in their efforts by the subcommittee staff.
>
> What I found equally incomprehensible is that the report makes only scant reference to the heroic actions of Thompson and his crew. Nothing is said about the dangers and skill involved in their marking the wounded civilians for medical assistance, rounding up the two VC suspects, locating the mortar site, investigating the situation at the ditch, rescuing approximately fifteen women and children from a shelter, and finally returning to the ditch to retrieve a wounded child and fly (her) to the hospital. Moreover, Thompson reported his observations and actions to his commanding officer and later to a chaplain.
>
> Of all those who participated in the operation, he was the only American who cared enough to take action to protect the Vietnamese noncombatants and to try to stop the wanton killing and destruction of property. Instead of being castigated, in my view he should have been highly commended. If there was a hero of My Lai, he was it.

Thompson may have been a hero, but it was a mantle he didn't particularly enjoy wearing. So far, being a hero had brought him a lot of grief and stress. It meant high pressure, cold stares and sleepless nights. He had been subpoenaed by the House Armed Services Committee, intimidated and embarrassed by its chairman, interrogated and bullied by its subcommittee chairman, cross-examined aggressively by defense lawyers, and ostracized by a good number of his fellow soldiers. Being the hero of My Lai was proving to be a tough, thankless job.

Chapter 10

A Nation Divided

IN THE SUMMER OF 1970, THOUGH HE WAS CONstantly on the go, continually busy working with the Army to prepare its case against Lt. Calley and the others, Hugh Thompson was experiencing a growing sense of loneliness and isolation. A mild form of depression was setting in as he realized that nearly no one with whom he came in contact was open and cordial toward him. Fellow soldiers seemed to be uncomfortable when they were around him.

He was aware that some servicemen viewed him as a "snitch," as the guy who "ratted-out" Charlie Company, the pilot who threatened his own kind in order to save foreigners. Some of those who held this view demonstrated their disapproval of him and his actions. One such incident occurred at the officers club at Ft. Rucker, Alabama. Thompson went into the club to have a few drinks and hopefully some conversation with fellow soldiers. Realizing who he was, they all got up and walked out, ten or twelve men.

As the months wore on and he found himself in officers clubs on different bases, where there were people he didn't know, he would introduce himself only as "Buck" and would avoid talking about Vietnam, except for passing references and broad generalities. Once he was asked directly whether he was any kin to "that s.o.b. Hugh Thompson," and he said he wasn't, that he'd never heard of him.

Thompson's sense of himself as a patriotic American who had fought honorably in Vietnam was taking a pounding on several fronts. He was developing a real complex about being unappreciated. Some of those who disapproved of his actions at My Lai expressed their feelings over the telephone, in the middle of the night. Others sent cards and letters. One anonymous postcard, postmarked Atlanta, Georgia, the city of his birth, stated:

> You should be stripped of your stripes, you chicken-livered traitor, for the trouble you have caused our country and our military. What do you think war is? A game of ping-pong? That village was a threat to our own men. Would you rather see our men mowed down by the enemy? Your kind is our worst enemy, the rat commie within our country....You are a disgrace to the South (which is a producer of patriots), a disgrace to the nation .... You are through in the service whether or not you get kicked out. If you were in the Marine Corps I don't think you would last very long. However, you will pay the full price of all traitors. For every man you have caused to be locked up and punished, you will walk in shame the rest of your days.... May our country always be right (which is not easy when dealing with international communism). But *our country right or wrong*. If you don't believe that way, you are no American; you are no better than the fanatic communist animals who have trapped and killed all the U.S. military to date. You are worse than they, as you are supposed to be an American. I was proud of my town until (now). You have disgraced us all.
>
> – *Jane Q. Citizen*

In the same months that Thompson was becoming increasingly sensitive to the disapproval of others, Lt. Calley was gaining the sympathy of more and more Americans, who held the viewpoint that he was a soldier who was just taking orders when he did what he did at My Lai. They saw Calley as a scapegoat for the transgressions of his superiors, a guy who was singled out to take the fall for the officers over him and the men around him on that day in March of 1968. Calley was, in the minds of many, a national hero.

The divergent views of Calley as a martyr by some and a murderer by others was reflective of a deeply divided U.S. citizenry, those for the war and those against it. Those who supported the war tended to see it as a means of stopping the spread of atheistic communism and protecting the people of South Vietnam from the oppression of a totalitarian government. Those who opposed it viewed it variously as a no-win war of attrition that was claiming the lives of tens of thousands of America's young men, an immoral war where hundreds of thousands of Vietnamese civilians – ninety percent of whom were women and children – were being killed in bombing raids and through other means by military people from both sides with callous disregard for the value of human life.

The gap between those in the U.S. who were for the war and those against it widened as the Calley trial got underway in November of 1970. A hue and cry to "Free Calley" was heard from throngs of people from one side of the nation to the other, with the loudest voices coming from the Southern and Midwestern states. There were bumper stickers on countless cars and trucks, resolutions of support for the accused from half a dozen legislatures, letters and telegrams by the boxful being received at the White House and at Calley's quarters at Ft. Benning, where he was under house arrest. A "Rally for Calley" was put on by the American Legion of Columbus, Georgia. A theme song that portrayed him as a martyr and scapegoat, titled "The Battle Hymn of Lt. Calley," could be heard on radio stations throughout the land.

The widespread and highly emotional campaign to free Calley brought him a substantial degree of comfort, so much so that he was starting to think he would be acquitted. But a jury of his peers thought otherwise and, in March of 1971, declared him guilty of murdering twenty-two "Oriental human beings" and sentenced him to life in prison at hard labor. The jury, by and large, regretted having to do it, but the evidence was overwhelming, the crime heinous.

Calley seemed stunned. A large percentage of the American public was outraged, angry and loud in expressing disapproval of the verdict. Thompson felt that at least in this one case justice was finally done, or so it seemed, for now.

But President Richard Nixon – who had literally cringed over the idea that U.S. soldiers would be court-martialed in connection with war crimes in Vietnam – stepped in immediately as Commander-in-Chief of the Armed Forces to release Calley from the stockade, pending the appeal of his conviction. Calley was placed under house arrest and allowed to live in his bachelor quarters at Ft. Benning.

The announcement of the guilty verdict brought on a convulsion of anger and protest among many U.S. citizens and a flood of emotionally charged letters and telegrams to President Nixon, Secretary of Defense Melvin Laird and other top-ranking government officials.

> Dear President Nixon:
>
> The Lt. Calley trial and conviction is a colossal miscarriage of justice and should never have taken place. Stop any more of the same, and grant Lt. Calley full pardon with honors for doing his duty to his country and protecting his men. This is the only crime he committed, and we need more men like him. Thousands of our men have been murdered....
>
> Correct this colossal error immediately and save the United States from disastrous reactions which could happen soon by the angry patriotic people of the country and relatives of the men ordered into the war and the men in uniform....
>
> *R.F.S. Harman*
> Jacksonville, Fla.

> Dear Mr. Laird:
>
> Killing innocent people is not to be condoned, but in the case of Lt. Calley, I feel that he is being made a scapegoat. To his knowledge and his judgment, these people were being used by the enemy to mine fields and used grenades against our troops. Should he have made his decision in favor of the civilians and against his men?
>
> In the Nuremberg Trials we, the United States, held mili-

tary leaders responsible for the actions of their men in the field even though these leaders were not present nor did they directly or indirectly order what we termed "atrocities," yet we hanged them. Do we have a different standard for trying our own country?

Our Air Force people are not prosecuted for dropping bombs and napalm on civilian areas so why should the foot soldier bear the brunt of the "sudden streak of national conscience"? It was his orders to carry out this dirty assignment. Now it's Calley, the little foot soldier, whose life is ruined....

Surely no sane young men will now volunteer for service, and you will probably find the draftees laying down arms, then where will your discipline be?

In view of all this, I hereby urge you to exert all the powers of your office, as the representative of the civilians of this country, to secure a full pardon for Lt. Calley. If this is not done, I'm afraid our defenses will fall apart and you can say good-bye to Indo-China and maybe much more. Will all our sacrifices be in vain? For shame!

Clarence K. Wilson
Santa Ana, Calif.
A Disgraced American

Many of the thousands of correspondences to the President and the Secretary of Defense called for "a full pardon" or "clemency" or "amnesty" – pleas for mercy for one of the men who showed no mercy to the women, children and old men who begged for their lives three years earlier in an irrigation ditch in My Lai. Telegrams to Secretary Laird were impassioned and to the point:

The undersigned Americans are alarmed and disturbed over the results of the Lt. Calley trial. We don't condone killing anyone. We particularly don't condone killing civilians during war.

But how in the heat of battle and under the conditions (in which) the Vietnam War is (being waged) could anyone take the time to determine whether an individual of Oriental extraction is friendly or an enemy? Soldiers are trained to kill or be killed when in combat. How can the leaders of this great nation be so blind as to even consider punishing a man who has devoted his life to the military to defend the things so many men have died for?

> If Calley is guilty so is every American who ever fought for his country. Calley is not only innocent, in our opinion, but a hero (and) should be decorated merely for risking his life for the country all Americans are supposed to love....
> *Frank Mason, Wiley Cox, John Corey, etc.*
> Birmingham, Ala.

Petitions seeking Calley's release were passed around in numerous states, and signatures were obtained from people from all walks of life, in the workplace, in bars, at basketball games, on street corners, even outside the doors of churches. In Indiana, the drive was particularly well-organized; petitions on American Legion letterhead were distributed and signed by tens of thousands of citizens. Addressed to Secretary Laird, these petitions stated:

> We, the undersigned citizens of the United States of America, petition you, as Secretary of Defense, to intercede immediately in the Lt. William Calley case and reverse the findings of the jury in that case. We believe that this is a wanton miscarriage of justice and we DEMAND that you, as a top military official in our country, a second only to the President, use the weight of your office to right a terrible wrong.

A Gallup Poll, commissioned by *Newsweek* Magazine and published in its April 12, 1971 edition, gauged the public reaction to the verdict and to Nixon's intervention. Asked if they approved of the verdict of premeditated murder, seventy-nine percent disapproved and nine percent approved. Those who disapproved were asked if they disapproved because they thought what happened at My Lai was not a crime or because they thought many others besides Calley shared the responsibility; seventy-one percent said others were responsible, while twenty percent said it wasn't a crime.

Asked whether they thought Calley was being made a scapegoat for the actions of others above him, sixty-nine percent said yes and twelve percent said no.

Was the sentence fair, too harsh or too lenient? Too harsh was the response of eighty-one percent, eleven percent said it was fair, and one percent said it was too lenient. Asked whether they approved or disapproved of President Nixon's decision to release Calley pending appeal of his conviction, eighty-three percent approved and seven percent disapproved.

One of those who vigorously disapproved of President Nixon's intervention in the judicial process was the prosecutor in the Calley case, Capt. Aubrey Daniel III. In a strongly worded letter to the President, the prosecutor, who had worked for a year to convict Calley, spoke his mind:

> Dear President Nixon:
>
> ...How shocking it is if so many people across this nation have failed to see the moral issue which was involved in the trial of Lt. Calley: that it is unlawful for an American soldier to summarily execute unarmed and unresisting men, women, children and babies.
>
> But how much more appalling it is to see so many of the political leaders of the nation who have failed to see the moral issue or, having seen it, to compromise it for political motives in the face of apparent public displeasure with the verdict.
>
> I would have hoped that all of the leaders of this nation – which is supposed to be the leader within the international community for the protection of the weak and the oppressed, regardless of nationality – would have either accepted and supported the enforcement of the laws of this country as reflected by the verdict of the court or not made any statement concerning the verdict until they had had the same opportunity to evaluate the evidence that the members of the jury had.
>
> In view of your previous statements concerning this matter, I have been particularly shocked and dismayed at your decision to intervene in these proceedings in the midst of the public clamor.
>
> Your decision can only have been prompted by the response of a vocal segment of our population who, while no doubt acting in good faith, cannot be aware of the evidence which resulted in Lt. Calley's conviction.
>
> Your intervention has, in my opinion, damaged the military judicial system and lessened any respect it may have gained as a result of these proceedings....
>
> Not only has respect for the legal process been weakened and the critics of the military judicial system been given

> support for their claims of command influence, but the image of Lt. Calley, a man convicted of the premeditated murder of at least twenty-one unarmed and unresisting people, as a national hero has been enhanced....
>
> I would expect that the President of the United States, a man whom I believed should and would provide the moral leadership for this nation, would stand fully behind the law of this land on a moral issue which is so clear and about which there can be no compromise.
>
> For this nation to condone the acts of Lt. Calley is to make us no better than our enemies and make any pleas by this nation for the humane treatment of our own prisoners meaningless.
>
> While in some respects what took place at My Lai has to be considered ... a tragic day in the history of our nation, how much more tragic would it have been for this country to have taken no action against those who were responsible.
>
> That action was taken, but the greatest tragedy of all will be if political expendiency dictates the compromise of such a fundamental moral principle as the inherent unlawfulness of the murder of innocent persons....
>
> Respectfully yours,
> *Aubrey M. Daniel III*

President Nixon read Daniel's letter, but he stood by his decision to keep Calley out of the stockade but under house arrest and confined to his quarters at Ft. Benning during the time his conviction was being appealed. (Four months later, in August of 1971, Calley's sentence would be reduced to twenty years by the Commanding General of the 3rd Army; then quietly in April of 1974 the sentence would be cut to ten years by the Secretary of the Army; seven months later the Secretary would decide to free Calley and place him on parole after having served one-third of his twice-reduced sentence.)

After all was said and done, in the effort to court-martial those who were responsible for the murder of five hundred and four Vietnamese civilians, and the coverup which followed, only one man was found guilty of anything whatsoever in a court of law. More than two dozen men had been recommended for court-martial for war crimes or related misdeeds.

Murder, maiming, assault, rape, scalping, torture, dereliction of duty, failure to report a crime, coverup, perjury, all of these things went unpunished. The deaths of women, children, babies, the lame, the feeble, the defenseless, all of them Oriental human beings, all seemed to fall under "the merely gook rule," which held that the lives of these people – the illiterate, unlanded, unadvanced – were somehow less valuable than their liberators from the West. The Geneva Conventions, the rules of land warfare, and the basic tenets of human decency, all of these were cast aside, broken and trampled into the ground in Southeast Asia.

Hugh Thompson, Larry Colburn and other men of goodwill – who cooperated in the Peers Inquiry and who testified repeatedly during the courts-martial and in the pre-trial hearings – had hoped to see justice done but ended up saddened and disillusioned at the outcome.

A near-total sense of futility came over Thompson. He had gone to a lot of trouble for nearly no result, except for what he considered a token conviction. It would be a long, long time before he would go to that much trouble again for anyone or any cause.

Calley was convicted, Nixon had made it easy on him, five hundred and four people were dead in Vietnam, it was a war crime, no one paid for it. Thompson was disgusted.

The hero of My Lai had had enough. He was worn down by the tension of the courtroom, angered by the lack of justice, wounded by the mean looks and cold shoulders he was getting while out in public. Now, he just wanted to go home, back to his base at Ft. Rucker, Alabama. He just wanted to be left alone.

Chapter 11

A Return To Obscurity

WITH THE VIETNAM WAR AND THE MY LAI massacre courts-martial behind him, Thompson was glad to get back to the relative calm of Ft. Rucker, Alabama, where he hoped to settle into his job as a helicopter pilot instructor. It was December of 1971.

Though he was less than pleased with the outcome of the trials, at least the stressful job of being a professional witness was over. He could now move on with his life and hopefully put the whole ordeal behind him – the war, the helicopter crash, the fear, the never-ending questions he had to answer under oath.

The very idea of a life of peace and quiet was immensely appealing. And it was a good thing for him that it was. Before he was able to settle in well at Ft. Rucker he received orders to ship out to one of the quietest, most distant fronts in the world where the American military had a presence. He was going to Korea. He would be accompanied by his new wife, Joyce (nee Miller), whom he had dated during his time in Washington and married toward the end of 1971.

Shortly after their arrival in Korea, in July of 1972, Thompson took over as executive officer, the second in command of B Company, Second Aviation Battalion. His was one of the northernmost American military units in South Korea, stationed just south of the Demilitarized Zone, which divided North from South. If any U.S. aviation company in the country was going to see combat action it was Thompson's.

But the North Koreans stayed home, and armed conflict never broke out in the thirteen months Thompson was there. Instead, he picked up where he left off at Ft. Rucker, spending most of his working hours training soldiers to fly helicopters.

Throughout his tour of duty in Korea virtually no one knew who he was, in terms of his connection to My Lai, nor was the subject of the massacre ever brought up in his presence. And that suited him fine. All was quiet on the northern front.

There was one small problem, however, which would grow into a larger one: The Army had recently started using a new, stricter Officer Evaluation Report (OER) form, and as a result many officers who had previously received only high marks began to receive lower grades. Thompson was one such officer.

Though Thompson worked at his job long and hard, his commanding officer, Donald F. Matson, apparently felt there was room for improvement. In the end, Matson gave him a low grade on his OER, a blemish on his record that would come back to haunt him later. Every OER prior to this one and every OER since showed Thompson to be a top-flight soldier who was a team player, a competent instructor and a soldier with a high degree of respect for Army protocol and traditions.

Thompson left Korea in August of 1973 and returned to the States to take on a new assignment at Ft. Jackson, South Carolina. Two years later, having moved up from battalion training officer to company commander, he received some bad news. With the Vietnam War having come to an end, the Armed Services were in the process of downsizing, or, in military terms, implementing a Reduction In Force (RIF). As a result, many men and women who were in the service would be dismissed, or "RIFed." Thompson was one of them. The Army, naturally, wanted to keep their best, most efficient people, and one of the arbitrary criteria they leaned on heavily to help them make that choice was the OER.

Thompson had no desire to leave the Army. This was his chosen profession, his career. It was his life. But here it was, July of 1975, light years before he planned to retire from active duty, and it looked as though that one bad OER he got while in Korea was going to do him in. To say that he was shocked and upset would be an understatement.

His anger and disappointment would be short-lived, however, as the Army sought him out and asked him to return to the service only three or four weeks after being released. He and his wife, Joyce, had moved to Stone Mountain, Georgia, and were staying with his parents when the Army's call came in.

Thompson, who was still feeling wounded and unappreciated, told the Army he would think about it. Then for several days he and his father discussed the pros and cons of going back into the service. Hugh Sr., who had spent much of his life in the military (five years on active duty and thirty years in the reserves), wanted his son to have the benefit of a more experienced man's viewpoint, whether the younger Hugh Thompson asked for it or not. With both of them being strong-willed individuals, their rational discourse sometimes became heated and evolved into rather loud arguments.

The elder Thompson reminded his son that since he had been in the service for twelve years already, if he would remain for eight more years then he could retire with significant and continual retirement pay for the rest of his life. Hugh Jr. agreed with his father but maintained that he would have to be offered a base with a location that was to his liking, or else he wouldn't be returning at all. This issue of location was resolved when the Army called back and told him in essence that he could go to any base in the world where the Army needed helicopter pilots.

Since he had never been stationed on the West Coast, he chose Ft. Ord, California, which at the time was a training base. His job would be to instruct soldiers to fly helicopters, or so he thought. By the time he reported for duty, in September of 1975, the Army had converted the base from a training facility to the new home of the Seventh Infantry Division. He was irritated and felt somewhat deceived that no one had told him of the impending change. Rather than being a flight instructor, his assignment was changed to flying a medical evacuation helicopter and taxiing military VIPs via helicopter.

One of the reasons Thompson had hesitated returning to the Army was that he would have to go back in with a lower rank and less pay. He had been a captain and company commander just two months earlier, but he would have to return as a warrant officer without a command if he were to re-join. He did accept the Army's terms, though he would harbor resentment over this matter for some years to come. He felt as though he had been manipulated.

Like other assignments that would follow, this one lasted three years, ending in September of 1978. Things ran smoothly for Thompson in his job, and he continued to receive good OERs throughout his time in California. Things had not been going smoothly in his marriage, however, and he and Joyce were divorced in 1977.

Not one who enjoyed being alone at night, Thompson was married again, to Kay (nee Fleming), the following year.

After completing his work in California, Thompson and his bride packed up and headed for Hawaii, where he was assigned to another medical evacuation unit. He would, in essence, be doing the same job he had done at Ft. Ord.

His job involved flying a Huey helicopter and rescuing soldiers who were injured while on maneuvers in the woods and on the mountains, as well as medical evacuations of civilians who were seriously ill, pregnant or injured in auto accidents. Stationed at Wheeler Air Force Base on Oahu, he was a member of the 68th Medical Detachment, a unit in which he thoroughly enjoyed serving.

His commanding officer, Major Don Conkright, was glad to have Thompson in his unit because of the high level of competence as a helicopter pilot he had built while in Vietnam and in the years that followed. This was one pilot he did not have to worry about when it came to aviation skills and critical decision-making. From the beginning, Conkright noticed that Thompson was a staunch supporter of military traditions and protocol. He thought of Thompson as "the consummate professional," a team player and a friend. Conkright called him "Buck." Thompson called him "Sir," even in off-duty situations, out of respect for his superior rank.

They spent a considerable amount of time working together and socializing regularly after hours, at the officers clubs, at company functions and on other special occasions. In the three years they were together in Hawaii, however, Thompson never mentioned his connection to My Lai. Nor did Conkright have any idea that there was a connection. The subject never came up.

When the Thompsons left Hawaii in September of 1981, they did so with an addition to their family: a frisky, bright-eyed two-year-old named Steven, who bore a strong resemblance to his father.

They were headed for Ft. Polk, Louisiana, which would be Thompson's final assignment, the last leg of his twenty-year odyssey as a member of the U.S. Armed Forces. There he would continue his work as a medical evacuation helicopter pilot. He would also train soldiers to fly helicopters, using both visual and instrument flight rules, as he had done for many years.

As before, he would go by the name "Buck" and not Hugh, and he would never initiate a discussion about his connection to My Lai, South Vietnam.

However, the circumstances at Ft. Polk were different: Some of the men with whom he was associated were aware of who he was, and they asked him about My Lai. One of these men was his commanding officer, Lt. Col. Nick Johnson. He had read articles about the massacre and had identified Thompson as the man who headed up the helicopter crew who risked their lives to stop the killing. He felt fortunate to have such a man under his command; his admiration for Thompson was considerable. He wanted to know more.

Johnson and his wife frequently socialized with Thompson and his wife while off duty. On several occasions Johnson tried to learn more about Thompson's heroic actions, but Thompson would never elaborate. Rather, he would shrug it off, saying that the incident happened a long, long time ago and that he was just doing his duty. Thompson would say that he didn't consider himself a hero, that he felt he had done nothing more than any other soldier would have done under the same circumstances.

Johnson never believed that for a minute. But he did quit asking questions when Thompson made it clear that he didn't want to talk about it. He felt proud to be in the presence of a true American hero, a man of extraordinary courage.

As Thompson's assignment at Ft. Polk was drawing to a close, so, too, was his military career. Johnson was sad to see him go. He felt privileged to have worked with this modest soldier whom he felt had brought a great measure of honor to the uniform of the U.S. Army.

On November 1, 1983, Hugh Thompson retired from military service. For the next eight years he would continue to make a living as a helicopter pilot, flying men and material from south Louisiana heliports to offshore oil platforms thirty, sixty, eighty miles out in the Gulf of Mexico. He settled down in Broussard, Louisiana, four miles from Lafayette, the unofficial capital of the Cajun country.

Within a year of the time that his military career ended, so too did his marriage to his wife, Kay. They were divorced in 1984, and Thompson realized now as never before that maybe, just maybe, he wasn't cut out to be a family man.

He was beginning to recognize that there was a pattern in his married life, just as there had been in his military life. He was married for five or six years then single for one; married for five or six years, single for one, etc. Similarly, he was assigned to one Army base for three years at a time then reassigned to another for three years, and so forth.

After three or four years flying offshore he started to feel an urge to move on, to another company or another kind of work or both. But there was something about this urge that was different; besides plain wanderlust there was an element of fear at work this time. A certain fear of flying was beginning to creep up on him, and he started to consider getting away from helicopters altogether.

Thompson told one of his buddies that he had come to believe that flying offshore over the Gulf of Mexico was more dangerous than flying over the jungles of Vietnam.

"The most dangerous flying I've ever done in my life is over the Gulf of Mexico," he said. "The weather, the fog, the treacherous winds that blow when you're trying to land that chopper on that little pad on those offshore rigs, that's dangerous. I just got scared after a while."

March 16, 1988 was the twentieth anniversary of the My Lai massacre. With two decades having passed since that day of infamy, and nearly seventeen years since the last of the courts-martial, the name of Hugh Thompson had all but disappeared from the American consciousness. His name and his good deeds were as distant and vague a memory as the massacre itself, if not more so. This soldier had succeeded in fading into obscurity.

He was now just a civilian leading a quiet life in a little town in southern Louisiana. His neighbors and co-workers knew little or nothing of his past.

But that was about to change.

The telephone rang in his home one weekend in the summer of 1988. On the other end of the line was a British journalist named Michael Bilton, who had developed a keen interest in the My Lai massacre. Bilton had happened upon a copy of the voluminous Peers Report, officially titled *The Department of the Army Review of the Preliminary Investigations into the My Lai Incident*. Once he picked up the report and started reading he found it difficult to put it down. He was so intrigued with the material and so curious to learn what happened to the people involved that he decided to write a book on the subject and to produce a documentary film. The vitality of the project would depend not only on the details in the Peers Report and the transcripts from the courts-martial, but also on first-person interviews with key players in the tragedy at My Lai. One of those interviews he considered indispensable was Hugh Thompson's.

Not knowing whether Thompson was even alive, Bilton and his research assistants went to the phone books and to directory assistance operators and began calling people with the same name all over the United States. The name is not uncommon, so they made dozens of calls.

This method failed to produce Thompson's phone number, and Bilton became frustrated. Thompson couldn't have disappeared from the face of the earth without a trace; he couldn't have just vanished into thin air. Where in the world was he?

Bilton dug deeper. He was able to ascertain Thompson's middle name – Clowers – from Army records in Washington, D.C., then he began calling the driver's license bureaus of several states around the country to try to match this particular Hugh Thompson with a name in their files. He failed to make the connection in several states, then finally his luck changed. He located the name of a Hugh Clowers Thompson Sr. in Mission, Texas. Bilton figured this was the father of the man for whom he was searching. He called the number, and Wessie Thompson answered. She informed him that her husband had died recently and that her son was living in Louisiana. Guarding her son's privacy, Wessie told Bilton she doubted he would want to talk to any media people, but she would pass along the number and that Hugh could decide for himself whether to return the call.

Bilton asked her to have her son phone him in Washington, where he was doing research. He also told her that Hugh's long-lost friend and comrade, Larry Colburn, had been trying to get in touch with him for some time and that he (Bilton) would pass on Colburn's number if Hugh would call him. Wessie relayed the message right away, and Hugh returned Bilton's call in a matter of minutes. Bilton introduced himself and started to explain that he was doing a TV documentary and wanted to interview him on camera. Thompson cut him off.

"Not interested," Thompson said in his characteristically blunt manner.

"But, but, Mr. Thompson, why?" an anxious Bilton stammered.

"I've had some real bad experiences with the press. They don't like me, and I don't like them. They haven't treated me well."

"But, I'm different," Bilton asserted, trying to regain his balance.

"Yeah, I've heard that before," Thompson shot back, with more than a little skepticism in his voice.

"No, really, I'm not like that..."

"Look, I'm tired of being made out to be the bad guy," the former Army pilot said, reflecting on some of the grief he had been through as a result of his actions at My Lai twenty years earlier.

"But, you're not the bad guy! You're the good guy. Who made you out to be the bad guy? That certainly isn't my intention," Bilton responded.

"Not interested," Thompson repeated in a gruff, dry voice.

"Well, look, if you should change your mind..."

"I won't."

"But, please, let me send you a copy of a documentary I did on the Falklands War and you can see the calibre of work that I do, and maybe..."

"Okay, send it along, but you're wasting your time. But I'll look at it."

"Fair enough," Bilton concluded.

Then Bilton said something that changed Thompson's uncooperative disposition:

"I understand you haven't talked with Larry Colburn in a number of years."

"Yes, I lost track of him fifteen years ago," Thompson responded.

"Well, if you have a pencil and paper handy, I'll give you his address and phone number," Bilton offered.

Thompson gladly wrote down the information, and as he did he felt his attitude toward Bilton shifting and a sense of gratitude beginning to form. Perhaps this guy was different than some of the pushy journalists he had encountered in the past. He rather liked this fellow with the British accent.

Colburn and Thompson talked the following day, and in a matter of a few months Bilton and his camera crew from Yorkshire Television were in Lafayette to interview and videotape the two surviving members of the helicopter crew that made a difference at My Lai. Also on the team from England was Kevin

Sim, who would co-author the book, *Four Hours In My Lai*, and co-produce the documentary, *Remember My Lai.*

Hugh Thompson's long period of obscurity came to an end, in rather dramatic fashion, when the documentary film was aired in 1989, first on British television then in the U.S. on Public Broadcasting System (PBS). The book would be published three years later. With the release of the film came a renewed media interest. Thompson and Colburn were asked to appear on *The Larry King Show*, on *Sonya Live* and on *The Charlie Rose Show* in Washington, D.C. TV audiences in America were thus reminded of the war that most of them would have preferred to have forgotten altogether, not to mention the massacre which had outraged people of conscience all over the world.

One of those who watched the documentary with extreme interest was Clemson University professor David Egan. He was deeply moved by the program and thoroughly impressed with Thompson's courage. He wondered whether Thompson had ever been decorated for valor, whether he had been recognized by the U.S. government in a manner befitting a soldier of such distinction.

Chapter 12

A Whole New Light

THE SKIES WERE CRYSTAL CLEAR OFF THE California coast on the morning of March 18, 1998 as the huge passenger jet began its descent into Los Angeles International Airport. A thoroughly exhausted Larry Colburn remained fast asleep on the big vinyl seat, his knees tucked under his chin. Hugh Thompson looked at him and thought about waking him.

His friend had had a rough time emotionally on the lengthy return flight from Vietnam. The tears he shed had gone a long way in relieving the pent-up emotions he had carried with him for thirty years, since his days as a soldier in the Vietnam War.

The trip back to Vietnam had been beneficial for both of them. To see the country at peace now, to be reunited with some of the women whose lives they saved, to see the children seemingly happy and smiling rather than fearing for their lives, all of these things had done their hearts good.

While the abundance of media attention had been stress-arousing, it had also been flattering. Both Thompson and Colburn were honored that TV and newspaper people from around the world had found their return to My Lai to be so newsworthy.

But now that the trip was coming to an end Thompson was feeling a sense of letdown, of withdrawal. It was time to come down to earth, time to go back to work, to the daily routine of an eight-to-five job. He felt mildly depressed.

He nudged Colburn, and Colburn woke up.

"What's up, Buck?"

"Time to wake up."

"Where are we?"

"Just a little way out of Los Angeles."

"You doing okay?" Colburn asked.

"Sort of. I was just sitting here thinking: They say that everybody has their fifteen minutes of fame sometime in their lives, and I think we've just had ours. So, it's all downhill from here."

"Oh, I wouldn't say that. Why do you say that?"

" 'Cause it's true."

"Well, we've still got '60 Minutes' coming up."

"Yeah, I guess so."

"And, there are several people back in Vietnam who are still alive because of us. We can hold on to that thought."

"Yeah, you're right. I just hope this all counts for something."

"What do you mean?"

"Just that. I hope that what we just did at My Lai and what we did during the war, I hope that counts for something in the long run. That's all I'm saying."

"Of course, it counts for something. It counts for a lot, Buck."

"Yeah, I reckon..."

Thompson was in something of a pessimistic frame of mind, feeling a little blue and out of sorts, when the jet touched down at the airport. He and Colburn gathered their carry-on luggage and headed into the huge terminal to wait for their suitcases and to clear customs.

Colburn reminded him of their pact to each see a counselor shortly after returning home. Thompson hadn't forgotten. If he had made a promise he would keep it.

They said good-bye and hugged one another before going their separate ways.

"You know, boss, I'd still take a bullet for you," Colburn told Thompson.

"And I hope you know I'd do the same for you."

"I know you would, Buck. I know you would."

"Give my love to Lisa and Connor," Thompson said.

"I will. God bless you, Buck. Let's talk soon."

Colburn walked away toward his gate, where he would board a plane to Atlanta. Thompson went in another direction to catch his flight to Lafayette, by way of Dallas.

Thompson slept on the plane to Dallas, but he was wide awake and keyed up on the final leg of the flight, to Lafayette. He was anxious to see his friends, and they were happy he was coming home. They had been watching him on TV and reading about him in the newspapers. He had been depicted as an international war hero, a man whose heroism transcended conventional dimensions, a defender of human rights, regardless of the human's nationality.

Thompson's friends had prepared a "Welcome Home" party for him at the Cajun Pier Restaurant, on the banks of Bayou Vermilion in Lafayette. This would be the hero's welcome he never got when he returned from Vietnam some thirty years prior.

The party went on for a few hours, until it was obvious that the man of the hour was about to drop from fatigue. He needed to go home and go to bed.

It was after midnight when he got home. His son, Steven, greeted him at the door.

"Dad, you got a bunch of mail," Steven pointed out.

There, on the coffee table, was a week's worth of mail. It was such a tall pile that some of the letters had fallen off the table and onto the floor. Thompson's eyes lit up.

"Boy, that *is* a bunch. Who's all this from?" he asked, with energy returning to his voice.

"People from all over the country. I think it's fan mail."

"How did they get our address?"

"Well, most of 'em don't have any real address, except Lafayette, Louisiana. Look how some of them are addressed: 'Hero of My Lai' or 'Soldier's Medal Recipient.'"

All of a sudden, the weary traveler didn't feel fatigued at all. Maybe his trip to Vietnam did count for something. Maybe his whole involvement in Vietnam was worthwhile. It certainly appeared so, judging from the volume of mail that had accumulated in his absence. If Thompson ever had any doubt about the value of what he had done at My Lai, that doubt was about to leave him. If he had been burdened over the years by some sort of complex about being unappreciated, his burden was about to be lifted. He sat down on his sofa with a handful of letters and started reading.

Dear Mr. Thompson:

I'm writing to you to thank you for making me proud to be an American. I was unaware until last week of your actions at My Lai, thirty years ago. I remember the massacre all too vividly, and I remember the trial, but unfortunately, the part of it all that represents what this country stands for was left untold until now.

Sincerely,
John Aiken
Irmo, South Carolina

Reading about what you did at My Lai released imprisoned emotions that I didn't know I had locked away all these years. I guess My Lai had hurt and shamed me more than I knew. Your heroism in the face of that terrific evil has renewed my faith in mankind.

I can't believe I'm writing this, because I am not at all emotional or morose or even deep-thinking, normally. But the description of what you did, and my spontaneous and involuntary reaction to it, has made me realize that I was deeply wounded by Vietnam, and My Lai in particular. I'll bet there are many more like me.

You have healed many of my wounds. I could feel it as the emotions broke free the day I read your story. Thank you for that.

Thank you also for showing all of us that man can perform moral and courageous deeds even if threatened by terrible and evil danger. You have given us all an inspiring lesson in how to live.

Sincerely,
Jim Gustin
Bridgewater, Connecticut

You make my heart sing!

Elizabeth Caffrey
Weaverville, North Carolina

In yesterday's newspaper I read an account of the action you took at My Lai, protecting the Vietnamese villagers from American troops. I cried. I'm near to tears again, writing this.

I'm not a Vietnam veteran. I've never served in the armed forces, and I've never been to Vietnam. But I am an American Jew who grew up in the wake of the Holocaust, studying history as an endless parade of massacres of the innocent....Usually the daily paper proves to me, over and over, that human beings would literally rather hurt each other than eat. I don't like feeling like this, but I think I always have.

But every now and then. Every now and then.

I collect these now-and-thens inside myself whenever and wherever I come across them. They may make me cry by day, but I cling to them at night, to keep myself warm remembering that – for all the horrors of history – human beings are capable of kindness, courage, love, self-sacrifice and passionate sympathy. It's terribly easy to forget that, and I usually do. You have reminded me....

Very sincerely yours,
Peter S. Beagle
Davis, California

Your action is an action that gives me unbelievable hope about the human condition. I have always admired courage and bravery.... I have and I do admire people who can stand in the face of opposition, against the status quo, people who can go against the grain to stand up for a Godly principle. I consider the highest Godly principle to be love for our neighbor, whoever that neighbor might be....

I am a firm believer that all of us, children and adults alike, need heroes in order to call the best from us. The problem today is that so many of the heroes presented to youth are so questionable in what they invite people to emulate.... It would be refreshing to have someone like yourself talk to students at Loyola... about a different kind of heroism, one that necessarily bucks "peer pressure" when higher values are to be followed and when one's conscience is to be listened to....

I am convinced that people are capable of great heroism, but they must first hear from people who have fought to the place of being considered heroic.

I do not want all this talk of "hero" to frighten you away, Mr. Thompson. It is just a code word for what you did, which was essentially loving your neighbor in a profound way under difficult circumstances.

Respectfully and in peace,
Michael Hugo
Loyola Academy
Wilmette, Illinois

I am writing this letter to thank you for what you did for the people in Quang Ngai, especially at My Lai. You and your gunners are true heroes. You not only saved those innocent civilians in My Lai, you also saved the soul of the American Nation....

I am from the Province of Quang Ngai. My village was close to My Lai. I have lived in the United States with my Navy officer husband and our six children since 1970....

When I read books about the events, I could not hold back my tears. I cried in my sleep. The books written about the monk that Calley tortured, about the mama-san on the ground that Calley killed, and about the little baby he killed. How can a little baby be Viet Cong?

I was not there when My Lai happened. But that mama-san could have been my mother. That little baby could have been my son. For weeks, I have had to fight against hate and rage. It was as if thirty years ago was yesterday.

I also read about what you did. Because of you and your men my mother lived long after the war ended. And my Vietnamese son joined us in the United States. You stopped the killing, otherwise the whole Province of Quang Ngai could have been destroyed. My family all could have been killed. Because of you I am able to tell our six children that, like their father, more American soldiers came to Vietnam to fight and to help, but not to kill like the mad dog. It is good that America remembers you now, because many times America forgets much too easily. It also sometimes forgets the good it has done.

My personal wish is to thank you and all of the Americans who came to Vietnam to help the South Vietnamese people, not to kill them. I would like to thank all U. S. soldiers who helped my mother and sister and relatives in our village because, according to my family, there were mostly good soldiers who came to our village.

You took a very big risk for humanity.... You are a brave man and a good one....

Mai Donohue
Barrington, Rhode Island

Thompson was touched by what he read. He cried tears of joy. The adulation was overwhelming. The positive tone and message of these letters were exactly opposite of what he was subjected to nearly thirty years earlier, when he was ostracized by some of his fellow soldiers and even branded as a traitor by some for not going along with the butchers at My Lai.

Enclosed in many of the letters were news clippings relating to his receipt of the Soldier's Medal and his return to My Lai. There were clippings from newspapers from all over the United States – North, South, East and West – from *The Detroit Free Press*, *The New Orleans Times-Picayune*, *The Boston Globe*, *The Los Angeles Times*, and dozens of others. Additionally, the media in Europe and Asia gave the story considerable coverage, and the travelers returned to the States with clippings from newspapers based in Ho Chi Minh City, Bangkok and Hong Kong.

Predictably, another wave of letters streamed in in the first few weeks of April, just after CBS television broadcast its segment of "60 Minutes," titled "Back to My Lai." Viewed by some twenty-two million people throughout the United States, the exclusive footage documented the historically significant and emotionally charged reunion between Thompson and Colburn and three of the women who survived the massacre. It told the heartrending story of the My Lai tragedy in a concise and moving fashion.

In addition to the letters of congratulations, Thompson was honored to receive several speaking requests, from high schools, colleges, law-enforcement organizations and military institutions. Among those inviting him to speak were the Vietnam Veterans for Peace, the Southwest Law Enforcement Institute, and Loyola Academy in Wilmette, Illinois. He was invited to participate as the honored guest in a major celebration of Native American Indian culture in Anadarko, Oklahoma; to be the marshal for the Fourth of July parade in his old hometown of Stone Mountain, Georgia; and to receive an honorary doctorate at Connecticut College.

The long-forgotten hero was invited to Sherborn, Massachusetts, to receive the Courage of Conscience Award, sponsored by the Peace Abbey, which is affiliated with Harvard Divinity School and Wellesley College. Thompson was flabbergasted to learn that the honor – bestowed upon people who have made major humanitarian contributions, particularly on behalf of the poor and the powerless – was previously given to world-renowned figures such as Mother Teresa of Calcutta and Mahatma Gandhi.

While the receipt of the Soldier's Medal had been most gratifying, Thompson felt an enormous sense of satisfaction when he received an invitation to speak on battlefield ethics from the U.S. Military Academy at West Point. Also forthcoming were invitations to address the Naval Academy at Annapolis, the Air Force Academy at Colorado Springs, and the Marine Pilots at Pensacola.

He and Colburn were invited, through the Norwegian ambassador to the United States, to address a major human rights conference at Levanger, Norway. While in that country they would also be guests of the Norwegian and International Red Cross organizations and would tell their story during a symposium attended by people with special interests in the Geneva Conventions, international law and human rights.

Thompson took the time to read every letter he received. While he appreciated them all, the ones from his fellow Vietnam veterans – from the men who knew what it was to watch their buddies die in combat – held a special significance.

Dear Mr. Thompson:

The news of your heroic actions sent chills up and down my spine. And news it was: Until I read about how you set your helicopter down in the midst of the mayhem, I had no idea that there had been an intervention.

Thank you for your words and actions then, and your "welcome home" words at the ceremony at the Memorial Wall, 30 years later.

In Peace,
Tom Verkozen
Vietnam veteran
San Rafael, California

I'm glad the Army finally honored you for the courageous act you performed in My Lai thirty years ago. I wonder how many of us other good citizens would have taken the trouble to stop, intervene, and save the lives of many innocent civilians. I was in Vietnam as one of the "Advisors," (before it became a shooting war) in 1962-63. I found the Vietnamese people to be kind, hard-working, honorable people.

It would seem repetitious to say to you, "God Bless You," for He already has. Great will be your reward when you meet God face-to-face after you...take up your other wings more reliable than chopper wings....

When I read of (My Lai) now it brings tears to my eyes without fail. Those folks you stopped were certainly not the US Army with which I served 23 years (1942-65).

Thank you again for showing us there are good men left in the U.S.

Sincerely,
Leo A. Hatten
Lt. Col., US Army (Retired)
Portales, New Mexico

All of us who served in Vietnam bore a sense of shame and indignity for the My Lai incident and the actions of our fellow soldiers. Until I read of you and your crew's actions in the newspaper, I was unaware that there was a positive side of that terrible incident.

Although a very long time in coming, I would like to add my sincere congratulations for the award of the Soldier's Medal to you and your crew. Additionally, I would like to thank you for the very difficult and brave decision you made on that fateful day....

It took a great deal of courage for you to make the stand you did thirty years ago. As a former soldier and Vietnam veteran, I extend to you and your crew (but especially you since you had to make the decision) my deepest gratitude, admiration, and respect. In anyone's description, you are a true American hero. It gives me a great sense of pride that we wore the same uniform.

Sincerely,
Gordon Hennessy
Colonel, USA (Retired)
Latham, New York

As a fellow veteran, I would like to thank you from the bottom of my heart for your courageous actions during this period of darkness in American history.

I'm sorry I never knew your story until two weeks ago. I never felt much pride in being a Vietnam veteran.... I always felt a certain amount of shame, especially after My Lai was brought to light.... I saw no difference between what we were doing and similar conflicts involving Third World dictators or even Nazi Germany.

It sent me into a deep depression for years and almost destroyed my marriage. I lived, slept and agonized over Vietnam for years. I joined Vietnam Veterans Against the War for a few years. Then after that I just drifted away from the war and blocked it out....

Your courageous story touched me and helped set my heart at ease. I'm so proud that they finally honored you and Lawrence Colburn and Glenn Andreotta. May God bless you.

With deepest respect,
Ed Laurson
Littleton, Colorado

One of the veterans who contacted him was so inspired by Thompson's heroism that he wrote not a letter but a song. Titled "Warriors for Humanity," the ballad sounded like it was straight out of the 1960s. The writer of the song, Fred Greco of Granite City, Illinois, called Thompson and asked if he could sing it to him. Flattered, Thompson told him to go ahead. The main verses include these:

Warriors for Humanity

...It takes some nerve to stick your neck out, people,
To make a stand that all the world can see.
'Twas the action of three heroes down at My Lai
I call them warriors for humanity.

Three people rarely spoke of were at My Lai.
They chose to stop that day and make a stand.
It takes us back some thirty years of memories,
To the war year '68 in Vietnam.

And I thank our weary stars for Lawrence Colburn of the crew,
That helped Hugh Thompson make his faithful stand.
And deep inside their hearts is Andreotta that they knew,
The crew chief of their ship in Vietnam.

We never like to face up to our downfalls.
And I'm sure Hugh Thompson's just like you and me.
And I'll make no mention of the bad guys that day
That hurt the helpless people on their knees...

It takes some nerve to stick your neck out, people,
To make a stand that all the world can see.
'Twas the action of three heroes down at My Lai
And I call them warriors for humanity.
And I call them warriors for humanity.
Yes, they were warriors for humanity.

Thompson liked the song. Greco promised to develop it further. He got with a friend of his in a local band, Eddie Starr, who put some music to the lyrics and recorded the piece on a demo tape. Greco sent copies of the tape to Thompson and together they began a search for a big-name entertainer to perform and record it professionally.

As the months rolled by, Thompson learned that his actions at My Lai had inspired not only a sixties-style ballad and a whole slew of letters but also poems, prayers, editorials, essays and even a symphony, written by Jonathan Berger of Stanford University in California. And, if that weren't enough to shore up a

– Photo by Danny Izzo, Nouveau Photeau, Lafayette, La.

Hugh Thompson, Vietnam War hero, as he appeared in February 1998.

Visiting Norway

Hugh Thompson and Larry Colburn traveled to Norway in October of 1998 as guest speakers for a major human rights conference, the Falstad Seminar, at Levanger. They were also guests of the Norwegian and International Red Cross organizations in Oslo and told their story during a symposium attended by people with special interests in human rights and the Geneva Conventions.

The Falstad Seminar was held near a building that served as a German concentration camp during World War II and that is used as a museum today. Local officials are planning to use some of the building for an international center for the study and promotion of human rights.

What prompted the Norwegians to invite the two Americans was that their heroic rescue of unarmed women and children at My Lai provided a shining example of legally and ethically correct treatment of civilians during wartime, as prescribed by international law and the Geneva Conventions. And it was through the initiative and leadership of the Red Cross that the Geneva Conventions were first written, in the mid-1860s, and expanded upon through the years.

Hugh Thompson and Larry Colburn answer questions concerning human rights during a news conference in Oslo, Norway, in October of 1998. The conference was sponsored by the International Red Cross. From right to left are: Thompson, Colburn, Dr. Astrid Nokleby-Heiberg, president of the International Federation of the Red Cross; and Terje Lund, special legal advisor to the Norwegian Red Cross. Lund, an assistant professor at Army College in Oslo, informed the two Americans that for ten years he had been using the story of what they did at My Lai to help teach battlefield ethics.

While in Oslo, Thompson and Colburn visited the Norwegian Parliament and told the story of the My Lai rescue to members of the Foreign Affairs Committee. **Above:** *The Parliament building.* **Below:** *Meeting with members of the Foreign Affairs Committee.* **Bottom:** *Thompson listens as Parliamentarian Agot Valle makes a point about Norway's form of government.*

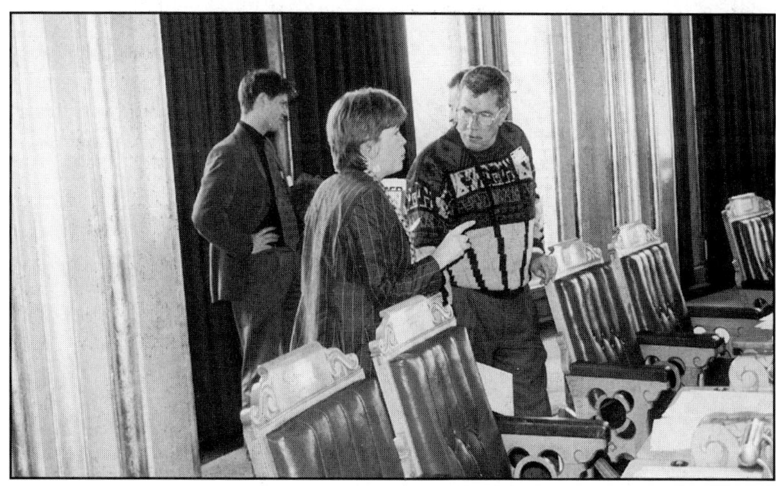

Colburn (left) and Thompson answer questions at a news conference in the Falstad Museum. Next to Thompson is a model of the World War II German concentration camp known as Falstad Prison, which was later converted into the museum.

Among the exhibits in the museum are pro-German, pro-Aryan posters used for propaganda purposes before and during the war. Commenting on the posters is Morien Rees, one of the people who helped establish the museum. Rees says the Germans tried to convince the Norwegians prior to the war that they were natural allies because of their common Aryan features. The Norwegians rejected the Germans and their logic.

Thompson (center) and Colburn (right) learn about the German occupation of Norway from Erik Lykke, a former Norwegian diplomat whose father was executed by the Nazis during World War II. The three are in the courtyard of the Falstad Museum, which was used as part of a concentration camp during the war.

In recognition of their heroic actions at My Lai during the Vietnam War, Thompson and Colburn received honorary doctoral degrees from Connecticut College in the fall of 1998. From left to right are: David Lewis, provost of the college, Claire Gaudiani, president of the college; Thompson;Duncan Dayton, chairman of Board of Trustees; and Colburn.

Photo by Jon Crispin, Amherst, Mass.

Thompson applauds Colburn after his brief remarks to the Connecticut College student body.

Michael Bilton (center) talks with Larry Colburn (left), as David Egan looks on, following the Connecticut College convocation. Bilton is co-author of the book Four Hours In My Lai *and co-producer of the documentary film* Remember My Lai. *Egan is the former Army officer who spearheaded the long campaign to have the U.S. government decorate Thompson for heroism; he became interested in championing this cause after viewing Bilton's film in 1989.*

– Photo by Danny Izzo, Nouveau Photeau, Lafayette, La.

Hugh Thompson with his Courage of Conscience Award, sponsored by the Peace Abbey, which is affiliated with Harvard Divinity School and Wellesley College in Massachusetts. Other recipients of this major humanitarian award include Mother Teresa of Calcutta and Mahatma Gandhi.

person's sense of self-worth, Thompson was approached by a dozen movie producers wanting to acquire an option on his life story.

Expressions of admiration and support continued to come in steadily for several months after Thompson's return from Vietnam. People he knew and people he didn't contacted him to thank him for what he did at My Lai or to ask him to speak to their institutions or organizations. They wanted to shake his hand, to touch him, to hear him tell his story. They wanted to be in the presence of this man of integrity, this American soldier who risked his life to protect the weak and defenseless, without regard for the consequences.

Epilogue

MORE THAN THREE DECADES HAVE PASSED since Hugh Thompson and his crew made their courageous stand on behalf of the defenseless civilians at My Lai. Until the story of their impending receipt of the Soldier's Medal broke in the media in November of 1997, only a small percentage of Americans were even aware that there had been such a rescue at My Lai.

Who would have thought that there could have been anything positive about the My Lai massacre, one of the darkest chapters in U.S. military history? What eternal optimist would have dreamed that there could have been a silver lining around this dark, dark cloud?

Even more obscured than the rescue itself has been the impact of the rescue, the far-reaching positive consequences, in terms of the good it has done, the lives it has saved, the soldiers it has enlightened and inspired.

Beyond the five hundred and four people who were killed on the morning of March 16, 1968, it is certain that more would have died at the hands of U.S. troops that afternoon and the next day and the day after that. Perhaps hundreds more would have died, perhaps thousands, had not someone taken a strong stand against the systemic evil which was running rampant under the code name of Task Force Barker.

My Lai was only the starting point. The task force had targeted two heavily populated areas with a total of more than ten thousand people, primarily women, children and old men. Those in charge made it clear to their men – before the first of what was to be a series of search-and-destroy missions – that anyone found in these villages and hamlets, in this free-fire zone, would be considered Viet Cong or Viet Cong sympathizers. It would be open season on every living thing in the soldiers' path.

But Hugh Thompson and his crew interfered. Their actions – putting themselves in harm's way and complaining of the killing of civilians over the airwaves – brought about a cease-fire and thus put a stop to the massacre. Thompson's loud and demonstrative protest put the officers in charge on notice that not all the soldiers under their command would participate in such barbaric, illegal acts, nor would they look the other way while unarmed, unresisting civilians were murdered.

The leaders of Task Force Barker realized that day, or very soon thereafter, that they would not be able to get away with the indiscriminate slaughter of civilians, even though some of the civilians were suspected of giving aid to the enemy. Soon after the massacre, strongly worded orders were issued by those in command of U.S. forces in Vietnam that all servicemen were to adhere strictly to the international laws requiring humane treatment of civilians and prisoners of war.

In addition to the Vietnamese lives saved as a result of the stoppage of Task Force Barker, many more lives have been saved around the world as an indirect result of the action of the three heroes at My Lai. Their good deed has provided an example for other servicemen to follow; their story is used in U.S. and European military ethics manuals as an example of the proper treatment of civilians in wartime. Their story also demonstrates the soldier's obligation to disobey illegal orders, a responsibility that was anything but clear in the minds of many of the U.S. troops at My Lai.

Thompson first learned that the rescue story was being used in U.S. military ethics manuals in the mid-1990s. He was informed by David Egan, the ex-Army officer who initiated the campaign to have the Army officially recognize him as a hero. Thompson was surprised and flattered by the news.

He learned that the story was being used in European military training manuals in October of 1998, when he and Larry Colburn traveled to Norway to participate as guest speakers in a major human rights conference, called the Falstad Seminar. It was there that Thompson met a man named Terje Lund, who informed him that he had been using the story of his heroic rescue at My Lai to teach battlefield ethics to Norwegian military men for ten years. Lund, an officer in the Norwegian Air Force, also pointed out that the rescue story was being used not only in Norway but in the military training manuals of other European countries as well.

An attorney and special legal advisor to the Norwegian Red Cross, Lund is well versed in the field of international law. His experiences include having worked for the United Nations as a war crimes investigator in the former Yugoslavia. As an assistant professor of humanitarian law and the law of war at Army College in Oslo, Norway, he told the Hugh Thompson story to soldiers-in-training countless times, not only in classroom lectures but also through the books and booklets he wrote on military ethics.

Lund explained that for him, as a teacher, the story of the My Lai rescue has provided a living example, a clear demonstration of legally and ethically correct behavior for other soldiers to see. This example has helped to take the meaning of the Geneva Conventions and international humanitarian law from the abstract and theoretical into the realm of the real and the concrete, thus enhancing the understanding of these rules by legions of military personnel who have been involved in armed conflicts around the world since the Vietnam War. And, he added without equivocation, as a direct result of the soldiers' better understanding of the laws, countless lives of civilians and prisoners of war, perhaps thousands, have been saved.

In conclusion, it can be said with certainty that the actions of Thompson and his crew resulted in the saving of not only nine or ten lives but, ultimately, many more. One can hope that the example they set will continue to be emulated by soldiers from many nations and that, as a result, humankind will continue to reap the benefits of their good deed long after they are gone.

Appendix 1

The 504 people killed in the My Lai massacre

Here is a list of the Vietnamese people killed in the My Lai massacre. The names of the deceased are followed by their age and sex. A brief tally shows that 50 of the people were three years old or younger, 69 were between the ages of four and seven, 91 were between eight and twelve, and 27 were in their seventies or eighties. (The list was provided by the Embassy of Vietnam in Washington, D.C., in response to a request by the author.)

Phạm Chồi, 59, m
Huỳnh Thị Hưng, 39, f
Phạm Thị Câu, 49, f
Phừng Thị Muông, 29, f
Phạm Thị Hoa, 10, f
Phạm Sinh, 5, m
Phạm Thị Huệ, 5, f
Phạm Thị Hồng, 1, f
Phạm Thị Thí, 39, f
Phạm Thị Dạng, 29, f
Trịnh Thị Thứ, 8, f
Dương Thị Chư, 69, f
Phạm Mùi, 43, m
Phạm Hưởng, 13, m
Đỗ Thị Mùi, 67, f
Đỗ Khanh, 80, m
Nguyễn Thị Đạo, 70, f
Hoàng Đích, 46, m
Võ Thị Tư, 40, f
Hoàng Văn Thứ, 7, m
Hoàng Văn Đủ, 5, m
Đỗ Thị Trị, 31, f
Bùi Thị Sản, 8, f
Bùi Thị Mán, 6, f
Lý Thị Đồng, 50, f
Quảng Em (Quặm), 49, m
Quảng Dũ (Vũ), 49, m
Quảng Xuất, 50, m
Quảng Thị Lũy, 6, f

Quảng Thị Bàn, 4, f
Quảng Cu, 1, m
Phạm Hòe, 30, m
Phạm Cu Ba, 4, m
Phạm Hoặc (Hược), 60, m
Phạm Xí, 18, m
Nguyễn Thị Chác, 40, f
Phạm Thị Cảm, 18, f
Phạm Thị Bảy, 10, f
Phạm Tâm, 8, m
Phạm Thị Chinh, 2, f
Phạm Đốc, 40, m
Nguyễn Thị Thậm, 35, f
Phạm Tài, 12, m
Phạm Xí, 10, m
Phạm Mẽo, 8, m
Phạm Đực, 6, m
Võ Thị Mại, 35, f
Lương Xí, 14, m
Lương Sáu, 11, m
Lương Thị Kiên, 37, f
Phạm Lương, 15, m
Phạm Mực, 13, m
Phạm Đực, 10, m
Phạm Thị Bê, 4, f
Dương Thị Khéo, 67, f
Phạm Thị Đằng, 17, f
Phạm Bồi, 8, m
Phạm Thị Bảy, 6, f
Nguyễn Khôi, 50, m

Nguyễn Thị Năm, 43, f
Nguyễn Nay, 12, m
Lê Thị Lệ, 48, f
Nguyễn Thị Thú, 32, f
Trần Thị Diêm, 48, f
Tô Giỏi, 10, m
Tô Một, 6, m
Phạm Thị Hiệp, 48, f
Nguyễn Thị Thanh, 48, f
Phạm Thị Giàu, 31, f
Lương Thị Hung, 71, f
Phạm Thị Văn, 61, f
Nguyễn Thị Sang, 29, f
Nguyễn Thị Sáo, 28, f
Nguyễn Văn Bốn, 27, m
Lương Thị Xanh, 8, f
Lượng Rừng, 11, m
Lương Tân, 5, m
Ngô Thị Tý, 9, f
Ngô Thị Mùi, 33, f
Lương Hai, 11, m
Lương Thành, 8, m
Lương Thị Diệp, 5, f
Lương Tào, 2, m
Ngô Thị Một, 10, f
Lê Tiểu, 11, m
Lê Thị Họn, 75, f
Nguyễn Thị Huệ, 39, f
Phạm Thị Chút, 39, f
Đỗ Thị Lấm, 9, f

Phạm Thị Rằng, 42, f
Lương Văn Hiếu, 10, m
Võ Cao Phúc, 9, m
Võ Thị Ánh, 7, f
Võ Cao Sáu, 4, m
Võ Nuôi, 76, m
Phạm Thị Lịch, 54, f
Từ Thị Y, 26, f
Võ Cu Tèo, 3, m
Phạm Thị Hược, 55, f
Nguyễn Thị Thiệt, 20, f
Võ Đức Tô, 2, m
Võ Mua (Mãi), 61, m
Phạm Thị Phán, 59, f
Võ Thị Mười, 15, f
Võ Thị Nhung, 2, f
Ngô Thị Ngon, 31, f
Nguyễn Thị Khi, 9, f
Nguyễn Khái, 7, m
Nguyễn Khối, 3, m
Nguyễn Thị Hóa, 28, f
Trần Hai, 9, m
Trần Ba, 7, m
Trần Tư, 3, m
Lê Thị Khứu (Lài) 42, f
Võ Thị Phụ, 30, f
Dương Thị Hà, 1, f
Nguyễn Thị Ba, 5, f
Cao Thị Em, 61, f
Nguyễn Thị Quyên, 32, f
Lý Thị Hai, 9, f
Lý Văn Sinh, 6, m
Nguyễn Thị Yên, 29, f
Ngô Thị Cát (Một), 45, f
Nguyễn Thị Một, 23, f
Nguyễn Duy Thanh, 15, m
Trần Thị Bé, 3, f
Ngô Đê, 6, m
Ngô Lê, 4, m
Ngô Xin, 15, m
Phạm Thị Đạo, 48, f
Đỗ Thị Kiêu, 70, f
Võ Thị Vai, 49, f
Nguyễn Thị Ty, 65, f
Nguyễn Nhơn, 50, m
Nguyễn Thị Bủng, 13, f
Nguyễn Thị Chúa, 10, f

Võ Song, 25, m
Ngô Ngọ, 55, m
Ngô Tự, 15, m
Ngô Sinh, 63, m
Ngô Đắc, 40, m
Ngô Thị Biết, 45, f
Ngô Các, 46, m
Phạm Hùng, 78, m
Lê Thị Dược, 36, f
Phạm Sẵn, 12, m
Phạm Thị Thanh, 6, f
Nguyễn Thị Phước, 62, f
Nguyễn Thị Ba, 12, f
Bùi Thị Biết, 37, f
Nguyễn Thị Muối, 3, f
Bùi Thị Bông, 76, f
Nguyễn Thị Chút, 24, f
Nguyễn Văn Chạy, 3, m
Đinh Thị Hải, 67, f
Nguyễn Thị Thông, 38, f
Nguyển Thị Dung, 6, f
Nguyễn Kỳ, 14, m
Phạm Quy, 80, m
Nguyễn Thị Quý, 76, f
Phạm Thị Có, 56, f
Nguyễn Thị Thắm, 12, f
Nguyễn Thị Hồng, 11, f
Nguyễn Thị Vân, 7, f
Đỗ Còn (Ngộ), 65, m
Đỗ Duy Hạt, 5, m
Đỗ Duy Thành, 11, m
Đỗ Thị Nhựt, 7, f
Nguyễn Nhiều, 47, m
Nguyễn Chốn, 68, m
Nguyễn Toàn, 21, m
Đỗ Xúc, 61, m
Nguyễn Thị Đây, 50, f
Phạm Thị Thịnh, 3, f
Phạm Thị Thư, 1, f
Đỗ Thị Bảy, 21, f
Nguyễn Thị Tương, 46, f
Trương Thị Đâu, 45, f
Lê Thị Tữu, 70, f
Phạm Thị Thơ, 64, f
Nguyễn Thị Bi, 17, f
Nguyễn Thị Thu, 8, f
Trương Nhị, 33, m

Nguyễn Thị Chấn, 31, f
Trương Bốn, 13, m
Trương Năm, 6, m
Trương Thị Sáu, 4, f
Trương Thị Bãy, 3, f
Nguyễn Thị Chua, 56, f
Nguyễn Thị Đào, 8, f
Lê Thị Thi, 30, f
Nguyễn Thị Thuyền, 5, f
Nguyễn Cu, 2, m
Nguyễn Hay, 57, m
Đỗ Thị Hành, 58, f
Nguyễn Hay, 21, m
Nguyễn Cương, 3, m
Nguyễn Giác, 1, m
Nguyễn Hân, 2, m
Nguyễn Thị Bảy, 19, f
Nguyễn Thị Dần, 18, f
Đỗ Thị Sương, 70, m
Trương Giảng, 55, m
Đỗ Thị Hiệp, 57, f
Nguyễn Thị Tưởng, 22, f
Nguyễn Ca, 2, m
Đỗ Cu Bảy, 9, m
Đỗ Cu, 3, m
Trương Thơ, 72, m
Trương Thị Mai, 43, f
Lê Thị Bày, 45, f
Trương Thị Sửu, 18, f
Trương Kiết, 18, m
Trương Thị Nếp, 9, f
Trương Thị Du, 1, f
Trương Sung, 62, m
Phạm Mục Lai, 70, m
Nguyễn Đa (Xí), 6, m
Trần Đâu, 80, m
Trần Đốc, 48, m
Lê Thị Tất, 43, f
Trần Hùng Sinh, 18, m
Trần Thế, 5, m
Đỗ Thị Xuyến, 68, f
Đỗ Thị Lợi, 34, f
Trương Thị Ba, 8, f
Trương Thị Khai, 6, f
Trương Tấn, 14, m
Trương Củ, 12, m
Trương Thị Xĩ, 8, f

Trương Thị Bích, 10, f
Trương Kích, 6, m
Phạm Thị Nhi, 65, f
Nguyễn Thị Cung, 57, f
Đỗ Trợ, 35, m
Đỗ Thị Nhành, 7, f
Dỗ Thị Bé, 9, f
Đỗ Cu, 5, m
Đỗ Thị Lộc, 7, f
Đỗ Cu, 1, m
Phạm Thị Em, 34, f
Đỗ Thị Hồ, 23, f
Nguyễn Thị Chúc, 55, f
Nguyễn Văn Đức, 3, m
Cao Thị Nhúng (Liệu), 62, f
Nguyễn Thị Đẩu, 36, f
Phạm Thị Mãi, 12, f
Phạm Phúc (Đùm), 26, m
Phạm Thị Nhỏ, 24, f
Phạm Thị Khánh, 6, f
Phạm Hòa, 4, m
Phùng Thị Lý, 24, f
Phạm Thị Dư, 1, f
Nguyễn Thị Sâm, 22, f
Đỗ Thị Nguyệt, 12, f
Đỗ Dược, 36, m
Đỗ Thành, 14, m
Đỗ Thị Nhựt, 7, f
Đỗ Cu, 1, m
Đỗ Thị Bé, 3, f
Lê Văn Mỹ, 8, m
Đỗ Thị Cân, 26, f
Đỗ Thị Thuộc, 45, f
Phùng Thị Liễu, 25, f
Phùng Thị Tiền, 5, f
Đỗ Đình Tư, 4, m
Lư Thị Xuân, 34, f
Nguyễn Thị Thuận, 60, f
Quảng Thị Vận, 55, f
Trương Đề, 30, m
Nguyễn Đá (Hòa), 50, m
Phạm Thị Lâu, 47, f
Nguyễn Hiệp, 40, m
Đỗ Thị Rí, 70, f
Đỗ Thị Chín, 49, f
Đỗ Thị Gái, 42, f

Phạm Thị Tình, 70, f
Phạm Thị Đạo (Lại), 75, f
Nguyễn Đối, 70, m
Nguyễn Thị Núm, 35, f
Nguyễn Thị Xí, 12, f
Nguyễn Tại, 72, m
Nguyễn Gặp, 68, m
Nguyễn Thị Lãnh, 30, f
Nguyễn Thị Thành, 28, f
Nguyễn Cơ, 28, m
Trương Thị Huyền, 65, f
Đỗ Ích, 56, m
Đỗ Dũng, 8, m
Đặng Hãnh, 63, m
Trương Thị Nho, 61, f
Đặng Thị Xí, 4, f
Đặng Đức, 2, m
Phạm Lân, 49, m
Lý Thị Ánh, 30, f
Phạm Hùng, 14, m
Phạm Thị Xí, 1, f
Nguyễn Thị Dận, 27, f
Phạm Cường, 1, m
Nguyễn Lựu, 55, m
Nguyễn Thị Nguyệt, 8, f
Phạm Thị Hoặc, 31, f
Nguyễn Thị Liên, 52, f
Nguyễn Thị Trí, 10, f
Nguyễn Hóa, 5, m
Nguyễn Danh, 2, m
Phùng Thị Hiệp, 30, f
Nguyễn Thị Huệ, 12, f
Nguyễn Thị Bé, 3, f
Lê Thị Bĩnh, 34, f
Đỗ Thị Nguyệt, 10, f
Đỗ Bạch, 8, m
Đỗ Cu, 4, m
Phạm Thị Ưng, 45, f
Nguyễn Thị Nguyệt, 8, f
Nguyễn Cư, 5, m
Đỗ Thị Mai, 42, f
Nguyễn Thị Ru, 11, f
Nguyễn Rân, 9, m
Nguyễn Cu, 7, m
Đỗ Phùng, 68, m
Đỗ Doàn, 20, m
Phùng Cu, 1, m

Phạm Thị Tuân, 28, f
Nguyễn Thị Huynh, 7, f
Nguyễn Chí, 44, m
Ngô Thị Tuyết, 46, f
Võ Thị Thìn, 68, f
Nguyễn Thị Bích, 45, f
Nguyễn Thị Bướm, 8, f
Bùi Tá, 60, m
Phạm Thị Sở, 50, f
Nguyễn Thị Lan, 19, f
Trần Lan (Hậu), 59, m
Đỗ Thị An, 42, f
Trần Thị Hương, 17, f
Trần Văn Khôi, 15, m
Trần Văn Sánh, 12, m
Trần Thị Thu, 10, f
Trần Thị Hoa, 1, f
Nguyễn Thị Dương, 12, f
Nguyễn Mai, 9, m
Nguyễn Đẹp, 7, m
Nguyễn Tinh, 4, m
Nguyễn Tư, 2, m
Nguyễn Khương, 25, m
Phạm Thị Tri, 23, f
Nguyễn Thị Bé, 1, f
Phạm Kỹ, 20, m
Phạm Thị Thân, 12, f
Phạm Thị Lành, 10, f
Phạm Cỗ, 60, m
Phạm Quới, 39, m
Nguyễn Thị Bộ (Tẩu), 49, f
Trần Thị Hồng, 11, f
Trần Thị Huệ, 7, f
Trần Thị Thông, 55, f
Ngô Da, 20, m
Ngô Thị Quan, 14, f
Ngô Thị Minh, 12, f
Ngô Thị Xí, 7, f
Ngô Thị Hoa, 8, f
Ngô Cu, 4, m
Lê Lý, 70, m
Võ Thị Bút, 65, f
Nguyễn Thị Luận, 34, f
Lê Cổ, 42, m
Lê Cu, 11, m
Lê Thị Danh, 9, f

Lê Thị Biết, 13, f
Đỗ Thị Dược, 70, f
Nguyễn Sương, 45, m
Phạm Nhỏ, 35, m
Lư Thị Quen, 42, f
Đỗ Thị Nguyệt, 9, f
Đỗ Cu, 5, m
Phạm Thị Xí, 20, f
Nguyễn Tấn Sanh (Gòi), 75, m
Võ Cu Tuấn, 10, m
Võ Phan, 11, m
Trần Ân, 45, m
Trần Chấn, 20, m
Trần Sương Kinh, 28, m
Phạm Nhất, 1, m
Phạm Xí, 9, m
Phạm Tân, 5, m
Nguyễn Kỳ, 52, m
Trương Luyện, 58, m
Trương Luyến, 12, m
Trương Công, 16, m
Trương Sung, 2, m
Trương Thị Nhơn, 6, f
Nguyễn Quyền, 46, m
Nguyễn Đức Huy, 32, m
Nguyễn Thị Một, 6, f
Đỗ Bồng, 10, m
Nguyễn Hiệp, 52, m
Đỗ Thị Thuần, 60, f
Nguyễn Oanh, 10, m
Nguyễn Thị Anh, 14, f
Nguyễn Hoàng, 60, m
Nguyễn Hà, 5, m
Nguyễn Đắc, 10, m
Đỗ Kỳ, 57, m
Đỗ Phước, 26, m
Đỗ Thị Bình, 12, f
Đỗ Thụy, 10, m
Phạm Chúc, 62, m
Phạm Chánh, 1, m
Phạm Cuộc, 12, m
Phạm Suy, 41, m
Phạm Khá, 68, m
Phạm Tòng, 38, m
Đào Sơn, 50, m
Phạm A, 6, m
Phạm Tuân, 12, m
Phạm Cổ, 49, m
Phạm Thị Sính, 19, f
Phạm Thí Bé, 1, f
Phạm Thị Em, 6, f
Nguyễn Thị Mười, 10, f
Nguyễn Thị Lùn, 13, f
Nguyễn Một, 50, m
Nguyễn Dân, 52, m
Nguyễn Cao, 64, m
Nguyễn Thị Hoa, 7, f
Lê Thị Cảnh, 14, f
Lê Thị Tương, 12, f
Phạm Thị Kiệt 26, f
Phạm Thị Thọ, 16, f
Phạm Thị Hoàng, 40, f
Nguyễn Văn Thanh, 5, m
Nguyễn Văn Cu, 1, m
Ngô Thị Thi, 7, m
Nguyễn Toán, 13, m
Nguyễn Nhiễu, 13, m
Lê Thị Minh, 2, f
Nguyễn Thị Kiên, 16, f
Lê Thị Được, 14, f
Nguyễn Thị Đụm, 38, f
Nguyễn Thị Hòa, 16, f
Nguyễn Thị Nga, 2, f
Phạm Thị Lưỡng, 2, f
Phạm Thị Toàn, 49, f
Đỗ Ngọc Nên, 50, m
Đỗ Thị Nhâm, 33, f
Nguyễn Thị Cải, 43, f
Nguyễn Cẩm, 19, m
Nguyễn Dưỡng, 39, m
Đỗ Thị Xí, 2, f
Dương Thị Hàn, 10, f
Trần Thị Sỏa, 6, f
Nguyễn Dương, 55, m
Trần Thị Phượng, 60, f
Nguyễn Mỹ, 21, m
Nguyễn Quân, 18, m
Nguyễn Thị Bườm, 12, f
Nguyễn Thị Phương, 10, f
Đỗ Hợp, 8, m
Nguyễn Thị Trương, 32, f
Trương Thị Ri, 2, f
Nguyễn Thị Bình, 6, f
Nguyễn Thị Bốn, 10, f
Nguyễn Thị Huỳnh, 15, f
Ngô Ngọ, 5, m
Phạm Chiêm, 45, m
Đỗ Thích, 6, m
Phạm Tằng, 59, m
Trương Hiệp, 18, m
Nguyễn Thị Ngộ, 45, f
Nguyễn Thị Một, 22, f
Nguyễn Vận, 15, m
Trương Thị Diễn, 67, f
Dương Thị Nhớ, 66, f
Nguyễn Sinh, 19, m
Trương Anh, 42, m
Đỗ Bang, 15, m
Đỗ Thị Sang, 13, f
Đỗ Thị Thành, 1, f
Đỗ Tất, 9, m
Đỗ Thị Thảnh, 7, f
Trần Sơn, 52, m
Trần Hỏa, 38, m
Trương Thị Châu, 72, f
Nguyễn Phương, 12, m
Phạm Hước, 50, m
Phạm Thị Mẫn, 10, f
Phạm Thị Vọng, 71, f
Võ Thị Cổ, 72, f
Nguyễn Thị Thiên, 32, f
Phạm Thị Mới, 70, f
Phạm Sơn, 42, m
Phạm Em, 18, m
Trương Thị Lân, 38, f
Đỗ Hạnh, 1, m
Nguyễn Cừ, 11, m
Phạm Tấn, 9, m
Trần Kình, 38, m
Đỗ Phượng, 19, m
Nguyễn Tâm, 48, m
Nguyễn Cươi, 10, m
Nguyễn Thị Tuất, 46, f
Đỗ Thị Xí, 1, f
Ngô Thị Biết, 45, f

Appendix 2

Letters To A Hero

Following his receipt of the Soldier's Medal at the Vietnam Wall in Washington, D.C., on March 6, 1998, Hugh Thompson received hundreds of letters of congratulations from U.S. citizens. All the letters expressed joy at hearing or reading the news; many of those who wrote stated they had no idea that there had been an intervention during the My Lai massacre. Following are excerpts from some of those letters; others can be found on pages 200 to 207.

Dear Mr. Thompson:

I was reading the local newspaper a couple of weeks ago. My eyes caught this article about you. I read on spellbound, with tears streaming down my cheeks. I tore the article out. I wanted to give it to someone. I wanted someone else to feel what I was feeling. I wanted to make the article bigger somehow. I wanted it to be on the front page. For the letters to be larger. I wanted it to make more noise. It's just so very rare to come even this close to integrity of this caliber....

Thank you so very much. I shall cherish that story of you always. It touched me deeply. You are a man worth knowing, Mr. Thompson. Thank you for fighting that dreadful war and thank you for being who you are. The saying is oh so true: The world needs so much more of the likes of you.

With highest regards,
Aisling McCallum
Santa Rosa, Calif.

We'll never adequately pay tribute to the dedicated and valiant service of so many so long forgotten. That's why it's especially pleasing to see your valor, your heroism, your incredibly brave stand for what is good and decent be recognized, albeit so late. Congratulations, sir. You are an American hero.

Sincerely,
Robert L. Livingston
Member of Congress

Thank you. For remembering your humanity in the midst of madness, thank you.... For remembering the divine spark, that still, small flame, thank you.

I have always been ashamed of this country that is always at war – either with itself or with others, ashamed of its banal absurdity of training boys into killers and then pinning medals on their empty breasts. With Thos. Jefferson, I, also, tremble for my country when I remember God is just.

For saving the lives of innocents, thank you. For following the highest orders of conscience and instinct, thank you.

With Schindler and Wallenberg, you may inscribe your name with the Righteous Among Nations.

Aloha,
Glenn Robinette
Kealakekua, Hawaii

Even though we have never met, you have touched my life very deeply.... As a mother, I could not help but think that if my children were ever victims of war, that they too would be saved from massacre....

Then I was overwhelmed with emotion again because human beings could kill innocent children, women, and elderly; it is nearly incomprehensible.

But more importantly, I was deeply moved by the action you and your fellow soldiers took to stop such an awful event. As an American and, in the broader scope, as a member of the human race, reading about your courageous acts brought on a tremendous feeling of pride and joy.

Sincerely,
Sandra Ploegert
Plano, Texas

The inner strength it took to defy the callousness that you witnessed, when it could have been easy to look away under the insanity of war, saved more than lives that horrible day. You redeemed the true spirit of mankind by placing your own life and limb in harm's way to reach out in compassion and justice. Mr. Thompson, although I have served on the National Security Committee for many years and seen all types of brave men and women pass before me, I feel as if through your selfless act I truly know what it means to be a hero. Peace and God bless.

Sincerely,
Robert A. Underwood
Member of Congress

...If courage is defined as grace under pressure, your actions many years ago require a re-writing of that definition. Your physical bravery and moral courage are even more extraordinary when considered in the context of conflicted loyalties, physical danger and the relative youth of a 24-year-old man. That strength of character is what every parent works for and prays for as they watch their children become young adults.

My husband and I recently had our first child, a son, and I have clipped your story from our local newspaper to save, and at the right time, to show our son, so he will understand moral courage and know that once this country was privileged to have a hero in its midst.

Jody Cramsie
Spokane, Washington

I want to thank you for what you did at My Lai 30 years ago. I wept when I read the story in the newspapers....You are a hero in the highest sense of the word; and I hope all this will help us heal....

God bless you and keep you,
Anne Morrison Welsh
Black Mountain, North Carolina

Appendix 3

Narrative accompanying Hugh Thompson's Soldier's Medal

SOLDIER'S MEDAL
HUGH C. THOMPSON, JR.
(THEN WARRANT OFFICER ONE, UNITED STATES ARMY)

For heroism above and beyond the call of duty on 16 March 1968, while saving the lives of at least 10 Vietnamese civilians during the unlawful massacre of noncombatants by American forces at My Lai, Quang Ngai Province, South Vietnam. Warrant Officer Thompson landed his helicopter in the line of fire between fleeing Vietnamese civilians and pursuing American ground troops to prevent their murder. He then personally confronted the leader of the American ground troops and was prepared to open fire on those American troops should they fire upon the civilians. Warrant Officer Thompson, at the risk of his own personal safety, went forward of the American lines and coaxed the Vietnamese civilians out of the bunker to enable their evacuation. Leaving the area after requesting and overseeing the civilians' air evacuation, his crew spotted movement in a ditch filled with bodies south of My Lai Four. Warrant Officer Thompson again landed his helicopter and covered his crew as they retrieved a wounded child from the pile of bodies. He then flew the child to the safety of a hospital at Quang Ngai. Warrant Officer Thompson's relayed radio reports of the massacre and subsequent report to his section leader and commander resulted in an order for the cease fire at My Lai and an end to the killing of innocent civilians. Warant Officer Thompson's Heroism exemplifies the highest standards of personal courage and ethical conduct, reflecting distinct credit on him, and the United States Army.

Sources

Books, newspaper and magazine articles, letters and other printed documents

AFP. "Thanks to them, I am alive." *The Bangkok Post*. March 16, 1998, page 6.

Ackerman, Maj. Gen. Michael. Keynote address for Thompson's and Colburn's Soldier's Medal ceremony. Washington, D.C., March 6, 1998.

Alexander, Paul. "The Burden of My Lai." *The (Baton Rouge) Advocate*. (Associated Press). March 16, 1998. Page 1.

Anderson, David L. (Editor). *Facing My Lai: Moving Beyond the Massacre*. Lawrence, Kansas: University Press of Kansas, 1998.

Auchincloss, Kenneth. "Who Else Is Guilty?" *Newsweek*, April 12, 1971, pages 30-32.

Bilton, Michael and Sim, Kevin. *Four Hours In My Lai*. New York: Penguin Books, 1992.

Calley, Lt. William. Transcript of Calley's murder trial, 1971.

Dagnes, Lt. Col. Peter. Internal e-mail to Assistant Secretary of the Army, Sara Lister, recommending that Thompson's Soldier's Medal be put on hold, July 1996.

Daniel, Capt. Aubrey M. Letter to President Nixon. April 1971.

Department of the Army. *Report of the Department of the Army Review of the Preliminary Investigations into the My Lai Incident (Volume I)- The Report of the Investigation,* Washington, D.C., March 14, 1970.

Gallup Organization. "A Newsweek Poll on Calley's Fate." *Newsweek*, April 12, 1971, page 28.

Goldstein, Joseph; Marshall, Burke; and Schwartz, Jack. *The My Lai Massacre and Its Cover-up: Beyond the Reach of Law?* New York: The Free Press (Division of Macmillian Publishing Co.), 1976

Greenhaw, Wayne. *The Making Of A Hero: The Story of Lieut. William Calley Jr.* Louisville, Kentucky: Touchstone Publishing Co., 1971.

Hebert, F. Edward, with McMillan, John. *Last of the Titans: The Life and Times of Congressman F. Edward Hebert of Louisiana.* Lafayette, Louisiana: Center for Louisiana Studies, University of Southwestern Louisiana, 1976, page 386.

Hoffman, David. "5 Quang Ngai Legislators Deny Atrocity Charges Against GIs." *Washington Post.* Nov. 24, 1969.

Investigation Of The My Lai Incident: Hearings of the Armed Services Investigating Subcommittee of the Committee on Armed Services, House of Representatives, Ninety-First Congress. F. Edward Hebert, Chairman. Hearings held April, May & June, 1970; transcript of hearings declassified and published in 1976, pages 224-248.

Koch, U.S. Rep. Edward I., et al. Letter to U.S. Rep. F. Edward Hebert urging release of secret testimony, Nov. 24, 1970.

McGaffin, William. "Rivers in Trouble Blocking My Lai Court-Martial." Chicago Daily News-Sun Times Service. April 18, 1970.

——, "Rivers vs. Army on My Lai." *New York Post*, April 16, 1970, page 17.

Mikva, U.S. Rep. Abner J. Letter to U.S. Rep. L. Mendel Rivers urging release of secret testimony, Dec. 7, 1970.

"My Lai: An American Tragedy." *Time*. Vol. 94, No. 23, Dec. 5, 1969, pages 23-34.

Nixon, Richard. *RN: The Memoirs of Richard Nixon.* New York: Grosset & Dunlap, 1978, pages 351, 499, 500.

Peers, Lt. Gen. W.R., USA (Ret.). *The My Lai Inquiry*. New York: W.W. Norton & Co., 1979.

Powell, Gen. Colin. Letter to David Egan regarding Thompson's award for heroism. Aug. 19, 1991

Resor, Stanley R. (Secretary of the Army). Letters to Congressman F. Edward Hebert. Dec. 19 & 29, 1969; Jan. 6, 1970.

Ridenhour, Ronald. Letter to President Nixon, Secretary of the Army, et al. March 29, 1969.

Rosenthal, Harry F. "Henderson report quoted: civilians not gathered, killed." *The Birmingham News*. (Associated Press) Sept. 2, 1971, page 14.

Shea, Maj. Gen. Donald. Invocation for Thompson's and Colburn's Soldier's Medal ceremony, Washington, D.C. March 6, 1998.

Taylor, Delphine. "We were supposed to be the good guys." *Memories*. Vol. 2, No. 5, Oct./Nov. 1989, pages 88-91.

"The Killings At Song My." *Newsweek*. Dec. 8, 1969, pages 33-41.

Varney, James. "A Hero's Welcome." *The Times-Picayune*. March 5, 1998, page 1.

Vistica, Gregory L. "A Quiet War Over the Past." *Newsweek*. Nov. 24, 1997, page 41.

VNS. "Village remembers day 30 years ago when over 500 were slaughtered." *Viet Nam News*. March 17, 1998, page 3.

Westmoreland, Gen. William C. *A Soldier Reports*. New York: Doubleday & Co., 1976, page 375.

Wilson, Col. William V. "I had prayed to God that this thing was fiction..." *American Heritage*, Vol. 41, No. 1, February 1990, pages 44-53.

Wilson, George C. and Homan, Richard. "Copter Pilot Tells House Inquiry of rescuing Vietnamese at My Lai." *Washington Post*, Dec. 12, 1969, page 1.

——, "Pilot's Story Leaves Rivers Uncertain on Viet Massacre." *Washington Post*, Dec. 11, 1969, page 1.

Wingo, Hal. "The Massacre at My Lai." *Life*. Vol. 67, No. 23. Dec. 5, 1969, pages 36-45.

Documentary Films

Bilton, Michael and Sim, Kevin. *Remember My Lai*. (Television documentary for British television, shown on ITV network's "First Tuesday.") Aired first in May 1989 in the United Kingdom, then in the United States on PBS.

Boehm, Mike. *The Sound of the Violin in My Lai*. Madison, Wisconsin, 1998.

McKenna, Terrance (Reporter) and Phizicky, Stephen (Producer). *Return to My Lai.* (Television documentary for Canadian Broadcasting Corporation's "The National Magazine") Aired March 31 and April 1, 1998.

Sim, Kevin (Moderator); Hugh Thompson, Ron Ridenhour, William Eckhardt (Panelists). *Experiencing the Darkness: A My Lai Oral History*. New Orleans: Fertel Communication. December 3, 1994.

Wallace, Mike (Reporter) and Anderson, Tom (Producer). *Back To My Lai.* (Television documentary for CBS News' "60 Minutes") Aired March 29, 1998.

Personal Interviews

Andreotta, David. Brother of Glenn Andreotta.

Andreotta, Joe. Father of Glenn Andreotta.

Andreotta, Ruth. Mother of Glenn Andreotta.

Berger, Jonathan. Stanford University teacher who wrote concerto about My Lai massacre and rescue.

Bernhardt, Michael. A soldier in Charlie Co. who refused to participate in My Lai massacre.

Bilton, Michael. Author and filmmaker who researched and documented My Lai massacre story in detail.

Blakesley, Christopher. Law professor at Louisiana State University Law School in Baton Rouge. (J.Y. Sanders Chair of International Criminal Law.)

Boehm, Mike. Former U.S. soldier and humanitarian who works to help My Lai citizens.

Brownlee, Gayle. Hugh Thompson's first girlfriend.

Carter, Donald. Hugh Thompson's best friend in high school and junior high.

Clement, Kevin M. U.S. Army officer who worked from within the Pentagon to help get Thompson the Soldier's Medal.

Colburn, Lawrence. Gunner on Thompson's helicopter at My Lai.

Conkright, Don. Thompson's commanding officer in Hawaii.

Creswell, Rev. Carl. Thompson's chaplain in Vietnam.

Crooks, Joseph. Hugh Thompson's Army-appointed attorney during some of the My Lai courts-martial, hearings and investigations.

Daniel, Aubrey M. III. U.S. Army prosecutor of William Calley Jr.

Eckhardt, William. Prosecutor in three of the five My Lai courts-martial.

Egan, David. Former U.S. Army officer who led the crusade for Thompson's Soldier's Medal.

Greco, Fred. Vietnam veteran who wrote song, "Warriors for Humanity," to honor Thompson and his crew for their heroism at My Lai.

Haeberle, Ron. U.S. Army photographer who photographed the people slaughtered in the My Lai massacre.

Johnson, Nick. Thompson's commanding officer at Fort Polk, Louisiana.

Jones, Mary. Sister of Larry Colburn, one of the crew who rescued civilians in the My Lai massacre.

Jordan, Robert. General counsel of the Army, working closely with Secretary of the Army Stanley Resor on legal matters, including those related to the My Lai massacre.

Lippman, Matthew. Professor of Criminal Justice at University of Illinois in Chicago.

Lloyd, Barry. Thompson's platoon leader in Vietnam at the time of the My Lai massacre.

Lund, Terje. Norwegian military officer and war college professor who used the story of Thompson's heroic rescue to teach battlefield ethics in Norway.

MacCrate, Robert. Civilian attorney who helped to spearhead the Peers Inquiry into the My Lai massacre coverup.

Paust, Jordan. Law Foundation Professor at University of Houston Law Center.

Pham Thi Nhung. One of the women rescued from the bunker by Hugh Thompson and his crew. (She was 46 at the time.)

Pham Thi Nhanh. One of the women rescued from the bunker by Hugh Thompson and his crew. (She was six at the time.)

Poche, Charlie. Vietnam veteran and one of Hugh Thompson's best friends.

Resor, Stanley. Secretary of the Army at the time of the My Lai massacre and subsequent courts-martial.

Rehm, Bruce. Glenn Andreotta's best friend in high school and junior high.

Thompson, Hugh C. Jr. U.S. Army soldier who intervened in My Lai massacre and rescued civilians.

Thompson, Tommie. Brother of Hugh Thompson.

Thompson, Wessie. Mother of Hugh Thompson.

Tucker, Palma Baughman. Thompson's second wife and mother of his two eldest children.

Watke, Fred. Thompson's commanding officer in Vietnam.

Westmoreland, Gen. William. Commander of U.S. Armed Forces in Vietnam.

References

Chapter 1. A Special Gift...

pp. 14-16 – *Egan's campaign for Soldier's Medal*: David Egan, personal interview.
p. 15 – *...given the same set of circumstances.*: Hugh Thompson, personal interview.
p. 16 – "*...chaos of battle.*": Gen. Colin Powell, Chairman of the Joint Chiefs of Staff, writing back to David Egan, Aug. 19, 1991.

Chapter 2. Quest for the Soldier's Medal

pp. 17-18 – *Why Army wasn't anxious to award medal for heroism*: Hugh Thompson, personal interviews.
pp. 18-21 – *Telephone conversation between Egan and Thompson*: personal interviews with Egan and Thompson.
p. 21 – *...troops who fought in Vietnam*: David Egan, personal interview.
p. 22 – "*...American soldiers and our country*": David Egan letter to Gen. John M. Shalikashvili, Chairman of the Joint Chiefs of Staff, Aug. 4, 1994.
p. 23 – "*...or legislation by Congress.*": David Egan letter to Secretary of the Army Togo West.
p. 24 – "*...All I need is your go-ahead.*": Lt. Col. Kevin Clement, internal e-mail to his immediate superior, John P. McLaurin, May 17, 1996.
p. 24 – "*...until clear of the election.*": Lt. Col. Peter Dagnes, internal e-mail to Asst. Secretary of the Army Sara Lister, July 1996.
p. 25 – "*...the accompanying narrative.*": Lt. Col. Kevin Clement, personal interview.
p. 26 – "*...in the near future.*": Lt. Col. Kevin Clement, internal e-mail to his superior, John McLaurin, Feb. 18, 1997.
p. 27 – *...without further delay.*: David Egan, personal interview.
p. 28 – "*...Thompson not...notified by the Army...*": Tom Bowman, *The Baltimore Sun*, Nov. 14, 1997.
p. 28 – "*...Soldier's Medal for his bravery.*": Gregory L. Vistica, *Newsweek*, Nov. 24, 1997.
pp. 30-31 – *Pentagon's plan for a private ceremony*: Hugh Thompson, personal interview.
p. 31 – *Vietnamese government's willingness to present medal.*: Ibid.
p. 32 – *Meeting in Atlanta*: Larry Colburn, personal interview.

Chapter 3. A Day of Triumph

p. 33 – "*He is with us.*": Hugh Thompson, personal interview.
pp. 34-36 – *Colburn biography*: Larry Colburn and his sister, Mary Jones, personal interviews.

p. 38 – *Why Thompson hadn't talked about massacre*: Hugh Thompson, personal interview.

p. 38 – *...choke up with emotion.*: The story of Thompson's and Colburn's receipt of the Soldier's Medal was published on the front pages of newspapers throughout the U.S., broadcast live on CNN, and given prominent coverage by the major television networks in the U.S. and some other countries. Hundreds of U.S. citizens responded to the news of the issuance of the medals – and to the news that Thompson and his crew had risked their lives to stop the My Lai massacre – by writing to Thompson and Colburn and thanking them for what they did. Dozens of those who wrote to Thompson stated they had no idea anyone had intervened to stop the slaughter; it was news to them, coming 30 years after the fact. (Excerpts from some of these letters appear on pages 200-203, 205-207 and 227-229.)

pp. 39-43 – *Andreotta biography*: Ruth Andreotta (mother), Joseph Andreotta (father), David Andreotta (brother) and Bruce Rehm (best friend in high school), personal interviews.

p. 45 – *Chaplain's prayer*: Maj. Gen. Donald Shea, read at Soldier's Medal ceremony.

pp. 45-46 – *Main address*: Maj. Gen. Michael Ackerman, read at Soldier's Medal ceremony.

p. 57 – *Former President Bush's letter*: George Bush's letter to Hugh Thompson was read at Ft. Belvoir reception following Soldier's Medal ceremony.

Chapter 4. Growing up in Stone Mountain, Ga.

pp. 59-60 – *Thompson interview*: Conducted in Washington, D.C., the day after Soldier's Medal ceremony.

p. 61 – *...interested in other mates.* Gayle Brownlee (Thompson's first girlfriend), personal interview.

pp. 62-63 – *...this pivotal virtue*: Tommie Thompson (Hugh's brother) and Wessie Thompson (Hugh's mother), personal interviews.

p. 63 – *...love, dating, marriage...*: Ibid.

p. 64 – "*...anything she didn't approve of.*": Hugh Thompson Sr., as quoted by Wessie Thompson.

p. 65 – *Motorcycle accident*: Don Carter (Hugh's best friend in high school), personal interview.

pp. 65-66 – *Auto accident*: Ibid.

p. 67 – *Thompson's first marriage*: Hugh Thompson, personal interview.

p. 68 – *...attractive to him*: Ibid.

Chapter 5. Mission to My Lai

pp. 69-86 – *Thompson's and Colburn's visit to Vietnam in March 1998.*: Unless otherwise noted, the description of the two war heroes' activities and statements while in Vietnam is based on the personal observations of the author, who accompanied them while in Vietnam.

p. 83 – "*...get me out of here.*": Hugh Thompson, personal interview.
p. 86 – *...good to be in Da Nang...*: Ibid.
pp. 86-100 – *Thompson's and Colburn's return flight to the U.S.*: Hugh Thompson and Larry Colburn, personal interviews.

Chapter 6. The My Lai Massacre

p. 102 – *...rid the area of Viet Cong...*: Lt. Gen. W.R. Peers, *Report of the Department of the Army Review of the Preliminary Investigations into the My Lai Incident (Volume I)*, March 14, 1970; Michael Bilton and Kevin Sim, *Four Hours In My Lai,* New York, Penguin Books, 1992; Bilton and Sim, *Remember My Lai* (TV documentary).
p. 102 – *...meet the enemy head-to-head...*: Ibid.
pp. 103-116 – *The assault on My Lai*: Ibid.
p. 107 – *...anything out of the ordinary.*: Ronald Haeberle, personal interview.
pp. 109-110 – *...group of bodies*: Ibid.
p. 110 – *...what had just happened.*: Ibid.
p. 112 – *...crimes against humanity.*: Michael Bernhardt, personal interview.
p. 113 – *...executioners from Charlie Company.*: Ronald Haeberle, personal interview.
p. 114 – *Medina shoots woman.*: Larry Colburn, personal interview.
pp. 116-117 – *How bodies ended up in ditch*: Hugh Thompson, personal interview.
p. 119 – *...brains had been blown out...*: Ibid.
pp. 119-120 – *Thompson's confrontation with Calley*: Ibid.

Chapter 7. A Daring Rescue

pp. 123-134 – *Rescue of civilians in bunker*: Hugh Thompson, personal interviews (except as otherwise noted).
p. 124 – *...seriousness of his intent.*: Larry Colburn, personal interview.
p. 126 – *...gotten myself into this time.*: Ibid.
p. 128 – *...showing his respect...*: Ibid.
p. 128 – *...experience it in her mind.*: Pham Thi Nhung (massacre survivor), personal interview.
pp. 129-131 – *Rescue of child in ditch*: Larry Colburn, personal interview.
p. 134 – *...one of those things...*: Chaplain Carl Creswell, personal interview.
p. 134 – *...cannot protect themselves. Amen.*: Hugh Thompson, personal interview.

Chapter 8. Hazardous Duty

pp. 135-151 – *Thompson's life after the massacre*: Hugh Thompson, personal interviews (except as otherwise noted).
pp. 136-140 – *Thompson and wife, Palma, in Hawaii*: Hugh Thompson and Palma Baughman Tucker, personal interviews.
pp. 140-141 – *Andreotta's death*: Larry Colburn, personal interview.

p. 143 – *...hung for murder.*: Michael Bilton and Kevin Sim, *Four Hours In My Lai*, New York, Penguin Books, 1992; and Bilton and Sim, *Remember My Lai* (TV documentary).

p. 143 – "*...a counter-propaganda campaign...*": Col. Oran Henderson's report on the massacre to Maj. Gen. Samuel Koster, April 1968.

p. 144 – *...would not go unpunished.*: Michael Bernhardt, personal interview.

p. 144 – *Bernhardt's punishment.*: Ibid.

p. 152 – *...the one at My Lai.*: Michael Bilton and Kevin Sim, *Four Hours In My Lai*, New York, Penguin Books, 1992.

p. 154 – *...besmirch the name...*: F. Edward Hebert (D-La.) and L. Mendel Rivers (D-S.C.) were among the Congressmen who had extreme difficulty admitting U.S. soldiers were capable of the atrocities committed at My Lai. Like President Nixon, at first they viewed the reports of the massacre as an attempt to undermine the war effort.

Chapter 9. The Pursuit of Truth and Justice

pp. 155-156 – *Thompson's first interview with Inspector General's Office*: Hugh Thompson, personal interview; and Col. William V. Wilson, "I had prayed to God that this thing was fiction," *American Heritage* Magazine, Vol. 41, No. 1, Feb. 1990, pages 44-53.

pp. 159-160 – "*...military justice proceedings.*": Stanley R. Resor (Secretary of the Army), letter to U.S. Rep. F. Edward Hebert (Chairman of Investigating Subcommittee of House Armed Services Committee). This was one of a series of letters Resor wrote to Hebert, pleading with him to hold off on his hearings until the My Lai courts-martial were completed, lest the Army's attempt to have justice served be thwarted.

p. 160 – "*...get away with this...*": U.S. Rep. L. Mendel Rivers, speaking to the Altus, Oklahoma, Chamber of Commerce in April 1970, as reported by William McGaffin (Chicago Daily News-Sun Times News Service) and published in the *New York Post* on April 16, 1970, page 17.

p. 160 – "*...come up with something...*": Ibid, April 18, 1970.

p. 161 – "*...I'm being fair-minded...*": L. Mendel Rivers, as quoted in article titled "Pilot's Story Leaves Rivers Uncertain on Viet Massacre," *Washington Post*, Dec. 11, 1969, page 1.

p. 162 – "*Col. Barker is dead.*": Capt. Ernest Medina, addressing the full House Armed Services Committee, as reported in *Washington Post*, Dec. 12, 1969, page 1.

p. 162 – *Men charged with war crimes*: Lt. Gen. W.R. Peers, *The My Lai Inquiry*, New York, W.W. Norton & Co., 1979, page 227.

p. 162 – *Men with command responsibility who were charged*: Ibid, pages 221-222.

p. 163 – *...no extradition treaty...*: Robert MacCrate (civilian attorney who helped head up the Peers Inquiry), personal interview.

p. 163 – *...most appropriate forum...*: Ibid; and William Eckhardt (prosecutor in the My Lai courts-martial), personal interview.

p. 163 – *...a public relations nightmare.*: Michael Bilton and Kevin

Sim, *Four Hours In My Lai*, New York, Penguin Books, 1992; and Robert Jordan (Army lawyer who worked closely with Secretary of the Army Resor on legal matters), personal interview.

p. 163 – *...any chance justice would be served...*: Jordan Paust (law professor at University of Houston Law Center), personal interview; and Matthew Lippman (professor of criminal justice at University of Illinois in Chicago), personal interview; and Christopher Blakesley (law professor at Louisiana State University Law School in Baton Rouge), personal interview.

p. 163 – *...violated the Geneva Conventions...*: Ibid.

p. 164 – *...whitewashing the chain of command...*: Gen. William Westmoreland, *A Soldier Reports*, New York, Doubleday & Co., 1976, page 375.

p. 164 – *...the uniform of the American soldier.*: Stanley Resor (Secretary of the Army), personal interview.

p. 164 – *...point their weapons...*: Hugh Thompson, personal interview.

p. 165 – *...Rivers took Thompson...*: William Eckhardt, personal interview.

p. 165 – *...Thompson...felt embarrassed...*: Hugh Thompson, personal interview.

p. 166 – *Thompson considers fleeing to Canada*: Ibid.

p. 167 – *...men accused of murder...*: William Eckhardt, personal interview.

pp. 167-170 – *Thompson's testimony before Investigating Subcommittee*: F. Edward Hebert (chairman), transcript of the testimony taken by the Investigating Subcommittee of the House Armed Services Committee, declassified and published in 1976, pages 224-248.

p. 171 – *...the case collapsed...*: William Eckhardt, personal interview.

p. 172 – *... sabotage the prosecution...*: Ibid.

p. 172 – *... set him up to be court-martialed...*: Ibid.

p. 173 – "*...what really happened at My Lai.*" : U.S. Rep. Edward I. Koch, et al, letter to U.S. Rep. F. Edward Hebert, Nov. 24, 1970.

p. 174 – "*...the very laws it writes.*": U.S. Rep. Abner J. Mikva, letter to U.S. Rep. L. Mendel Rivers, Dec. 7, 1970.

p. 174 – *...to exonerate the U.S. Army...*: William Eckhardt, Robert MacCrate, Robert Jordan, personal interviews.

p. 175 – *...tried to discredit Peers Inquiry...*: Robert MacCrate, personal interview.

p. 175 – "*...antiwar propaganda...*": Ibid.

p. 175 – "*...unacceptable in their minds.*": Ibid.

p. 175 – *...their game plan...*: William Eckhardt, personal interview.

p. 176 – "*...a hero of My Lai...*": Lt. Gen. W.R. Peers, *The My Lai Inquiry*, pages 242-243.

Chapter 10. A Nation Divided

p. 177 – *...they all got up and walked out...*: Hugh Thompson, personal interview.

p. 177 – *...he'd never heard of him.*: Ibid.

p. 178 – "*...disgraced us all.*": Anonymous letter from "Jane Q. Citizen," postmarked Dec. 3, 1969 at Atlanta, Georgia.

p. 178 – *Calley...a national hero.*: Michael Bilton and Kevin Sim, *Four Hours In My Lai*, pages 339-340; also, this viewpoint is expressed in numerous letters and telegrams to President Nixon and Defense Secretary Laird, housed in the National Archives at College Park, Maryland.
p. 178 – *...throughout the land.*: Ibid.
p. 179 – *...a flood of...letters...*: Ibid.
p. 181 – *A Gallup Poll...*: *Newsweek*, April 12, 1971, page 28.
pp. 182-183 – "*...the murder of innocent persons.*": Aubrey M. Daniel III (prosecutor in Calley court-martial), letter to President Nixon, protesting his release of Calley from the stockade.
p. 184 – *...his twice-reduced sentence*. Michael Bilton and Kevin Sim, *Four Hours In My Lai*.

Chapter 11. A Return to Obscurity

p. 187 – *...accompanied by his new wife...*: Hugh Thompson, personal interview.
p. 188 – *...training soldiers to fly...*: Ibid.
p. 188 – *...poor grade on Officer Evaluation Report...*: Officer Evaluation Report dated June 4, 1973, signed by Donald F. Matson.
p. 188 – *...Army protocol and traditions.*: Thompson's Officer Evaluation Reports from Jan. 1, 1973 to Sept. 1, 1983.
p. 188 – "...RIFed.": Hugh Thompson, personal interview.
p. 189 – *...an understatement.*: Ibid.
pp. 190-191 – *Thompson stationed in Hawaii*: Major Don Conkright (Thompson's Commanding Officer), personal interview.
pp. 191-192 – *Thompson stationed in Louisiana*: Lt. Col. Nick Johnson (Thompson's Commanding Officer), personal interview.
p. 192 – *...a family man.*: Hugh Thompson, personal interview.
p. 193 – *...knew little or nothing...*: Ibid.
pp. 194-195 – *Bilton's and Thompson's phone conversation*: Michael Bilton and Hugh Thompson, personal interviews.
p. 196 – *...One...who watched...*: David Egan, personal interview.

Chapter 12. A Whole New Light

p. 197 – *...done their hearts good.*: Hugh Thompson and Larry Colburn, personal interviews.
p. 199 – *...the volume of mail...*: Thompson received hundreds of letters of congratulations and admiration from March through June of 1998. See samples on pages 200-203, 205-207, and 227-229. Colburn received many letters of a similar nature.
p. 200 – *...about to be lifted.*: Hugh Thompson, personal interview.
p. 204 – *...some twenty-two million people...*: CBS spokesman, in phone interview.
pp. 207-208 – "*Warriors for Humanity*": Lyrics by Fred Greco, Granite City, Illinois.

Epilogue

p. 219 – *...only a small percentage of Americans...*: The horrific nature of the My Lai massacre, coupled with the public outcry over the William Calley court-martial and subsequent conviction, all but eclipsed the story of the helicopter pilot and his crew who intervened in the massacre. Dozens of those who wrote to Thompson after he was awarded the Soldier's Medal made specific reference to the fact that they were unaware there had been an intervention at My Lai.

p. 219 – *My Lai was only the starting point.*: The game plan of Task Force Barker was to permanently get rid of the Viet Cong from a large area of Quang Ngai Province. My Lai-4 was but one subhamlet of one hamlet in one village in the target area. According to a story in *The Washington Post* by David Hoffman (Dateline: Saigon, Nov. 23, 1969), one of the members of the South Vietnamese House of Representatives, Quang Ngai Deputy Tran Van Phien, confirmed that there were approximately 10,000 people living in six villages in the target area when the U.S. search-and-destroy mission was launched.

Further evidence of the broad scope of the operation was given in open court by Lt. William Calley when he was on trial for murder in the early part of 1971. Referring to the briefing he received from Capt. Ernest Medina, he said: "We were going to start at My Lai 4 and would have to neutralize My Lai 4 completely.... Then we would move to My Lai 5 and neutralize it and make sure there was no one left in My Lai 5, and so on until we got into the Pinkville area. Then we would completely neutralize My Lai 1, which is Pinkville.... So, it was our job ... to go through, neutralize these villages by destroying everything in them, not letting anyone or anything get in behind us, and move on to Pinkville."

Additional evidence of the scope of the operation – and the near-total disregard for the safety of any civilians who would be encountered during the assault – is provided by Gen. Peers in his *Report of the Department of the Army Review of the Preliminary Investigations Into The My Lai Incident (Volume 1)*, Chapter 5, pages 1-25.

p. 220 – *...put a stop to the massacre...*: Lt. Gen. W.R. Peers, *The Peers Inquiry*, New York, W.W. Norton & Co., 1979.

p. 220 – *...U.S. military ethics manuals...*: David Egan, personal interview.

p. 220 – *...European military training manuals...*: Terje Lund, (officer in Norwegian Air Force and assistant professor of humanitarian law and the law of war at Army College in Oslo, Norway), personal interview.

p. 221 – *...countless lives...have been saved.*: Ibid.

Index

About the Author

TRENT ANGERS is a veteran journalist who has authored thousands of published news and feature stories, as well as three books, in a writing and editing career that has spanned four decades.

His books are: *The Truth About The Cajuns* (1989); *Dudley LeBlanc: A Biography* (1993); and *The Forgotten Hero Of My Lai: The Hugh Thompson Story* (1999).

Angers graduated from Louisiana State University in 1970 and was named the Outstanding Graduating Senior in Journalism by Sigma Delta Chi, professional journalism organization. He also won the Hodding Carter Award for Responsible Journalism. He served an apprenticeship at *The Palm Beach* (Florida) *Post*. In the early 1970s he was a staff correspondent for *The Times-Picayune* of New Orleans and *The Beaumont Enterprise*, and he wrote free-lance articles for a dozen other Louisiana newspapers.

Since 1975, Angers has been editor and publisher of *Acadiana Profile*, "The Magazine of the Cajun Country," based in Lafayette, Louisiana; it is one of the longest-running regional publications in the United States.